Regionalism among Developing Countries

Regionalism among Developing Countries

Sheila Page
Research Fellow
Overseas Development Institute
London

in association with
OVERSEAS DEVELOPMENT INSTITUTE

337.1
PI3M

First published in Great Britain 2000 by
MACMILLAN PRESS LTD
Houndmills, Basingstoke, Hampshire RG21 6XS and London
Companies and representatives throughout the world

A catalogue record for this book is available from the British Library.

ISBN 0–333–77486–8

First published in the United States of America 2000 by
ST. MARTIN'S PRESS, INC.,
Scholarly and Reference Division,
175 Fifth Avenue, New York, N.Y. 10010

ISBN 0–312–22660–8

Library of Congress Cataloging-in-Publication Data
Page, Sheila.
Regionalism among developing countries / Sheila Page.
p. cm.
Includes bibliographical references and index.
ISBN 0–312–22660–8 (cloth)
1. Developing countries—Economic integration.   2. Regionalism—
–Developing countries.   3. Trade blocs—Developing countries.
4. Developing countries—Commerce.   I. Title.
HC59.7.P283   1999
337.1'1724—dc21   99–33860
                                                                      CIP

This book is printed on paper suitable for recycling and made from fully managed and sustained
forest sources.

10   9   8   7   6   5   4   3   2   1
09   08   07   06   05   04   03   02   01   00

Printed and bound in Great Britain by
Antony Rowe Ltd, Chippenham, Wiltshire

Contents

Part III   Other Regional Linkages

List of Tables

Preface and Acknowledgements

My interest in developing country regional groups goes back to my earliest research and first job in development economics, so it is more than usually impossible to identify all those who have contributed to what I know and think about them. The research for this book formally began in 1994, with the support of a grant from the Economic and Social Research Council (L 120 25 1015), under its Global Economic Institutions Programme. The formal and informal discussions and differences I had with David Vines, the Director of the Programme, and the other participants made a major contribution to clarifying my understanding of the topic. During the period of the research, I also received financial support for related research from UNCTAD, the European Commission, the Department for International Development, and the Trade and Industrial Policy Secretariat of South Africa.

I am grateful to all of these for comments on my preliminary work on the subject, and also to participants in conferences organised by the European Association of Development Research and Training Institutes and the Project LINK forecasting group. I am particularly grateful to all the government officials, researchers, and people in private industry who allowed me to question them about how regions actually worked and what they were trying to do.

Margaret Cornell edited the final text and compiled the index, clarifying the content as well as the style. I am very grateful for her help.

None of these is responsible for any of the views expressed here.

Sheila Page

Part I
Defining Regions

1
What is the New Regionalism?

What is new

Why do countries form regions? How do these affect their members, those excluded, and the international system?In the last decade, new developments in trade and in the institutional structure of international economic relations have brought these questions back on to the international policy and research agenda. The multilateral trading system has been extended to new subjects and strengthened, with the completion of the Uruguay Round of trade negotiations and the implementation of the World Trade Organization (WTO) in January 1995. National governments have changed how they intervene and regulate. Between these, at the regional level:

- in some regions, the share of intra-regional trade has increased strongly;
- the number of formal regional organizations has increased at an unprecedented rate, with new groups emerging and old ones reviving;
- many have shown a commitment to other forms of cooperation in parallel with the extension of the coverage of 'trade' seen at the GATT/WTO level;
- the European Union already acts as a single unit in some cases rather than as a group of members with some common interests, although the members still act separately in other circumstances. Other regional groups are now following its example. The multilateral organizations and non-members of regions are having to adapt to new links among their members and to new counterparts: to a more diverse international structure, with a mix of countries and groups at various stages or degrees of integration.

The most conspicuous new trading area is the North American Free Trade Area (NAFTA), consisting of the United States, Canada, and Mexico. The most conspicuous adaptation is the EU's membership of the WTO, although the member states also remain members in their own right. If the new bodies prove to be more than expressions of regional goodwill or temporary cooperation, and particularly if they follow the example of the EU in deepening their structures, then countries may face a new environment in which to develop and the international organizations may face a new type of member, which is not simply a larger country. All will need to operate in a new system, dealing with a variety of levels of cooperation and with conflicts of responsibility within and between them.

Some of the administrative and regulatory issues which this raises are similar to those raised in the context of federal countries or multinational firms, where there are conflicts or overlaps of responsibilities. This may suggest one type of solution, that the international organisations should have a strong regulatory role in supervising the regional groups. Three basic questions are: whether the new system is, on balance, favourable or unfavourable for individual countries and for development; whether there is a need for stronger international regulation of regions; and whether the new structure will in fact be very different from the old which was never simple – there have always been entities which would not fit a simple model of 'country' and 'the rest of the world'. In the past, almost all groups have failed; a few have moved forward to become more like nations than groups of countries.

Although there has always been some concern for the external effects of regions, the current revival of interest can be dated to the beginning of the European Community's move towards a Single European Market, and then European Union (EU). This started in 1985: the SEM was formally completed on 1 January 1993; the moves to monetary union and coordinated foreign relations are reinforcing it. At the same time, there has been growing discussion about the appropriate trading policies for individual developing countries and how to improve their trading opportunities. Improving access to neighbours has been a traditional step.

During the Uruguay Round, the question was raised of whether regionalization was or should be an alternative to the international system, especially at points when the Round seemed on the point of failure. But it continued to develop even after the Round's successful conclusion. We must now ask: not whether regionalization or multilateralism, but how to reconcile and balance the two trends. Are they complementary or in conflict? Does their simultaneous emergence create problems or opportunities? And what are the implications for the developing countries?

If we look at what actually exists, the evidence casts considerable doubt on the view, popular in the early 1990s, that the world is being divided or will divide into regions based conveniently on the continents. There is one industrial country region, the EU, which is becoming increasingly integrated, and has already reached a stage approximating to the competencies usually found in a country rather than in a trading area. There are two other regions (MERCOSUR and SACU) which are formal regions, with clear integration programmes for the future and the past, respectively, and the potential to move to cover new responsibilities. There are some areas (NAFTA, northern South America, the Caribbean, South East Asia) where there have been some moves, some results, and many of the apparent conditions for regions. There are other areas, including Africa, where there are proposals, but where the political and social conditions seem no easier to meet than those for global integration. In these, it is difficult to see any argument (except perhaps that of limited bargaining ability) for regions as an alternative or supplement to global integration. In Asia, Africa and Latin America there are overlaps and inclusions of regions. There are also a variety of groups for special purposes, including some of those in Africa, where there are joint interests and there will be practical benefits from joint efforts, but not the continuing identity and progress over a range of issues which regionalization implies.

The regional response

This raises the question of what a region is. One purpose of the present research is to clarify this, so it will be refined in the course of this book. The basic definition is a group of countries which have created a legal framework of cooperation covering an extensive economic relationship, with the intention that it will be of indefinite duration, and with the possibility foreseen that the region will evolve or change. The criterion of extensive economic linkages (a major share of trade or trade linked with regulation or infrastructure, for example) is intended to exclude single issue alliances. The criterion of permanence reinforces this, and seems uncontroversial, although judgement can of course only ever be provisional (even the limiting form of region, the country, can break up). Evolution may seem less obvious as a criterion, but the intention is to reinforce the exclusion of groups formed for and limited to a single purpose, or a single period. It is precisely those groups which attempt to be more complex which raise the interesting questions. The need to evolve is inevitable over time because countries' economic structures change, and with them the nature of their linkages. But beyond this, just as has occurred at the multilateral level, the economic and regulatory links between trade and the rest of the economic system mean that a trading relationship will lead to other policies. The spread of the responsibilities of both the EU and the WTO to 'trade-*related*' areas illustrates how, for two of the longest established groups, lowering conventional barriers to trade brings to the fore a sequence of other differences among countries which affect trade, and in turn other differences which affect these. The paths are obvious from goods to services to the right of establishment and capital and labour movements; from tariffs to non-tariffs to non-border measures; from tariffs to other taxes and other policies; from trade classifications to standards; from trade competition to competition policy; the connections across to currencies, political decisions, and from services to language and entertainment.

It could also be argued, however, that the importance of the EU and WTO, whose legal competence is now based on trade, has distorted both policy and analysis. There are other models. Joint infrastructure (power, transport and communications being the most obvious, with examples among both the Latin American and the Southern African countries) or joint economic interests in promoting new industry (common among the import-substituting regimes of Latin America in the 1960s, but also in South Africa and its neighbours in the 1990s) are as important as they were in stimulating the European Coal and Steel Community of the 1950s. All successful regions, and most others, not only allow early links to evolve, but have objectives other than freeing trade, and this may be essential for the will to evolve. Trade may well be secondary to political or security objectives or a tool rather than an objective: it is difficult to find any groups which have only a strictly trade agenda.

The existence of regions and the recent changes pose a range of theoretical, empirical, and organizational questions. Why do countries form groups below the multilateral level? Is there a special nature of regions, or are they a form of federalism? Is there a regional equivalent to national loyalties or identities or are they purely instruments for a purpose?

Why do countries form particular groups, and how do they select their fellow members? Is there a sufficiently common pattern for the responsibilities the groups cover or how they behave that enables models of 'regions' to be usefully defined and added to our analysis of countries? In what fields are groups likely to be effective? Are they formed for traditional production development purposes, with motives like complementary production or economies of scale, or the traditional international trade agenda of improving efficiency, or for other reasons? What are the non-economic motives and conditions of success?

Do the increasing economic linkages of trade, capital flows, and other contacts, lead to or follow from more formal institutional linkages? Has the relationship between economic and political linkages changed? At a practical level, whether (or when) groups act as a unit is determined by the subjects they cover, but are there more significant differences in their choices of how to act? Some groups may have an explicit objective of using a joint approach, but for others it will emerge out of an interest in fostering intra-group relations.

If the answers to these questions suggest that there has been a significant move to a more organized regional approach to action at the international level, at least in some areas and some subjects, what are the implications for those in and outside the regions? How can those outside participate? Or how can they manage or mitigate the effects from regions?

The multilateral organizations have until very recently taken no official notice of 'regions'. Multilateral will be used here to mean organizations with a universal membership, or potential membership. Regional will normally be used for groups above country but below universal membership, not for divisions within countries, unless this is specifically indicated. As this has changed, the lack of a strong framework within which to analyse individual regions has become a problem. It is difficult to define how 'regions' fit into the traditional economic, political and institutional view of countries as the basic units of the international system and of multilateral organizations. In practice, there has always been a variety of institutional arrangements among countries, and these do not fit this black-and-white pattern, but we lack an understanding of the nature and possible roles of intermediate-level organizations. In economics and in political analysis, the issues can be discussed in terms of sovereignty, but this again may imply too precise a border line among levels of organization.

A fundamental difficulty is to know whether or at what point it becomes appropriate to look at the region as the appropriate unit of aggregation of individual interests, whether economic or other, rather than the countries which are its members. Implicitly, most of the literature still takes the country as the unit, as would be correct in determining whether countries should join, or leave, but becomes decreasingly appropriate as cross-border interests develop. The simultaneous emergence of new forces for sub-national regionalism presents parallel choices.

Beyond trade

Both the conventional economic classification of free trade areas, customs unions, and common markets, and the only fully developed regulatory structure for regions, under the World Trade Organization, assume that trade is the basic motive and characteristic and, by implication, the most important potential source of effects on third parties. They also assume a continuum from less to more integrated, along a single path. The briefest look at the empirical evidence, or the literature from disciplines other than economics, shows that neither assumption is true.

The fall in tariffs significantly weakens the trade motive for regions. In a regime where Latin American tariffs typically averaged at the high two-digit, if not over 100 percent level, to secure more favourable access was clearly a major benefit, both directly and in terms of preference relative to the rest of the world. This held until the 1980s; countries with protective regimes might have been prepared to make limited exceptions, for others judged not much more competitive than themselves, while not extending this to industrial countries. Similarly, it can explain the popularity of preferential access to the industrial countries, in schemes such as the Generalised System of Preferences (GSP) and more specialized ones like Lomé for the European Community's smaller ex-colonies. But improving access is a less obvious objective when the tariff levels of the industrial countries have come down to an average of under 4 percent, and those of Latin American countries to 10–15 percent. Preferences may still be worth having, especially as there are peaks and non-tariff barriers as well, justifying some continuing interest in regionalism, but this certainly does not explain why it should increase.

Regions have become more numerous and possibly more significant while tariffs were falling, a strong indication that they are based on other elements. As tariffs are effectively removed from the available policy instruments, future regions, or the future development of some of those that are evolving, may be based only on other economic linkages or on non-economic ones. The elimination of trading barriers makes other differences in market conditions more apparent, both as barriers to trade and as 'unfair' differences between firms in different countries. At a regional level, this phenomenon helps to explain the transformation of the European Community into the Single European Market; and at a global level, the new responsibilities attached to the WTO. The inclusion of services, investment, intellectual property, non-trade subsidies, and the other new issues in the WTO offers evidence that countries are finding these non-trade barriers more important and the existing mechanisms for regulating them unsatisfactory. Those areas where trade or other links are greater than average will find this force more powerful, potentially leading to a need being felt for regional cooperation or regulation. This could explain why a smaller increase in regional trade than in the past could be enough to trigger a policy response, and could imply that regional organisations may prove more stable than in the past. But it also suggests that exclusion may be more painful.

The non-trade economic and the non-economic elements of regionalism mean that the analysis of regions' needs to be extended in two ways. The other aspects need to be brought into the analysis of the region itself, why it formed, what it covers, how it evolves, whether there is a continuum. It also becomes necessary to look at the non-trade effects on non-members and the international system and not just the traditional 'trade-diversion' effects.

At the level of a single region, it makes sense to see it repeating the process followed by countries and international organizations, of moving to take on more responsibilities, because of the advantages of scale and because one subject is related to another. Obvious examples are services following trade in goods up from individual countries to the EU to the Uruguay Round and the WTO, labour standards and the environment moving to NAFTA and now on to the agenda of the WTO. But these examples are also warnings about the potential difficultly once there is more than one significant region. There is no reason why one region should have the same customs or forms, or division of responsibilities between the centre and the members as other regions. NAFTA has made much less progress on integration of services than the EU, and the EU less progress on labour or the environment than NAFTA. Both have probably made less progress on some aspects of payments and currency than some of the African regions (or on investment coordination than the Andean Pact attempted in the 1960s). The EU stresses labour mobility while NAFTA excludes it. The arrangements each has made on those subjects which they do share, whether border arrangements, industrial regulation, disputes settlement or standards, are very different. How important is this, given that countries also differ? It is feasible, although sometimes painful, to persuade applicants to an existing region to accept its rules. It has proved possible for the weight of world negotiations to persuade individual countries to adapt their procedures sufficiently to enable world agreements to be made. The question of whether regions, which are larger and which already embody painfully negotiated compromises, can negotiate and accept international standards remains open. If the negotiations are in fact the formal responsibility of the regions, which have the greatest interests in preserving their level and their arrangements against the pressures which, it has been argued, are normally in favour of size (and therefore ultimately the world), this may distort solutions away from welfare-maximizing. Allowing intermediate levels to choose how to allocate responsibilities among levels could create a bias against the better outcomes of moving responsibilities further up or further down.

A corollary of the observation that there is no simple definition or path of integration is that groups move in different ways towards more, or perhaps different forms of, integration. An analysis of their impact must therefore also try to define whether the nature of this evolution can be predicted, and thus what the future effects will be.

Regional organizations, particularly those among developing countries, have a history of enthusiastic formation followed by dissent and either dissolution or lapsing into purely formal existence. If we are to ask whether what is happening now is different from what happened in the past, we must ask whether there has been a change in the external conditions to make them more favourable or to make regional schemes more desirable, as well as looking at internal conditions.

There is growing integration of economies (what Oman, 1994, has called 'deep international policy integration'). This may require a more contractual response to any degree of *de facto* regional integration, whether trade or non-trade, than in the past. Some of the agreements required are not yet regulated by the WTO, although they are already moving on to its agenda. The environment and labour conditions are examples. The regulatory and long-term issues which they raise cannot be met by normal trade bargaining procedures. Where the regional organizations do now cover these questions, as the EU and NAFTA do, the standards and regulations which they set, and the implicit or explicit discrimination against or among non-members, are not subject to GATT/WTO obligations of most favoured nation (MFN) treatment, so that any adverse effects on non-members cannot be challenged. There is also no formal obligation to notify or explain them to non-members.

A second change is the increasing role of private actors in international economic relations. A third is the role of international contacts in the activities of smaller or more local economic interests than would have been affected in the past. There are now not only the traditional multinational companies carrying out traditional trading and investment, but new forms of international division of labour within these and an increasing number of smaller companies trading and investing abroad as part of their normal operations. The reduction of international barriers has made international trade more a matter of everyday economic activity. The increased importance of cross-border trade leads to other contacts, notably in the areas of services and intellectual property, which in turn leads to new linkages. The growth in foreign investment, and an increased perception of the possible choices between trade and investment, and the greater linkages implied by the choice of investment, are also important.

International, often regional, links among groups other than countries should also not be ignored. Professional groups and non-governmental interest groups of all types have greatly increased their contacts, formal and informal, partly because of the increase in the importance of trade which has made them identify common interests, partly because of greater ease of communications. Such interests may also see a need for greater regional economic contacts to be accompanied by more formal institutional structures than in the past.

Some larger (or geographically isolated) countries entering into regions have had less experience of 'closer than normal' economic relations with trading partners, because of their size and lack of dependence on trade (the US and Australia, for example). For these, there has been an element of learning which has perhaps led to a more formalistic approach to regions than by the more experienced. The newness of regional links for them may help to explain the perception that regions have suddenly become more important. There is also an element of terminological fashion. Just as companies have always had reciprocal trading relationships, but only in the 1980s were these classified as 'countertrading', so many forms of cooperation among countries have existed. For countries with less of a history of cooperation, the questions of 'sovereignty' may present themselves more forcibly because they are less accustomed to economic (and perhaps to political) dependence on their neighbours, leading again to more perception of regions as innovations. If the motives for regions were purely economic, this would suggest a choice between sovereignty and greater potential for economic gain through globalization. But if the motives go beyond this, then the past precedents, of alliances for political or military purposes, may provide useful precedents.

Structure of the book

A satisfactory framework for analysing regions should allow us to answer the questions: why countries form regions and, at the empirical level, why a particular group of countries has formed a region with a particular coverage of responsibilities at a particular time. Part I of this book will therefore examine the theoretical analysis of regions (Chapter 2): the different approaches, economic, political, cultural, geographical and institutional, which have been used for regions, and what the implications are for regions' effect on trade or other economic linkages. It will then look at the historical background of those regions which seem to meet the minimum definitions of a viable region, a group which is intended to have indefinite duration with the possibility of change (Chapter 3). This will indicate the wide variety of regions, and the large degree of 'overlap' in membership of different regions. The question of whether there are general characteristics of countries or preconditions which lead them to form regions will be examined in Chapter 4. Such characteristics could help to define both the choice of regions and the timing of regional formation. Chapter 5 outlines the regulatory structure for regions, which is largely trade-based.

Part II examines the trade and investment aspects of regions. For each, it analyses first what is liberalized at the regional level, compared with countries' policies towards the rest of the world, and then data on trade and investment. This will permit comparison of what the different regions cover. An examination of how much is traded or invested within regions, compared with the rest of the world, and of whether new trends in the direction or composition of flows have emerged, provides evidence on whether the trade effects predicted by theory are occurring and whether the pre-region linkages were strong. The short periods for which most regions among developing countries have had effective trade policy linkages and the range of other trade policy changes make this at best indicative.

Part III details the other types of institutional linkage which regions have, both economic and other. Do their objectives go beyond trade or investment, and do they follow the pattern of the multilateral institutions? These include other elements of production and trade, including services, intellectual property, and industrial laws and regulations. Going slightly beyond economics, there are linkages in sectoral or national or macroeconomic policy or planning. There are also semi-political links, and semi-judicial, particularly in settling disputes among members, or between different actors within the region, on matters of regional responsibility. The types of link cover the range of what national legislation can include.

This section will also look at regions' relations with the rest of the world: other countries, other regions, and the multilateral system. For some regions, there is an additional group, their potential members.

This is important to indicate how far they see themselves as a group with an identity, as well as to study their effect on the international system.

Part IV summarizes the results in order to examine the two fundamental issues for the developing countries: the interaction between regions and development, both in economic results and in the implications for policy design and implementation; and the relations between regions and the multilateral system. Does the present system of regulation need reform or extension? The section also looks at the implications of a regional approach to international economic regulation for one based on income or development needs.

2
Why Should Countries Form Regions?

Analysing groups

What is the advantage that countries see in a region, over the country or global level, and does the region damage non-members? These are long-standing problems in both economic and political theory. A region combines internal liberalization and external defining or strengthening of a unit within the multilateral system, and is therefore very different from either single-country or multilateral liberalization. Analysis must look at both aspects, at the effects of each on the members and on the rest of the world, and discover the balance of the positive and negative results.

Without clarity on why countries form regions, there is no criterion for what benefits to look for. The number of different motives and types of regions makes it difficult to generalize. This book, however, looks only at regions with some trade content, and the criterion of a continuing group implicitly requires some political commitment. Given this common core, it seems appropriate to look at all the arguments together, while recognizing that some will be more relevant to some regions. One distinction which needs to be introduced is that between customs unions and free trade areas. This is important because customs unions must act jointly relative to the rest of the world, at least on tariffs. Most existing groups are free trade areas; the only customs unions are the European Union, the Southern African Customs Union (SACU), MERCOSUR in South America, and CARICOM in the Caribbean. The Andean Pact and the Central American Common Market have partial common tariffs.

For countries to join together to form a region, it is normally assumed that all must gain relative to not joining. We also need to ask whether all will gain more than from other possible regions. This raises the difficult question of what the 'non-economic' or 'other' factors are which determine which regions are feasible or not. One important 'other region' is the world: when is this a possible solution? Once a region is formed, the questions are different. Gains from extending membership are perceived if the new member and all the existing members gain. Changing or doubtful advantages will produce unstable regions. That moves to regionalism, especially among developing countries, were high in the 1960s, then lower, and are now high again suggests that some of the groups are not regions in the rigorous sense used here, but more like the temporary alliances seen among large companies, perhaps for a particular product development or in particular markets. The analogy to a region would be a merger.

A region may be stable if there are a range of objectives, and if, while the initial advantages may become less important, new ones emerge, as in a merger of companies with a variety of objectives. Alternatively, it may be stable if there is an overriding long-term advantage or commitment. In analysing regions, we must ask whether we are looking at groups with concrete objectives or at a more general commitment, even a sense of regional identity. In the case of groups with only a limited set of objectives, it may be that different groups will be more appropriate for a country's other objectives. This gives rise to the phenomenon of 'overlapping' or tangled regions; are these stable?

Agreements where gains from trade seem very small, or where some countries actually receive payments to compensate for trade losses, are evidence that a variety of motives are present. If trade were the sole motive, the only reason for any compensating payments to be made would be if some countries gained much less (or lost) but needed to be included to provide gains to others. Formal compensation payments are included in very few regional agreements, but they are rarely based on trade.[1] The agreements which provide for payments are the EU, with its regional and agricultural funds, and SACU, with its allocation of customs revenues by South Africa to the poorer members. For the EU the payments are not tied to identified and quantified trade or other disadvantages of being in the group, but are determined by occupation, income, development, or other need. In SACU, the justification given for the payments is the cost-raising effect of South African tariffs and the loss of trade-policy independence by the smaller members. But the level of the extra 'enhancement' payment made, the change to a guaranteed rate in 1976/7 and the current proposals to reduce the subsidy have all been related to South Africa's willingness to subsidize the others, determined by its own economic situation and its interests in their political support, not by calculations of the costs.

Customs unions have to find a formula for allocating revenue, because in most of them duties are collected by the country of entry, not the final importing country. MERCOSUR still collects revenue at the final destination, and therefore has not yet needed or prepared a formula. Examination of free trade agreements, however, shows clear cases where provisions, on trade or other subjects, have been put in on the initiative of one member, and at a perceived cost to the others, so that these could be viewed as *de facto* payments. An example is the case of NAFTA. For all three countries, the potential gains from trade are small. Mexico gained little relative to its existing access from the GSP and the *maquiladora* arrangements. The US had gains relative to the unilateral reductions which Mexico had already offered but on a much lower share of its trade. Canada traded little with Mexico. Trade seems insufficient to explain NAFTA. 'Payments' include some concessions on investment and services by Canada and most notably the labour and environment agreements with Mexico. We must therefore ask: what did the three countries want from the agreement, if it was not an exchange of freer access to markets? There are similar cases in some of the less well known agreements, and the suggestions which are made here for NAFTA have many parallels.

These suggestions include: that Canada and Mexico feared that, in the absence of a special access agreement, the US would increase its barriers unilaterally (through anti-dumping, removal of privileges, etc.). If this is true, the correct calculation is not the small difference between trade with NAFTA and trade under existing policies, but the much larger one between trade with NAFTA and trade with reduced access. The gain came from not losing access, rather than from new access. Arithmetically, this gives the required higher numbers in the calculations, but it depends on the assumption that a commitment by the US to a regional agreement is more credible to its trading partners than one to the GATT/WTO. This is a direct contradiction of the usual argument for the advantage of GATT, namely, that especially for small countries trading with large, a commitment to an international agency and its membership is more credible than a unilateral concession. (It also contradicts the empirical evidence that most countries are at least as ready to evade or avoid bilateral commitments as multilateral.) A similar suggestion is that Mexico wanted to 'bind' itself to its current open trade policies by making a commitment to NAFTA. The same doubt holds here about relative credibility, especially as Mexico joined the GATT during the Uruguay Round explicitly to signal its commitment.

A third argument is that the smaller countries wanted international recognition as mature trading partners, or as specially favoured in a 'special relationship'. Analogues exist in many other trading groups, including some current applicants to the EU, and perhaps also South Africa's interest in the Lomé Convention. Once these more foreign policy-based gains are introduced, they need not hold only for 'small' countries tying themselves to 'large'. Many of the specially tailored trade agreements which the EU has signed, and which it continues to pursue, seem as much to show interest or friendship as to make absolute gains. SACU, especially in the past, contained elements of South Africa buying support. And in NAFTA, showing concern, insuring against future changes, and buying support could help to explain why the US wanted it. This leaves two problems. First, if NAFTA is basically a purchase of insurance against future loss in return for policy concessions on labour and the environment, with some gains in terms of special relationships (on all three sides) and if it is typical of other agreements in having non-trade motives at its core, then calculating its trade (or investment) effects may be interesting, particularly to third countries, but is not central to the analysis either of whether it is a stable solution for the participants or (given that other countries also have non-trade objectives) of its costs or benefits to non-members. Secondly, if a trade agreement is a position good, a 'special arrangement', then increasing the number of such agreements lowers the value of the existing ones doubly, not only by whatever 'undiversion' of trade, in the traditional model, may take place, but also by reducing exclusivity.

It is interesting how many objectives, other than trade, are used to explain what are conventionally analysed (and regulated internationally) as trade agreements. (A similar observation could be made about analysis of the Uruguay Round settlement.) If trade effects do not measure all the benefits to the member or the potential harm to the excluded, they should not be the only criteria for regulation.

Why regions rather than global?

The benefits to the inhabitants of a country from removing its own barriers to trade are well established in economic theory. The benefits of a multilateral regulatory system to ensure that liberalization is implemented and maintained, and that trade takes place under equitable conditions are also well supported. The costs or obstacles to freeing trade are (except for a few special cases) normally attributed by economists to non-economic reasons. Sectoral interests, combined with the political strength of individual producers may be difficult to combat; the gains to a country from regulation may be harder to achieve where there are fewer common objectives; political or social sympathy or similar tastes may be greater among those who are 'near' each other than among those who are more distant. Thus the economic benefits derived from greater liberalization by a country on its own or the security and certainty from greater regulation at the world level are to be balanced against the assumed non-economic costs of domestic politics or of lack of international compatibility.

This analysis of the benefits and costs of liberalization and multilateralism could give some intermediate level between 'the country' and the world as an equilibrium solution. The fact that regions seem to have become more attractive in recent years means that it is not possible to assume a static balance between those interests which benefit from larger areas and those which suggest smaller. In principle, this could be accommodated by altering the implied either–or choices into some model of demand and supply curves, with declining marginal benefits from liberalization as distance or size increases and economic contacts decrease and from regulation at growing levels of diversity, and rising 'non-economic' costs as more industries are affected at home and more political interests have to be reconciled abroad. Specifying how the curves are derived would explain why one or both could shift over time, occasionally giving a 'solution' at a point above the country but below the world level. Economic explanations might include changes in production conditions, altering scale economies, types of competition, etc., and also changing tastes, whether to greater uniformity because of communications changes, or more desire for variety because of rising incomes.

This type of analysis will raise a variety of questions. First, the traditional method of simply assuming 'political obstacles' to reducing 'national sovereignty' or special interests opposed to competition has always been weak in empirical and analytic content. Trying to stretch it to analysis of different and shifting degrees of opposition, to give a possible intermediate zone of regional arrangements, brings out these weaknesses. It also ignores the possibility of non-economic motives for external agreements.

The obvious question of whether any solution is an equilibrium suggests that we must ask whether there are inherent advantages in particular levels and whether arrangements tend to persist. If the underlying conditions leading to their choice at one period then change, will the institutions themselves become special interests and obstacles (the 'building blocks' or 'stumbling blocks' argument)? Should we consider the choice of level for each type of liberalization or regulation separately? To what extent is it feasible to have various regional regimes at different levels between the country and the world (and within countries)? Can there be different, overlapping, regions, for different issues? There is potentially a trade-off between choosing the best level or regional group for each decision, and the potential efficiency advantages of having a restricted number of levels and avoiding the potential inconsistencies of overlapping regimes. A final question, at a political level, is the 'sovereignty' choice of who decides the level.

The analysis of optimum currency areas offers both a precedent and a warning of the difficulties of trying to look at regional groups in this way. Effectively, we are asking for the optimum trading area (perhaps subdivided into different types of good and/or service), the optimum capital or labour mobility area, the optimum regulatory area for anything from intellectual property to competition policy, and the optimum areas for all public goods, whether of regulation, fiscal and monetary policy, or of economic inputs like education or infrastructure, and then the optimum number of levels of responsibility. As well as economic determinants of size we must consider the constraints which economists call on to explain smaller-than-efficient solutions; cultural, social, and historical factors. And then we are also asking for the optimum number and arrangement of areas. At sub-national level, countries frequently need different levels of organization for different purposes, so it is not surprising that it should be true at the international level as well.[2] The appropriate size for any individual region may give rise to a number of regions within the WTO or other international group which is not, in theoretical terms, optimum for reaching solutions to common problems.

This chapter can only summarize the major arguments which have been suggested for choosing the appropriate levels for economic liberalization or regulation, and the assumptions about criteria for choice or behaviour which each embodies, identifying some apparent contradictions, and also identifying whose interests are being taken as the target, in order to suggest how we should look at the stability and effects of the new regions.

The conventional analysis of trade diversion and trade creation logically comes second. The analysis of creation and diversion starts from the existence of a region (or proposed region). It does not attempt to explain why that region, rather than another grouping, was chosen,

and cannot explain why a region rather than full multilateral liberalization was chosen: any trade creation effects will be largest at the world
level, where diversion will be zero.

The trade-creating or diverting effects may appear instead as invest-
ment-creating or diverting, if investment moves to take account of new
market and cost structures. But more fundamentally, if the objectives of
the region are not only to improve welfare through trade, but include
other development or strategic purposes, and if other countries also
have non-trade objectives, then diversion and creation must be extended
to non-economic results. Measuring the quantifiable trade and
investment effects nevertheless remains a useful check on the economic
costs of other objectives to members and gives part of the effects of
regions on third parties.

For all types of effect, it is important to look beyond static gains. Recent
studies of the creation of the single market in the EU or of NAFTA, for
example, have also looked at the trade-generating effects if liberalization produces not only a one-off rise in income, but a dynamic contribution to growth. In principle, analogous benefits to outsiders could be
found from non-trade elements.

Geography

The conventional word for the groups which form between the country
and global levels is 'regional', but we need to ask how far they have a
geographical coverage, and whether there is any consistent geography.
It will become clear that many of the other conditions and criteria discussed here and in Chapter 4 on pre-conditions need not hold among
all countries which are geographical neighbours, and may hold among
those which are not. At the empirical level, Chile's negotiations to enter
a North American area rather than the Market of the South (MERCO-
SUR), or the absence of Switzerland from a Europe whose boundaries
have moved sharply to the east since 1989 are obvious examples of
strong interests which override geography and warnings not to take
geographical names at face value. The contorted definitions of the various Asian and Pacific areas, with and without South Asia, normally
without South America, are evidence that geography follows from other
interests. The following sections will consider other criteria for grouping. But many regions are 'near' and economic geography is a characteristic which we can identify as potentially changing. Thus it could be
relevant to identifying regions, and consistent with finding new regions
or with changes in the appropriate level of decision-making.

A shift in the relative costs of different types of transport, shifts between sea and land and between loading and distance costs, can alter the balance among ocean, continental, and simply distance-based regions. The nature of transportation costs, where the fixed costs are high, suggests a reason for believing that there may be high costs in moving from a local market or source of supply to a new transport type permitting a slightly larger (district or country) area, but then a low marginal cost of moving to larger areas within this form of transport, giving a series of steps as limits of particular forms of transport are reached. This could suggest a clustering of advantages at the points immediately before the next shift, which could correspond to countries, regions, and eventually the world. A reduction in the average cost of transport relative to other costs would reduce the costs of moving to larger areas and scales. It is difficult, however, to use this to explain either the present or the past. The two surges of regionalism (the 1960s and the current one) have occurred when transportation was relatively low-cost, and expected to remain so, while the 1970s and early 1980s, when there was a shift to a more multilateral approach, were periods of high actual and expected prices. The costs would be more consistent with a shift from country to world emphasis.

If the steps are present, it suggests that the regions themselves would tend to be consistent across periods (except when there is a technology change), while relative costs would alter the appropriate size. But transportation costs vary greatly as a proportion of total costs among different industries, between industry and other activities, especially services, and at different levels of production. This could imply that regions would be formed differently among different types of country or at different levels of development. A change in the type of production could change both the scale of the appropriate region and (combined with technological changes in transportation itself) the appropriate grouping. As geography is at first sight the most fixed of the explanations to be considered here, it is important that we can conclude that it is not immutable.

Geography and transport costs cannot explain a maximum size of regions. Like most of the basic economic costs, transport may suggest a minimum efficient size, but as production can be at more than one location as easily within a region as in different countries, it does not suggest any maximum limit. Given the possible changes in scale and grouping and advantage from stability, this would strongly suggest that appropriate geographic size will lie beyond the minimum.

Economics

The traditional approach is to ask what are the static advantages over the *status quo* of removing the costs of tariffs and other border barriers to production and to competition in international markets. What is more relevant here is to focus on the regulatory function of regional (and global) institutions. The phenomenon we are trying to explain is new organizations, not simply a series of liberalizing agreements or treaties among countries, or unilateral liberalization. It is not only the prospective market advantages which are being sought, but also institutions. In analysis of the various Asian groups which tends to emphasize their 'open' and market nature, this is characterized as 'market-driven policies' rather than 'policy-driven economic changes', but this is purely descriptive. The important question is whether the demand for regional regulation and institutions comes from the economic actors, who want the same institutions which they find useful at the national level, or from the political authorities, which see their control over economic actors diminishing and which therefore want to combine with other governments to restore their authority.

Trade

The simple argument is that the benefits (to competitiveness within and outside the region) in terms of reducing costs and producing without cost disadvantages from trade barriers all go up continuously with larger areas of free trade. A greater weight in trade flows for 'nearer' regions may mean that the marginal benefits decrease; a region can therefore give a high, and perhaps sufficient, share of the benefits from multilateral liberalization.

Whether this is true will depend on the type of production in the potential member countries: whether they are dependent on inputs from other members, or on their markets, and whether they are competing in similar goods or are complementary. The traditional arguments of improved efficiency and static income gains from liberalization assume similar production patterns. In this case, the region might tend to be trade-creating, through increased competition between production in other members and in each home country, not diverting, because they will have the same imports from non-member countries. The possibilities for efficient large-scale production to meet the larger market will be enhanced. As only similar countries are included, the market will still be homogeneous. If it is assumed that increasing returns characterize a large proportion of production, then increasing the size may produce greater efficiency, even if the countries are complementary. There are, however, three strong reservations about the role of economies of scale. For the large countries in the most studied regions, it is difficult to find industries where expansion to the region is important. For any region, accepting such expansion requires taking a 'regional' view of decisions on production and the distribution of benefits, which in turn requires a strong commitment or regional identity of interest. As trade barriers come down, a formal region is less necessary to gain market size. In contrast, if a region offers more opportunities for firms which are not competitive with outside producers to gain new markets, this will divert trade from the excluded countries and increase costs within the region.

It may well be necessary to distinguish between developed countries, which see integration as reinforcing, and removing distortions from, existing linkages between essentially unchanging domestic economic structures, and developing countries, which may have the intention of restructuring their economies and their linkages, and see integration as an aid to this. This may imply a stronger role for the state.

Special interest groups may have less power at the regional level than the national if they exist in only one member, but a region may create the possibility of new pressure groups, or give a weak one new allies. It has been argued that regions provide an external protection against domestic interest groups (Krugman in de Melo, and Panagariya, 1993, p. 58), but this does not seem to be an argument specifically for regions, but for any binding agreement which could be at national or multilateral level. A variant of this argument is that regions strengthen government (Oman, 1994, p. 99). These views suggest that the regulatory and institutional aspect of regions is their primary purpose, not the liberalization or other economic ends, and provide an interesting point to analyse particularly for developing countries. It is difficult, however, to distinguish from an alternative view that only governments with the confidence and strength to bargain and consider reducing their formal sovereignty can form regions.

A slightly different argument sees regions as a stage in production: industries can be competitive on a local, then national, then regional, then world, scale. This is plausible, on an infant industry protection view that they learn from experience, in a steady transition, but is not consistent with the alternative view that they learn by example from coming into contact with better technology and more efficient firms. It also needs to be offset by the costs of this learning to those consuming the products.

In looking at the composition of regions, it is necessary to ask what the economic objectives of the members are: efficiency or developmental? And in looking at the scale it is necessary also to consider two types of decision: whether to form a region in the first place, and then whether to expand it to new members. At the second stage, the question already raised of whose welfare we are considering becomes important, because individual members may have different interests from the region as a whole. Some members may lose from expansion in a region where some products are not produced in all members but the non-producers nevertheless have a tariff on imports (or if there is a common external tariff). Any gains in some industries from access to the new members may be diminished if other producers are also admitted to the region (the gains to the producing members from trade diversion are reduced). The gains to the non-producer are of course increased. As scales of production increase, and choice and variety become more important, the benefits of improving access increase, as does the risk of a single producer dominating the region, so a larger region is necessary to avoid monopoly. This suggests increasing advantages for regions over time.

For developing countries, particularly since most of those which have joined regions have been smaller, in population and income, than the major developed countries in regions, the scale arguments suggest an important reason to liberalize their own markets and to seek liberalization from others. Combined with their increasing emphasis on trade and liberalisation, this can explain the country and multilateral liberalization of the last decade.

One basic difference between developing and developed countries is that the economic structure of developing countries changes more rapidly and more fundamentally. This applies to sectors, to technologies, and to the macroeconomic variables such as trade, the role of government and the fiscal and other balances of the economy. This frequently entails changes on the monetary side as well, in the institutions, in the role of exchange and interest rates, and in inflation rates. All of these, however, are areas in which conventional criteria for successful regions look for complementarity, congruence, or convergence.

An examination of trade structures for complementarity, to find the potential advantage for the area itself of trade creation, and the possible damage for it and for the rest of the world of trade diversion, normally looks at existing structures, with some allowance for how these will change, given present industrial structures, if barriers are removed or altered (see, for example, World Bank, 1995). This is potentially inadequate for any group which is intended to be permanent, and the uncertainties are greater for countries whose trade and industrial structures are changing more rapidly, indeed for which change is actively sought in development policy. In practice, complementarity measures tend to produce higher numbers for trade groups among industrial countries or between industrial and developing (EU and NAFTA) than for developing (MERCOSUR) (World Bank 1995, p. 20). But they will, of course, always give the maximum index of 1 for a trading group defined as the world. Complementarity cannot therefore explain why countries should form regional groups rather than moving directly to full international trade.

Using complementarities may not suit the motives of developing countries. Industrial countries can look at the traditional efficiency advantages of removing barriers to current economic activities. After years (centuries) of development, their industrial structure is a major characterization of the economy, and changing it in response to an integration programme can be expected to have a significant effect on economic performance. The entire internal analysis of the effects of the Single European Market, for example, as done by the Commission itself, was in these comparative static terms, while some external analysis went one step beyond, to identifying potential dynamic effects if efficiency led to higher output and potential savings from efficiency-stimulated growth. But this type of gain would be unlikely to have as strong an effect in developing country integration, and it has not normally been the objective of developing country groups. Their existing industrial structures are small relative to their economies or to their planned development, and the static gains from rationalizing these among member countries by easing flows of trade are correspondingly small.

The objectives of a developing country group may be structural. They have included development of new industries through the cross-border coordination which economies of scale, a broader home market and better access to inputs might permit. By avoiding completely the high costs of establishing some industries, they would avoid the inefficiencies which industrial country integration is expected to eliminate *ex post*. It is this purpose of regional organization which was behind the 1960s attempts and which UNCTAD still stresses as important for developing countries, citing 'large economic spaces ... which could foster competitiveness, contribute to trade liberalization and help impart new dynamism to international trade' (UNCTAD 1995) and which should encourage investment cooperation and the setting up of joint ventures between firms in their regions and in developing countries.

The implicit assumptions behind the structural arguments for early regional integration are that there are no costs to early specialization to offset the saving from later shifting out of an inappropriate choice of industry or inefficient diversification, that the choices made within the regional context will be efficient, and that the countries will accept specialization. These assumptions could be violated by mistaken decisions, either by the market or the governments, or if the region subsequently breaks up. There may also be benefits from moving through a variety of industries and stages of production in offering experience in responding to changing demand and opportunities. The conclusions about whether regions among developing countries benefit development, even more than among industrial, are highly sensitive to the probability of permanence. Given that the potential structural advantages for developing countries tend to derive from individual projects or opportunities, and that the static efficiency arguments are weak, this argues more for one-off agreements on joint projects than for a trade area set up as a permanent link.

The problems of finding continuing advantages in joint development without coming against irreconcilable differences over the direction or rate of development, or the allocation of benefits among countries with potentially different objectives, have not been solved by any existing group of developing countries. They require a higher degree of long-term common interests for continuing integration than do industrial countries because the degree of structural change is greater. The changes in industrial and in macroeconomic structure over time could imply changes in both the 'optimum' size and the appropriate partners of a developing country trading group. Technical conditions also change. Different industries require different sizes to achieve appropriate economies, and there seems to be no regular evolution towards ever greater scale.

Even if simple trade and welfare objectives are accepted as the measures of a region's effects, analysing these is too demanding of data and forecasts to be practical. A full analysis of the trade effects would require data on:

- Each country's imports and exports from the region and from the rest of the world, classified by product: how important is the region to each country and in which products?
- Unrecorded border trade: one effect of a free trade area might be simply to bring into the open existing trade flows.
- Tariffs, by product (including allowance for existing or preferential arrangements within the region): how much difference would tariff

removal make to relative costs? If imports from the region differ in composition from average imports, the effect on each country's tariff revenue will need to be calculated across the relevant products, allowing for trade creation and diversion. This requires good models of demand and supply by product and source.

- Non-tariff barriers, with the same detail, but calculating their 'tariff equivalent', requires knowledge of both the demand and prices structures and assumptions about how these will change. If they are completely removed, the administrative costs must also be calculated as there will be an additional gain from removing these.

- Actual costs of production, for present and potential production, i.e. full supply curves for actual and potential exports to the region for all members. For some products in some regions, it might be possible to assume that the region is too small relative to the rest of the world to influence the prices of other suppliers, but where any country is a major supplier of a product this may not be valid.

- If demand and supply elasticities indicate that for some products the effects will be large, relative to production in either a country or the region as a whole, it would be necessary to examine the production conditions and efficiency gains possible if output changes significantly.

The calculations would need to consider a variety of indirect effects if any member countries have ties to the same third countries, but not within a single regional group (a hub and spokes arrangement with the EU, or the US, for example) or if the regions include members of existing free trade areas or preference groups. Here, the indirect effects of creation or income effects could circulate through the partner country.

These data would, however, produce only a limited answer. Particularly for countries which are developing rapidly, the structure of production and demand will change rapidly, so that it is, in principle, not the present answers to all these questions that are needed, but the expected answers when the region comes fully into effect (after transitions of ten years, plus ratification delays), and then in the years after that. These must then be compared with how the countries would have wanted their industries to develop, not with the present structure, taking into account the fact that a region will restrict some types of planning.

A country considering joining a region should compare the outcome not merely with not joining (or with the present situation) but with other potential regions or with a different trade policy, for example multilateral liberalization. It may or may not be legally necessary to choose to join just one region (different regions have different rules), but in terms of policy and commitments it is normally desirable.

Analyses of the effects of regional groups (*ex ante* or *ex post*) are rarely uncontroversial. (Examples are the debates over each new member in the EU; the recent controversy over the World Bank assessment of MERCOSUR; assessments of the effects on the EU and on the rest of the world of the Single European Market.) Most countries have neither the data nor the trade and production models to make firm calculations even for the immediate static effects, and no region has done them *ex ante*. In addition, the aggregate figures, whether for the world, for the excluded countries, or for the region, are not decisive; the effects on each country, often each interest within a country, must be considered.

As well as any internal controversies, analysis (excluding dynamic effects) cannot give a positive number for the rest of the world, so there will inevitably be potential opposition on purely trade grounds. This may be small if the region is small or the elasticities of substitution are small. Allowing for income effects which increase demand in the rest of the world can reduce any loss (while requiring more data), but then it is necessary to take a view on whether outsiders will treat their relative loss, gaining less than the members of a region, as a real loss.

Investment

The arguments here are the same as for trade, although the existence of choice between the two needs to be watched in using data on either to identify the potentials and effects of regions. If capital is mobile within a free trade area (the international regulations do not require this and it does not always hold in actual areas), opening the region will give greater freedom to choose the location of production, as well as increasing the potential returns to investment. As changes in technology have led to more advantages in breaking up processes, these increase the advantages of liberalizing, whether to regions or the world; on the other hand, reduction, in all countries, of standard barriers to investment has reduced the potential benefits of regions. From a market point of view, regions with purchasers similar to one's own country may be preferred, but to lower costs of production, countries with access to different raw materials or factors of production at lower cost may be an advantage. As with trade, benefits will increase with size, although at a decreasing rate. But the 'regions' which an analysis on the basis of above-average bilateral flows will identify for capital are very different from those for trade. Within developed countries, the EU will still prevail for most of its members, but with the next logical partners being the US and Japan, not other European countries. For developing countries, a cluster can be identified among the NICs and South-East Asian countries, but the US and Japan are also major partners, and the US would dominate Latin American bilateral flows. Thus, even for trade and investment, the apparently appropriate regions may differ. Whatever the group, as for transportation and trade, the composition and the necessary minimum size may change over time with new types or technologies of production.

Policy arguments

These are the convenient residual for economists: the problem, as Krugman (in de Melo and Panagariya, 1993) points out, is that there are

> no widely accepted positive models of policy formation. And the multilateral-regional debate hinges crucially on how the institutions of the trading system will affect not just the consequences of given trade policies but the choices by governments of what policies actually to adopt.

The general assumption behind the arguments that policy is the constraint on which regions can form, or for choosing regions rather than global agreements (or countries rather than either regional or global) is that political or institutional factors tend to give advantages to smallness or to limited groups. This is normally presented as a general argument, that decisions among nearer or fewer people are preferred because of more similar interests. Alternatively, it is assumed to be easier to reach agreements in 'small' groups, ignoring the evidence on trade-offs among large groups and instability in small groups. There is also an extensive political science literature on the types of cohesion which lead to possible or stable groups (see Zormelo, 1995 for a discussion of MERCOSUR in these terms). But there are some specifically economic, public sector, responsibilities with scale implications which an economics paper can at least enumerate.

Whose interests?

In analysis of trade policy it is frequently unclear whether we are looking at the advantages to individuals, as producers or consumers, or to countries. This becomes crucial when we are talking about the costs and benefits of transferring control from one level of government, which represents one group, with the normal qualifications about aggregating individual welfare functions, to a different level, representing a larger group. It is obvious that it is not sufficient to assign each country equal weight, or even to assume that the weights can be determined by relative size of population or income, without taking account of the differences and distributions within countries, although in fact this is what is normally done. It may, however, also be illegitimate simply to reaggregate across the new space, because there is a potential trade-off between a set of solutions which meet the tastes of several groups more closely and one which satisfies a collective group on average; this suggests a different rule for aggregation.

This is the problem of whether larger areas increase or reduce choice. The trade-off just identified is based on an assumption, frequently advanced as a non-economic reason for regions below the global level, that similarities of tastes, in the consumption sense, and perhaps also in terms of choices of appropriate economic, regulatory and political regimes, decline sharply with distance with no overlap between groups, so that aggregating over a larger group is likely to have a less satisfactory outcome than over a smaller. This seems to contradict the economic assumption that a larger level of production can permit more different tastes to be met because the diseconomies of small scale are avoided. It may be true that it is possible to offer two different car models from a total production of two million more cheaply than when production is only one million, but it is harder to offer two different intellectual property regimes in a larger area. Alternatively, however, it may be feasible to offer a more complex regulation, perhaps to justify more detail to suit different types of intellectual property. If 'common tastes' is not a simple concept, but rather a set of preferences varying among individuals, it cannot be known in advance whether regulations are like or different from car models.

If there must be a choice, are the potential trade and investment benefits greater than the cost of what may be considered less satisfactory policies? One case would be if people have an active preference for local decisions, even if those decisions have a cost. Models of extreme chauvinism implicitly assume this. For policy to be a problem implies that countries do not have only one objective, namely, to maximise economic income or that there are unresolvable uncertainties at any time about how to do so. It is these assumptions which mean that it is impossible to devise 'compensation' for policy differences.

A related question is that of the number of participants. If countries are assumed to be entirely similar within themselves, then fewer participants (if appropriately chosen), increase the advantages of similarity but a reduced number of countries reduces the range of trade-offs that may be available among the members. The balance between a reduced need for and a reduced availability of bargaining possibilities can lead to either a higher or a lower number of countries being 'easier' to deal with; the literature on this is only beginning to be applied to regions.

Countries which are more similar and also relatively advanced are less likely to change and therefore diverge in the future. This suggests that where the groups are diverse – in southern Africa or NAFTA, or the larger Asian groups which take in not simply ASEAN or Australia–New Zealand, but these plus the new NICs and South Asia – either there must be particularly strong common interests which offset economic diversity or they will not prove durable.

Is regulation seen as a benefit or a cost?

Is increased regulation at regional (or country or global) level seen by firms as an unnecessary cost, effectively a tax (the strong market approach), or as a necessary part of the infrastructure, as much worth paying for as good communications or water supply?

Both assumptions are used, implicitly or explicitly, in much regional analysis. Globalization of production and sales can be seen as carrying a risk that firms operating at international level can escape from national controls on the environment, competition policy, minimum product (or labour) standards, and perhaps also from taxation. Alternatively, firms may want a stable and universal regulatory environment, predictable access for trade and foreign investment; similar treatment of intellectual property and profits and remittances. One of the most conventional benefits cited in analyses of the role of the WTO and of the Uruguay Round outcome is the limits which they impose on unilateral changes in access to markets through tariff and non-tariff measures. Whether it is countries attempting to pursue escaping companies or companies attempting to find common standards abroad, the focus here is on regulating a process which is happening, not encouraging new access and static efficiency gains. If the regions are where above–average trade or investment growth has already occurred, then this could provide an explanation for them. They will feel the need for such new regulation, whether at the demand of firms or governments, sooner or more strongly. In other words, growing and concentrated trade leads to new organizations, rather than being the result, although clearly there may also be causation in both directions.

If the demand for regulation increases with trade, then this influence will work in parallel with the economic arguments developed above. It is only if there is strong and effective opposition to regulation that it would be an obstacle to regions.

It is difficult to know whether the assumption that firms are basically risk-avoiding good citizens, with the international ones too big to want to risk shady deals, or the alternative, that they are villainous, control-evading unregulated multinationals, is more likely to produce regional regulation. The former is likely to make it easier to introduce, because firms will not resist government efforts, but the latter is likely to make governments more likely to want it. Data suggest, however, that multinationals are taking a falling share of world trade, with small firms becoming more important, particularly in the new industries and in Asia, so their interests and governments' fears of them may be of decreasing relevance. Small firms may be more anxious to have common controls and regulations, not because they are necessarily more virtuous, but because they are more vulnerable to both large firms and government policy changes, their own and foreign. Large firms, in contrast, have more experience and expertise in dealing with international uncertainties, as well as perhaps more opportunity to find their own solutions. This could suggest an increased demand by the new firms entering trade for regional and global institutions. But concentration of such trade is greater in Asia (with weak regions) than in Latin or North America.

For many regulatory services, the arguments for public intervention are likely to suggest a necessary minimum scale, if only to reduce the costs per unit regulated. The greatly increased regulation at the world level, in the Uruguay Round settlement and in other international institutions (for transport safety and standards, telecommunications and other electronics standards, health, etc.), and the number of these issues now considered sufficiently 'trade-related' to fall under the WTO, strongly suggest 'the bigger the better' in setting common standards. Here, there are clear reasons for believing that the groups should be related to those for trade and investment. There is also the countervailing power argument. The larger are private interests, including economic interests, the greater is the need for powerful regulators, with a remit at least as broad as the private interests (multinationals require international regulation). There is a risk of regulatory capture if the regulatory agency is too small. For others, for example, regulation of natural monopolies, increasing the size of units can reduce some needs for regulation.

In principle, the setting of the price for the exchange rate falls under this heading. The large literature on optimum currency areas can probably be viewed as a case within this wider debate.

Traditional public services

Many public services are closely related to directly economic needs, not just in broad terms, but with more specific sectoral or production factor interests in the cases of social, educational, and health provision, etc., so that it seems plausible to expect some congruence between the groups. If there is a tendency for public services and trade to cluster together, with the same coverage, their appropriate scales and any changes in them will influence economic regionalism. The traditional view, with some empirical support from recent reorganizations within countries, is that economies of scale become increasingly important, so that the appropriate level moves up, although some larger countries see some reaction against this. The same characteristics which make such services 'public goods' – the external economies arising from universal provision – explain this. But as the size of the unit increases, the number 'near' boundaries, and therefore wanting the size to increase, will become a decreasing proportion of the total, so that there are diminishing returns to expanding.

Fiscal and monetary policy; taxation; redistribution; other macro-economic action

Again, the arguments for seeing these as appropriate ways and purposes for public provision are also arguments for increasing scale (the difficulties of 'small' countries in having independent policies). Redistribution in particular, like its economic analogues of variety and complementarity, will have its potential scope and benefits maximized at the largest feasible scale. But again, the inter-personal benefits may diminish if each individual's concerns for others are assumed to diminish with 'distance'.

How policy decisions can be divided

The arguments about appropriate size differ depending on whether one is building up, from spreading responsibilities, or scaling down, to find those groups which will operate efficiently. In the absence of any overriding international organization or rules, or of universally held views at the national level, there is no single answer to the question of appropriate size or appropriate composition, and no answer to the prior question of who should make the choice of level for decision-making. The system is inevitably one of bargaining, in which economic strength, political strength, alliances, and in many cases interest groups outside national governments will have a voice. Once one goes beyond either a purely individual country approach or a universal international one, any intermediate grouping or choice of level for decision-making is a compromise. This should not be surprising in view of the number of different ways in which individual countries choose to organise their own internal regions and decision-making. Many of the same questions have long been raised in this context, and remain open to debate there as well.

Within countries there are two ways of approaching the problem. What is sometimes confusingly called functional federalism (messy regionalism may be a less misleading term) implies finding the appropriate level and area of coverage for each service (based on a hypothesis of economic costs declining with scale while efficiency costs from sacrificing nearness or smallness rise), with differing, overlapping jurisdictions expected and accepted. More formal decentralization, in contrast, seeks the district (and other subdivision) levels which give the best balance across a range of public services, i.e. with nesting, but not overlap, of regions. In putting these choices into practice, it is also necessary to ask who makes them. A federal system assumes that decisions about the competence of the higher levels are made at the lower levels (districts about allocation to the centre; countries about allocation to the region); a centralized one assumes that decisions are allocated down.[3]

At the global level, responsibilities are separated into different organisations (WTO, ILO, IMF, etc.), but countries are (normally) members of only one region. The WTO has taken on increasing responsibilities in what are traditionally considered to be public services, such as intellectual property, regulating standards, rights of establishment, and publicly regulated services, like telecommunications or transport, while such non-trade interests are frequently the basis for nominally trade agreements.

Social and other conditions

It is necessary to have a combination of agreement on common political assumptions and sensitivity and responsiveness to the political and economic objectives of the partner countries. Members of a region must agree, at a minimum, on how much the international economic contacts among the member countries should be regulated. Over time, countries will need compatible views of how far the various domestic interventions which affect traded goods and services and other international transactions should be regulated, and on the forms which this regulation should take. Some agreement is needed on what types of economic or other interest group should be responded to at the regional level, and how this should be done. As with the economic conditions, policies cannot vary too greatly, or change at very different paces within a region if a group is to continue to meet the conditions. The importance of permanence implies the need for some belief that the other members of the group are following stable and compatible policies. At a minimum, countries must be able to assume that their partners will want to continue the policies, including liberalization, that are agreed in the region. The more extensive the coverage of the group, the more specific the conditions become, to include a common attitude to trade policy, to some types of industrial development policy in so far as they use trade policies, and to at least the institutions of macroeconomic policy, as these may impinge on trade. This can become very extended, and the literature on Europe has dealt extensively with what needs to be included on the macroeconomic, monetary, financial, and other elements.

The evolution of those organizations which have survived shows how 'deep' this integration can become, but also indicates how shallow it can be at the outset. Regional organizations need to allow formally only for the 'shallow' at the beginning, but especially with the example of more mature organizations before them, they cannot ignore the probable future evolution. It is possible, therefore, that, as with 'latecomers' in industrialization and trade, progress through the stages will be faster than for the early regionalizers. The existence of provisions for investment, dispute settlement, labour standards, and the environment from the beginning in NAFTA makes a sharp contrast with the early years of the European Community or the GATT/WTO. The expanded coverage of the WTO may in turn influence new regions. Countries which have already accepted global intervention on these subjects may be more ready to accept greater intervention at regional level. If, however, there are some questions on which national differences are so strong that regional groups are unlikely to be allowed to intervene, at least in the foreseeable future, the greater coverage of the WTO may have reduced the range within which progress can be made at the regional level in this area, as it has in tariffs and other economic barriers.

At a deeper level, members of regions require consistent views on what issues are important, how much to regulate and what are the appropriate institutions with which to regulate. These arise out of basic assumptions about how national systems should operate. Regions depend on trust that the same formal institutions will operate consistently across the member countries; this may in practice require some common background. How deep this commonality needs to be, and on what subjects, will depend on the nature of the group, and will change with the 'depth' of integration which it reaches, and, like the political and economic constituency, it may itself be strengthened by integration. Negotiations on some of the new issues in the WTO have revealed different attitudes very clearly, for example on how to regulate intellectual property and over what subjects, on environmental choices, and on labour issues.

The need for common approaches reinforces the policy argument that groups may be able to integrate sooner than at global level. On the other hand, if the existence of global links has a parallel effect of accelerating the process of creating the conditions for further global integration, it may reduce the scope for regionalization. The 'new issues' have spread rapidly from the regional groups to the international level (services from the EU, labour and the environment from NAFTA) and then from it to other regions and back to the original regions in a harmonized form.

Do political or social requirements imply a geographical condition? Political requirements seem unlikely to do so, as institutions have spread among countries because of past associations or example more than because of geography, although historical common backgrounds are found in some regions.

The extent of congruent interests, economic, political, and other, which are required grows with each new issue covered by a region, particularly with those which lie on the border with non-economic questions. It took many years for tariffs to be fully accepted as appropriate areas on which to give up some sovereignty in negotiation, effectively until the establishment of the GATT in 1948. Still, only a few of the regional groups have moved to a common external tariff, and fewer (effectively only the EU) to accepting a common negotiating position on this tariff in all international negotiations. Non-tariff barriers began their transition to universal acceptance as suitable for regulation in the late 1970s, but remain sensitive within all regional groups as well as the WTO. Tariffs and NTBs depend mainly on how governments (or regional or world institutions) weight different economic interests within their countries, and therefore on the economic conditions. But some NTBs, and many of the new areas (investment, labour, intellectual property, the environment, common standards) are affected not only by how countries weight some economic interests against others, but also on choices among non-economic interests. They therefore require a wide range of the conditions for cooperation. Because this makes them unlikely to be fully accepted soon at the global level, it is here that opportunities may exist for regions to move further. It is here also that some regional groups are showing the most progress, but also the most divergent performance relative to each other. As long as these remain largely outside the WTO, it is also here that the effects of regions on non-members are least regulated.

Macroeconomic stability may be a condition for regions. If countries suffer high instability or vulnerability to external or domestic shocks, then their trade flows may be erratic, and either the uncertainty or the measures they may take to counteract the instability can have an unforeseen effect on neighbouring countries. This has been a common theme in European discussions (and conditions) for integration.

For developing countries, the problem of different levels of development may be considered a subheading of stability. If the structure of the economy is to be transformed, this may require, or lead to, major changes in the direction of policy and in attitudes to trade or other policies. More practically, it may have significant effects on infrastructure which alter the economic geography, and therefore the plausible regional partners, of a country.

On a political level, regions clearly need commitment by the governments because of their official nature. This commitment can be reinforced by, and perhaps may depend on, commitment to the region on the part of economic decision-makers or the public more generally. The government's commitment requires countries to have confidence in their own and their partners' political stability. This suggests that governments must have stable authority within their countries at a practical level in order to be able to carry through regional commitments, but also to be able to have the confidence to give up some sovereignty to the region. Interest groups with common interests and cross-border contacts between unofficial groups, business, labour, social, or consumer, have a role in regions which needs to be examined.

The relative size of the countries will influence how alliances are formed and policy established among the members. The question to be asked is whether it is more stable to have a group led by a single hegemon, which can impose its policy on the others but which may create resentment; a mix of large and small countries, giving a possibility of shifting alliances; or a group of countries of approximately the same size, giving a competitive or democratic model. Both political and economic analyses contain arguments for seeing a more stable outcome from either the first or the last, but what we observe belongs entirely to the first or the second.

Security

Forming alliances for military purposes is not normally considered a form of regionalism, but the two are not entirely separate. If countries believe that regions bring economic gains, at a minimum they will be unwilling to include countries that are potential enemies. Countries with a strong level of fear or distrust are unlikely to have the necessary degree of confidence to sign any long-term agreement. The association, however, is closer. The argument that trading binds countries together and therefore increases security dates at least from Adam Smith's view that commerce promoted peace. A complementary argument was that discriminatory trade could create tensions (Schiff and Winters, 1997, p. 5). This motive can also can be used to explain initiatives by an outside country to encourage regions, even when it is not itself a prospective member.

Bargaining power

The difficulties of the Uruguay Round of trade negotiations encouraged regions not only as alternative approaches to lowering trade barriers and achieving the other aims of individual countries within the negotiations, but also because groups might be better able to secure their objectives within the Round. In addition, forming groups might act as a signal to other participants that the members had an alternative, and thus provide credibility to a threat to withdraw from the negotiations if they did not proceed satisfactorily. Bargaining power could also be a motive in bilateral negotiations. For small developing countries, it may be particularly important. On the other hand, perception of weakness may be a problem in joining a region. Countries must feel reasonably strong relative to their potential partners before they are willing to negotiate at the regional level. While they are still developing and changing their own political institutions, they may hesitate to enter regional organizations. The empirical evidence on this is contradictory, and the existence of countries of widely varying economic and political size makes it complicated. The European countries' initiative succeeded among countries that had all reached a high level of national political development, and the recent surge of Latin American groups followed the political reforms of the late 1980s. The entry of Mexico into an agreement with the US would have been almost inconceivable in earlier periods. Earlier Latin American initiatives failed. On the other hand, the apparently stable Asian countries have not formed strong regions.

It is probable that at least some of the regionalization activities of the last ten years have been the results of pre-Uruguay Round efforts to increase bargaining power. The European Community's initial impulse to the Single European Market exercise was in part explicitly an attempt to increase its economic power, as well as its competitiveness, against the larger industrial countries, the US and Japan. NAFTA, it has been argued, was in part the response of the US to the SEM, in part a result of loss of patience with the GATT, and in part a warning to other countries negotiating within the Uruguay Round. The sequence continues, with MERCOSUR perhaps a counterweight to NAFTA, and the EU forming links with both Mexico and MERCOSUR as balances to NAFTA, while some Asian groups appear to have little content other than fear of being left off the regional bandwagon. Similar sequences can be seen in groups formed around sectors within and related to the Uruguay Round (notably agriculture and clothing, but also on shipping and intellectual property).

Merging is one possible outcome: for example, the EU's takeover of EFTA, founded explicitly as an alternative and SADC's (*sic*) admission of its original opponent, South Africa. Successful completion of the Round and more realistic views of the potential effects from the regions originally seen as threats may reduce the pressures for this type of counterweight region. As both economic and political power increase with size, such bargaining regions presumably have an interest in being as big as possible.

It seems possible that the present combination of publicity for the WTO and the number of new regions has provoked a terminological effect. Countries wishing to sign friendly agreements with each other appear to be choosing to call these 'free trade agreements' where in other periods they might have been called cooperation, defence, energy-sharing or cultural agreements. This is in part fashion, in part the result of the Uruguay Round assumption that all regional agreements are primarily trade agreements, with regulation of them based on the criterion of a free trade target. This makes a nominal free trade target seem mandatory.

In some cases, as noted above, there are also special interests in acquiring international recognition: Mexico seeking recognition as developed and creditworthy, by joining the OECD as well as NAFTA; South Africa as developing and aid-worthy by joining the EU's Lomé area as well as SADC; Australia and New Zealand as Asian (in APEC) rather than displaced European; the ex-centrally planned as European. In the case of these regional-as-label groups, there may be an interest in restricting rather than expanding membership, and therefore an offset to the other forces for size.

Forming regions for the purpose of increasing bargaining strength reveals a clear difference in possible motives between a regional and a multilateral approach. This motive is more important for smaller countries. These also, however, are those with a higher participation in international trade and investment flows. If bargaining power is only for the purpose of altering other countries' tariffs, it would apply fully only to countries in a customs union, and thus to only one of the new regions, MERCOSUR.

A different type of outside influence can be identified. Good economic performance and growing markets or political and military security or peace are desirable not only for countries themselves, but frequently for their trading partners or allies. Therefore, countries which are vulnerable to pressure from stronger countries may find themselves encouraged to form a region because the outside countries consider a region to be a useful instrument. Lack of bargaining power may therefore mean that countries are encouraged into regions.

The *Acquis*

Much of the discussion so far has been based on the implicit assumption that we are seeking to understand the initial formation of a region. Alternatively, we can ask whether the present organisation should change, and whether a move towards regions will help or hinder a move to the 'final' stage at multinational level. Here, the question of whether we are looking at the interests of countries or of individuals potentially regrouped into different interest groups in the alternative becomes important. If the region is long-lasting, the fact of having been grouped together may itself have created common interests, if only some common types of experience and relationships which may work against the advantages of changing to a new organization.

Those who are within an existing region, like those in a country, will have developed both formal and informal institutions with which they are familiar. Standards will have been set for those subjects and in those manners which are most suitable for the present members. Mild preferences for certain choices will have become more strongly established as adaptations are made. These include economic legislation and regulation, industrial and other organizations, customs concerning how certain types of business are done, relationships between the economic system and training, education, and the political system: broadly speaking an acculturation to a particular system. Within the EU, the whole system of how these have developed and now exist is called the *acquis*, and it is well recognized that for each new member joining is potentially more difficult than it was for earlier members because this *acquis* is constantly increasing. For countries which normally have longer histories and more responsibilities, the *acquis* is likely to be greater, and so the difficulties of amalgamating regions into a world system might seem less than of forming a region from individual countries in the first place. However, the nature of the bargaining process within regions and the attachment to compromises negotiated with difficulty (and recently) may militate against this.

Trade creation and trade diversion

The basic analysis of the effect of regional groups on their members and the rest of the world dates from Viner (1950). By liberalizing trade among themselves, countries are able to substitute for home production by importing goods produced at lower cost in other members. This increases both production and consumption and creates trade. Income is increased by the availability of the lower cost goods, and production is shifted from the less to the more efficient location. If, however, one country previously imported from a non-member country, but the removal of tariffs on imports from fellow-members means that imports from them are now cheaper to the purchaser, then trade will be diverted from the more efficient outside producer to the less efficient one within the group. The country loses: although there is a consumption gain from the cheaper imports, it does not receive the tariff revenue, while production is shifted from a more efficient to a less efficient location. Clearly, analogous arguments can be used for other economic linkages and barriers. The possible cost of diversion because of the effective increase in protection against the rest of the world is what make liberalization within a region likely to be damaging to the rest of the world (unless efficiency or growth effects outweigh the cost) and even potentially damaging to its members, unlike multilateral liberalization.

Trade diversion unambiguously damages countries not in the region, and this is an important reason for international concern and justification for international regulation to limit the diversion effects or compensate for them (see Chapter 5). Trade creation does not directly affect those outside, but the income effect can be positive, if some of the demand goes to goods produced outside the region. If the increase in income and efficiency in turn has dynamic effects, this effect is reinforced.

Particularly since the analyses of the effects of the Single European Market in the mid-1980s, this effect has also, confusingly, been called trade creation, although here it will be called trade generation.

Work on calculations of trade diversion and creation has gone in two directions, theoretical considerations of the conditions required for different results and actual empirical studies of changes in trade flows after a region has formed. Neither is wholly satisfactory, because of the large number of assumptions which must be made. In two recent studies, Laird (1997) and Schiff (1996) present virtually opposite summaries of the conditions for a group to be welfare-enhancing (and this is before considering how the increase in welfare is distributed). Laird (p. 5) argues (these are the conventional results) that

> welfare gains will be greater
> > the higher the trade barriers being reduced;
> > the higher the share of pre-existing trade between the partners;
> > the larger the partner countries;
> > the more diversified the partner countries' economies; and
> > the more closely the partners' domestic prices resemble world prices.

Schiff, after accepting that for exports the benefit is larger the larger the trade and the higher the existing trade barriers (p. 4), looks at the import side and finds that a country within a region benefits 'if it imports less from its partner countries', but it gains more from a union with a large country. The Laird conclusions are logical as the size of the trade barriers clearly has a scale effect, although it could operate to increase a loss as well. Schiff's conclusions do not look at export effects, but concentrate on the loss of tariff revenue and the costs of diversion. (They also suggest that, if all countries believe them, it will be difficult to find partners.) Laird points out that 'trade creation outweighs trade diversion in products where the import demand elasticity is high relative to the elasticity of substitution between different sources of supply' (p. 5). This suggests that manufactures, and perhaps services, are more likely to show trade creation, while primary products may show more diversion.

The problem with theoretical speculation is the wide range of possible assumptions about elasticities, about whether goods are produced at home, in the region or outside it, and on what scale, and the wide variation in tariffs and other taxes. It is not possible to be sure that low pre-region trade will be low post-formation, or that products which do not appear to be traded pre-region will remain untraded when (possibly

high) tariffs are removed. The higher the initial tariffs, the more necessary it may be to study not just trade flows, but domestic production
and prices. If agriculture, for example, is highly protected, there may
appear to be low primary trade, and hence low risk of diversion (on the
Laird argument), but reducing regional tariffs could markedly change
this. The size of very small partner countries may be a constraint, but
again it must be remembered that for both elasticities and welfare distribution calculations it is individual products and suppliers that matter;
even in a large country small producers may predominate.

Whether the creation or diversion effects will be more important for
the members of a region requires empirical analysis. It will depend on
the similarity and competitiveness of the members' economies and may
also depend on their size. Similarly, trade diversion and trade generation effects can be compared for those excluded. Here, it is important to
remember that each of the excluded countries must be considered separately, as it is not possible to assume that whatever transfers or other
compensations occur will produce a similar net effect for all.

The analysis of creation and diversion can be extended to other factors of production. Investment will be created or diverted into the region
to meet the new production demanded by the changes in trade flows.
Labour may follow a similar pattern. The effects of the other non-trade
elements on non-members will eventually appear in trade effects (for
example, outsiders disadvantaged by regional standards or intellectual
property rules). It is even possible to extend it to policy-making: members may be more interested in improving trade flows within the region
as these are a high share of their total trade, and this will increase if the
share increases. An interesting extension is to diversion of attention:
that joining a group 'tends to reduce the incentive to take a world view'
(Winters, 1993, p. 7). The simplest form of this is that countries may
not have the negotiating capacity to negotiate a regional and a multilateral agreement simultaneously. The stronger view is that this affects the
strategy of trade, but, as with trade creation and diversion, it must be
balanced against the possibility that regions may be an alternative to a
country view (strategy expansion) rather than an alternative to the
world (or other countries: strategy diversion). There may be declining
rates of return to policy-making as the intra-regional barriers become
smaller relative to the external.

If a group is formed with more structural motives for integration, and
if it is successful in implementing these, the effects on outsiders would
need to be analysed much more in the traditional terms of the effects of
development on trading partners, rather than concentrating on trade

(or other) diversion effects. In broad terms, the effects to be looked for would be faster growth and a changed composition of trade, rather than 'diversion' in the traditional sense. Some of the macro effects of investment diversion in response to faster growth might hold. If other countries also have growth or composition of output objectives, the effects on these rather than the simple diversion effects would also need to be examined.

This analysis holds where countries do not raise their actual barriers against the rest of the world; they merely do not lower them as they do for the other members of the group. An alternative strand of analysis asks whether the group is more likely to raise barriers than an individual country (or a larger group more likely than a smaller). For example, an argument for gains from setting the optimum tariff, the level which maximizes a country's income from terms-of-trade gain, suggests that a larger group will be more likely to raise this. This type of argument will not be discussed in detail here partly because multilateral regulation (for tariffs, binding under the WTO) has made clearly identifiable cases of this type increasingly rare, but also because there is little evidence that countries do follow optimum tariff policies. A related argument arises from the fact that it is easier to take protective action in response to any interests which consider themselves damaged against countries outside the region. Within the region, institutional constraints or greater sympathy for the interests of fellow members may prevent action. Either policy effect is likely to be negative for outsiders (unless also constrained by international policy).

A weaker argument would be that regions are less likely to liberalize; this would also be true of large countries relative to small. It could hold if optimum tariff considerations determine policy. But if larger countries or regions are less affected by the economic advantages and costs of trade, they may take a weaker bargaining approach to trade (or be prepared to make trade concessions for other purposes) or they may take less interest in any negotiations. These bargaining questions are indeterminate, and need specific analysis.

Implications of the arguments

These arguments suggest that regions can have a variety of explanations (and results), using different approaches: geographic, economic, political, and cultural. Clearly, different influences can operate at different times in a region's history and most of the explanations involve influences that can change over time. This is consistent with the observation that neither countries nor regions have ever been permanent. Hurrell (in Fawcett and Hurrell, 1995, p. 73) suggests a 'phased or "stage theory" to understanding regionalism', although even here it is necessary to ask whether the stages will be similar for all groups. A central question to be asked is whether any of the types of explanation seem to have priority, whether temporal or in ranking; are groups normally first political, or first economic?

A problem with most of the factors discussed here is that it is difficult to see any durable reason for preferring regions to a world approach. This is particularly true of the trade motivations, but also of the other economic and some of the non-economic. The explanations could hold at least as strongly at a world level. This suggests that regions may form out of a deep common interest, whether permanent or at a particular period, and have trade or other economic cooperation as an auxiliary benefit, not the fundamental motive. Where the interest is a long-term one, and the region survives for decades, other links follow, including trade and other economic cooperation, and continue to evolve, as they do within a country. Where the interests were weaker or transient, and the countries have developed differently, regional organizations have faded. Chapter 4 will examine some ways of classifying, if not quantifying, such an interest, but any reasoning is largely circular (as it is for a sense of 'national'): if a region survives is the only test.

These rather negative results for a general answer on what regions are and what they are intended to be suggest that the approach to analysing their likely permanence and effects must look also at the intentions of those who form them, in order to identify and describe, if not analyse, the common interest. The importance of not being broken up by a change of objectives also suggests the importance of history, and the evolution of their economies and policies. It is important that the forces remain favourable for some period.

The analysis from the conventional economic point of view of trade or investment liberalization is basically that of moving to parity with the national level by removing barriers which do not exist within countries. But the act of forming an institutionalized region (in contrast to an agreement for simultaneous tariff reduction) goes beyond this, to establishing at least some of the policy interventions and regulations which exist at the national level, but not normally at the international level. This means that any explanation of why regions form must go beyond the simple economic advantages of trade or investment liberalization.

If a region is seen as a continuing and evolving institution, and if among its effects are changes in industrial structure, then, particularly for a developing country region, its long-term effects on the countries within and outside the region are necessarily unpredictable. Singer (IDB, UN ECLAC, 1995) argues that a trading agreement for the American continent 'will be a far greater change in economic trading relations than theories and economic models are able to deal with' (p. 109). This implies that any group must be at least in part an act of faith, of confidence that the common interests, whether economic or political, of the members will remain strong. This again suggests that some other deeper integration is at work. Analysis of regions tends to treat deep integration as a result of the removal of barriers and then the establishment of common institutions, as an economic region goes beyond simple trade relationships. But this analysis suggests that some implicit deep integration must precede the formal integration. This suggests that there is a process by which the past decisions and existence of a region generate new forces of cohesion, a more biological, less mechanical analogy. If there are a variety of explanations, how do these interact in the interests of countries to produce the decision to form a region, to join one, or to stay out? Are there single or repeated calculations of gains and losses, producing one-off, or changing, decisions? Or can strategic choices be traced?

Notes

1 One exception was the compensation to food-importing countries for higher prices in the Uruguay Round settlement. This, however, provided only for the principle; the WTO had no funds or provision for obtaining them. It had only symbolic value, suggesting that the countries affected did see other advantages from the settlement.
2 Cooper (Garnaut and Drysdale, 1994, p. 18) notes that 'there is no such thing' as an optimal region. 'Optimality calls for a much more complex array of jurisdictions, compromising between the desire for greater decentralisation and the technical need for greater centralisation.'
3 The EU sometimes seems to confuse a criterion for decision, 'subsidiarity', namely, that decisions be made at the lowest practical level, with the institutional question of who makes the decision about which is this level.

3
A Brief History of the Regions

The regions chosen for this study, according to the criterion specified in Chapter 1, are, in Europe: the European Union; in North and South America: NAFTA, MERCOSUR, the Andean Group, the Group of Three, CACM, CARICOM, and the FTAA (and the Latin American Integration Agreement); in Africa: SADC, SACU, and AEC; in Asia: ASEAN, SAARC, ANZCERTA, and APEC (see Table 3.1).

APEC, FTAA, and the AEC are included, although they do not yet have any contractual arrangements, because of their potential importance if there is a move to a regional structure for the whole of world trade. All have targets of free trade, and the FTAA has working groups to prepare an agreement. They are also important in their implications for the existing regions, as they would include as subdivisions all the others (except the EU and SAARC). SADC is also a prospective, but not actual, region for trade. It does have economic cooperation in non-trade projects, including infrastructure projects, and has begun to negotiate trade arrangements. The LAIA is included because it still imposes formal legal obligations on how its members can form regions within it or with others.

The regions in the Middle East and North Africa are excluded partly because of lack of information, but also because of their limited liberalization and trade flows. There are groupings in western and eastern Africa, but the trade arrangements for these have not progressed far enough to be effective. COMESA, the Common Market for Eastern and Southern Africa, is excluded because its future is very unclear; several members are leaving, and the remaining members are turning more to SADC for trade policy. There are arrangements among some of the East European countries, but these are clearly in transition to EU membership, not permanent groups.

Table 3.1   Membership of regional groups included

EU	European Union. Belgium, Denmark, France, Germany,Greece, Ireland, Italy, Luxembourg, Netherlands, Portugal, Spain, United Kingdom (EU 12); Austria, Finland, Sweden from 1995 (EU 15)
NAFTA	North Atlantic Free Trade Area. Canada, Mexico,United States
MERCOSUR	Southern Cone Common Market. Argentina, Brazil,Paraguay, Uruguay (MERCOSUR 4); Bolivia, Chile from1997 (MERCOSUR 6)
Andean Group	Andean Common Market. Bolivia, Colombia, Ecuador, Peru, Venezuela
Group of Three	Colombia, Mexico, Venezuela
CACM	Central American Common Market. Costa Rica, El Salvador, Guatemala, Honduras, Nicaragua
CARICOM	Caribbean Community. Antigua and Barbuda, Bahamas, Barbados, Belize, San Cristobal, Dominica, Grenada, Guyana, Jamaica, Montserrat, St Kitts and Nevis, St Lucia, St Vincent and the Grenadines, Trinidad and Tobago
LAIA	Latin America Integration Agreement. Latin America
FTAA	Free Trade Area of the Americas. All Western Hemisphere except Cuba
SADC	Southern African Development Community. Angola, Botswana, Lesotho, Malawi, Mauritius, Mozambique, Namibia, South Africa, Swaziland, Tanzania, Zambia, Zimbabwe; Congo and Seychelles from 1997 (not included in data)
SACU	Southern African Customs Union. Botswana, Lesotho, Namibia, South Africa, Swaziland
AEC	African Economic Community. All Africa
ASEAN	AFTA: ASEAN Free Trade Arrangement. Brunei, Indonesia, Malaysia, Philippines, Singapore, Thailand, Vietnam from 1995 (not included in data), Myanmar and Laos from 1997 (not included in data)
ANZCERTA	Australia – New Zealand Closer Economic Relations Trade Agreement. Australia, New Zealand
SAARC	South Asian Association for Regional Cooperation. Bangladesh, Bhutan, India, Maldives, Nepal, Pakistan, Sri Lanka
APEC	Asia Pacific Economic Cooperation. ASEAN members,NAFTA members, ANZCERTA members, Chile, China,Hong Kong, Taiwan, Japan, South Korea; Russia, Vietnam and Peru from 1997 (not included in data)

This structure may seem very restricted compared with some analyses which attempt to show the wide range and complexity of arrangements by listing every bilateral trading arrangement. Some of these will be discussed in Chapter 11 on the relations of the regions and their members with the rest of the world, but most of the others are either not effective (the Indian Ocean or Black Sea arrangements, for example) or fall into the category of simple one-off agreements, not continuing arrangements (Chile–Canada, and many of the other Latin American bilateral agreements), often intended as transitions to other groups. There are also the preferential arrangements between developed and developing countries, and successors to these in EU and US 'free trade' relationships with some of the Mediterranean countries and Israel. Most of the preferential ones are not contractual, and the exception, the Lomé agreement between the EU and the ACP states which includes some of Europe's ex-colonies, is not seen as permanent; it expires in 2000 (or at latest 2005). It may be replaced by regions; this is discussed in the context of relations with the rest of the world. The line is necessarily arbitrary, because some of those excluded may evolve into regions, and some which are included may disappear.

Two of the regions include only developed countries: the EU and ANZCERTA. The EU must be included because it is the implicit model (or counter-model) for many of the other regions, and it and SACU are the only current regions with a long history (other arrangements which have lasted have become countries, for example Germany and Italy). ANZCERTA will be discussed only briefly, but provides an example of a small developed-country region, nearer in size than the EU to the developing country regions. It is also part of APEC.

This chapter will consider the history of these regions, including the declared motives at the time of their founding or major developments. It is summarized in Table 3.2. The order of integration of the regions (used in most of the summary tables) is defined by their degree of reduction in trade barriers, as analysed in Chapter 6.

Previous regions

Customs unions date from the nineteenth century, the first period in which countries themselves had become single markets, and therefore able to negotiate trading arrangements (Irwin in de Melo and Panagariya, 1993, p. 92). SACU, which began among British colonies, dates from this period. After the period of protection of the 1930s, when countries either retreated within their borders or developed relations with their colonies, the formation of the GATT in 1948 brought an emphasis on multilateral, rather than regional, arrangements. The

Table 3.2 Summary of history of regions

	EU	SACU	MERC-OSUR	CARI-COM	Andean	CACM	NAFTA	G3	ANZC	ASEAN	SAARC	SADC	LAIA	FTAA	APEC	AEC Score
	1956	1910	1991	1968/73	1967/85	1960/90	1994	1995	1965/88	1977/92	1992	1980/92	1960	2005	1989	
FTA	yes	yes	yes	partial	partial	yes	yes	yes	yes	target	no	no	no	no	no	
CU	yes	yes	yes	partial	partial	target	no	no	no	no	no	no	no	no	no	
Capacity to change																
coverage	yes	no	yes	yes	yes	no	no	no	yes	yes	no	yes	no	?	no	
members	yes	no	yes	yes	partial	yes	?	no	no	yes	no	yes	no	?	yes	
Motives	11	7	8	8	6	6	5	2	5	8	5	10	5	5	7	
Trade access	yes	yes	yes	yes	yes	yes	yes	no	yes	yes	yes	yes	no	yes	no	13
Investment access	yes	yes	yes	no	no	yes	yes	no	no	no	no	yes	no	yes	no	6
Dvlpt, industrialization	no	no	no	yes	yes	no	no	no	no	no	no	yes	yes	no	no	4
Economic restructuring	yes	no	yes	no	no	no	no	no	no	no	no	no	no	no	yes	4
Sectoral planning	yes	no	yes	yes	yes	no	no	no	no	no	no	yes	no	no	no	5
No other possible regions	yes	yes	no	no	no	yes	no	no	yes	yes	yes	yes	yes	no	no	7
Recent history of war	yes	no	yes	no	yes	yes	no	no	no	yes	yes	yes	yes	no	no	10
Reaction to others	no	no	no	no	no	no	yes	yes	no	yes	no	no	yes	yes	yes	7
Bargaining power	yes	no	no	yes	no	no	no	yes	yes	no	?	no	no	yes	yes	6
Military, security	yes	yes	yes	no	no	yes	no	no	no	yes	no	yes	no	no	no	7
Political cohesion	yes	yes	yes	yes	yes	yes	no	no	yes	yes	yes	yes	no	yes	no	13
Outside encouragement	by US	no	after EU	EU	after EU	after EU	no	no	no	no	no	no	opp. by US	no	no	5
History of political cooperation	no	yes	no	yes	no	no	no	no	yes	yes	no	yes	no	no	no	5
History of economic cooperation	yes	yes	no	yes	no	no	yes	no	no	yes	yes	yes	no	no	yes	8

colonial arrangements continued to exist, however, as did SACU (see below).

The EU

The European Coal and Steel Community was formed in 1951, but had several precedents. From 1948, the US Marshall Plan had encouraged countries which received assistance in 'cooperating with other participating countries in facilitating and stimulating an increasing interchange of goods and services among the participating countries and with other countries and cooperating to reduce barriers to trade among themselves and with other countries' (quoted in Viner, 1950, p. 132). The smaller countries, Belgium, the Netherlands and Luxembourg had a customs union from 1948, Benelux. The ECSC was intended not only to revive the coal and steel industries, but to link them across Europe in order to make war 'not only unthinkable, but materially impossible' (Winters, *World Economy*, 1997 p. 891). In 1957 the six members, Benelux, France, West Germany and Italy, joined to form a common market. Thus from the beginning they had the target of not only eliminating barriers but having a common trade policy *vis-à-vis* the rest of the world, and internal measures (as they already had with joint regulation of the coal and steel industries). It was also explicitly stated by the founding negotiators that preventing war between France and Germany, after the two world wars of the twentieth century, was the overriding objective.

During the next 40 years, the European Community increased in size, admitting Ireland, Denmark, and the UK in 1972, then Spain, Portugal, and Greece in the 1980s, and finally from 1995 Austria, Sweden, and Finland. Six more countries (Cyprus and five from eastern Europe) are formally expected to become members, and others are informally on the agenda. Here also the ending of war or the threat of war remains an explicit motive. For the southern European members and the Eastern prospective members, encouraging and preserving democracy were also motives, and explicit conditions for membership. After completing the common market in goods, the EU has extended it to services, capital and labour movements, and other types of regulation. It introduced exchange-rate coordination in the 1970s, and after progressively increasing this, is now moving towards monetary union. There are no provisions for withdrawal. The EU is thus following in the steps of the customs unions of the nineteenth century in Germany and Italy which moved from coordination of trade policy to deeper integration.

North and South America

Latin America has offered the most examples of regional groups (and more *ad hoc* cooperation agreements), while the US, until the 1980s, remained ostensibly opposed to them.

Influencing all the Latin American regions is the fact that a continental body for coordinating international economic policy has existed since 1960. The Latin American Free Trade Area (LAFTA) (which never actually became one) was established shortly after the first stage of European regionalism. It was intended to promote industrialization, by providing larger markets, but did not lead to liberalization on a continental basis. It came at a time when the major countries were pursuing industrial strategies which required managing their imports, including those from other Latin American countries. It was opposed by the US, which wanted its own arrangements with Latin America, and disliked its protectionist stance (Ffrench-Davis, in Teunissen 1995, p. 93). LAFTA was succeeded in 1980 by the Latin American Integration Agreement (LAIA) (or ALADI in Spanish). While not itself a trade group, it requires all arrangements among its members to be notified to it and to conform to certain rules. Of the groups examined here, CARICOM is not within the LAIA area, the Andean Group predates its rules, and NAFTA required Mexico to obtain a waiver because it was signing an agreement with two non-members without offering equal access to the Latin American countries. All the others are formally subgroups within LAIA. Most of the members of the groups already had agreements on a bilateral basis not only with each other but with other Latin American countries. Forming regions required them to renegotiate those with non-members on a regional basis, so that LAIA has meant significant opening in parallel with regions. By 1994, when MERCOSUR and NAFTA came into effect, there were 20 trade agreements under LAIA, but only four covered all goods: the Argentina–Brazil agreement which became the nucleus of MERCOSUR, and Chile's agreements with Mexico, Venezuela, and Colombia (UN ECLAC, 1994, p. 3). LAIA had standard rules of origin (including special sectoral provisions), model safeguard clauses, and rules for admitting new members (other Latin American countries cannot be excluded if they apply), but only some of the agreements under it have used these (ibid, p. 10).

The 1980s saw not only the economic groups discussed here, but other alliances among Latin American countries, particularly those arising out of the debt crisis. These brought sub-regional collaboration in the Central American, Contadora, and Cartagena groups, and then regional collaboration in the Rio group (Bouzas, 1995). All the Latin American and Caribbean countries except Cuba are members of at least one of the organizations described below.

Central American Common Market

Like LAFTA, the CACM was founded in 1960, but it was preceded by the Organization of Central American States, created in 1951 (Caballeros, 1992, p. 125). In spite of its name, it remains a preferential trade area, although with a target of a customs union (originally, the target date was 1966, OAS Compendium 1996). It has had a history of other types of link, including in debt and peace negotiations and regional payments. One member, Honduras, has left. During the 1980s, both the institutional structure and intra-regional trade declined sharply. The decision to revive it came in 1990, and Honduras was readmitted in 1992, with an FTA then targeted for 1993. The objective is economic union.

Andean Group

The next oldest of the existing Latin American groups is the Andean Pact, which dates from 1967. This puts it in the period of LAFTA, and it had an even stronger import substitution and industrial planning basis. Its membership has been modified over the years, with Venezuela joining in 1973 and Chile leaving in 1976, while Bolivia, Colombia, Ecuador and Peru have remained members. As well as the changing membership, different members have accepted different obligations.

In its original form, it provided centralized planning of the location of industry, and common rules on foreign investment and repayments. The objective was a customs union and harmonized economic and social policies (OAS, Compendium, 1996). These arrangements functioned for a few industries, but broke down in the 1970s. Chile left because it opposed government planning of economic policy. The Group was originally founded for 20 years, with a notice period of five years for withdrawal, but this has not been observed. It was revived in 1987. The old restrictive provisions, notably on foreign investment, were modified. It again adopted, in 1991, the goal of a common external tariff, and by 1994 it had achieved this although with exclusions. Effectively this was confined to Colombia, Venezuela, Ecuador and Bolivia. Colombia and Venezuela moved further, beginning in 1990 (see Chapter 6). In 1996, Bolivia formally joined MERCOSUR. Peru did not join in any of the tariff arrangements, but arranged bilateral agreements with the others. It considered leaving in 1997, but eventually remained a member, at least in part because of the trade concessions granted to the group by the US and the EU, a particularly clear case of outside intervention strengthening a region.

The Group of Three

The Group of Three is an interesting offshoot of the Andean Pact, with its two most integrated members joining with Mexico. The three had come together as a group in the Contadora group, which also included Panama, established by Central America's neighbours to work for and maintain peace in Central America (Vega Canovas, 1993). Although the Central American countries are not members, the Group gives Mexico some access to them, because of their joint agreements with Colombia. For Mexico, negotiating the agreement at the same time as NAFTA gave it a counterbalance to the US through access to South America. For Colombia and Venezuela, it provided an alliance with another middle-income country, in contrast to their existing partners in the Andean Pact (ibid.). The agreement came into force in 1995. It was intended only as a free trade area but it also included some health rules, standards, services, and other matters, thus going beyond the standard trade agreement. It has a very short notice period for withdrawal: six months (Echavarría in Lipsey and Meller, 1996, p. 145).

CARICOM

Three Caribbean countries came together in 1965, followed by the Eastern Caribbean Common Market in 1968, and CARICOM with the whole of the anglophone Caribbean in 1973. Integration thus dates virtually from independence, and the assumption throughout has been that common action is inevitable. Although not part of Latin America, CARICOM also had economic coordination and import substitution as its objectives. It made little progress during the 1980s, and was revived in 1989. It has had free trade among its members, and after first proposing a CET in 1991, by 1995 it had established it (UN ECLAC, 1995, Integration, p. 15). This was to be brought into effect in stages in 1993, 1995, 1997, and 1998, but still excluded agricultural products. Exchange-rate coordination remains only a goal, but integration has gone far in a variety of social and welfare arrangements, discussed in Chapter 10. Discussions are in train with other Caribbean countries, helping to establish the Association of Caribbean States, and with CACM, Panama,

Colombia, Venezuela, and Mexico, and possibly Peru. All the CARICOM members are also members of the EU's Lomé Convention. This expires in 2000, and the EU has proposed replacing it with regional agreements (see Chapter 11). One of these would be with CARICOM.

MERCOSUR

MERCOSUR dates from a declaration of intent between Argentina and Brazil in 1985, followed by a series of protocols in 1986–9 (Zormelo, 1995, p. 5). But even before that, Argentina had proposed a customs union with Brazil in 1939–41 (Bernal, *Trade Blocs*, 1997, pp. 27–8). The 1989 treaty had the target of a common market by 1995. This has now been put back to 2001. The two countries had a history of distrust and preparation for war (although no recent conflicts), but had acquired common interests in the 1980s as they returned to democracy and suffered from heavy foreign debts (Hirst 1992, pp. 141–2). The agreement was seen as a way of defusing regional tension as each country tried to integrate itself into the international economy. Although intra-regional trade was low (see Chapter 7), both countries were liberalizing trade and restructuring their economies. Argentina wanted to reduce its dependence on primary exports (ibid., p. 143). MERCOSUR therefore came at a time when they were changing development strategies; it was not seen as an institutionalization of pre-existing trends. Brazil also needed to reduce the distrust caused by its nuclear advances (ibid, p. 142), and a nuclear agreement was part of the cooperation (Schiff and Winters, 1997, p. 6). This group was therefore formed in a very different context from the other groups, which rose out of traditional trading and other relationships or from the industrial planning objectives of the 1960s. While increasing trade and some sectoral objectives were important, and there were significant changes in trade and other economic policies, it was very much led by political decisions, more specifically by the presidents and foreign ministries, not by economic interests. Economic policies remained very different; Brazil had an industrial strategy, promoting particular industries (notably cars in the context of MERCOSUR), while Argentina had had a more open approach since the 1970s.

In 1991, the Argentine–Brazilian agreement was extended to Paraguay and Uruguay, with the Treaty of Asunción; this is formally permanent. Uruguay had little alternative to joining with its two neighbours. Paraguay saw possible problems from being the least developed member, and suffering from imports from the two principal members (Breuer in Lipsey and Meller, 1996, p. 233), but nevertheless chose to join. The four had cooperated with Bolivia on developing their rivers and other infrastructure, but they deliberately excluded Bolivia and all other new members apart from Chile for five years, with a rule, technically contrary to the LAIA, that members of other trading groups were not allowed to join Brazil, however, proposed from 1993 a possible link with the Andean Group (Oman, 1994, p. 123). With the expiry of the five years, Bolivia joined in 1997. Chile has signed a free trade agreement with MERCOSUR, and also joined in some of its working groups and joint initiatives, but it is not formally a member because it did not want to raise its tariff to the planned CET of MERCOSUR. Bolivia's location and trading interests are as tied to MERCOSUR as to the Andean, and its infrastructure is probably more closely related. Chile's declared interests, however, were entirely in market opening. Both countries also have a history of armed conflict with the existing members, as recently as the 1970s.

The 1997 summit brought major steps toward greater integration. A target date for liberalizing services was finally agreed, a common anti-dumping policy was planned, and there were the first discussions of the possibility of transfer payments from the richer countries to the poorer. Chile was given observer status in the institutions, although still without a vote. In contrast, the summit saw little further progress toward broadening associate membership to other Andean Pact countries or to Mexico. Chile now no longer rules out full membership (van Klaveren, 1997), and has sought MERCOSUR support in trade disputes with the US outside current MERCOSUR obligations.

MERCOSUR was not designed to promote internal intervention, on the Andean Pact model, but did include three sectoral exceptions: cars, to protect Brazil's planning; and sugar and wheat, to protect Argentina's agriculture. The treaty did, however, exclude the use of safeguard clauses (except for the years up to 1994), so limiting future protection. Of the Latin American groups, only the Group of Three has safeguard clauses (Echavarría in Lipsey and Meller, 1996, p. 150). Both Argentina and Brazil, however, have found ways of taking temporary measures (see Chapter 6).

NAFTA

The US and Canada had had free trade in cars since 1965, and signed a full free trade agreement in goods in 1988. The US had had special arrangements with Mexico for processing goods on the border (*Maquiladora*) since 1966, and Mexico had had access for most of its exports to the US and Canada under their respective Generalised System of Preferences (GSP) arrangements. The initial proposal by the US was for an agreement with Mexico in parallel to that with Canada, but Canada then associated itself, and NAFTA was signed in 1992, to come into effect in 1994. In 1993, with the new US presidency, 'side agreements' on labour and the environment were added. NAFTA included staged liberalization of trade in goods, in four stages in 1994, 1998, 2003 and 2008. It also included investment provisions, and public procurement, although it did not cover services. There was strong government support in both Mexico and the US for NAFTA, but the explicit arguments for it were based on trade and investment gains. Only NAFTA, of all the American agreements, was subjected to any form of pre-signing calculation of trade and investment gains (of the type familiar in European integration stages). In Canada, in contrast, support came principally from traders (Molot in Lipsey and Meller, 1996, p. 331), although there was probably also an unwillingness to see the US–Canada becoming a hub and spoke arrangement, with the US as the hub.

For the US, signing these FTAs was a major innovation, although it had had a limited FTA with Israel from 1985. It had supported European integration in the 1950s for security reasons, but became disturbed by its protectionist and competitive implications in the 1980s. The agreements with both Mexico and Canada went well beyond traditional US trading agreements both in what they covered and in institutional strength. For Mexico, the agreement was part of the opening of its economy which had begun with unilateral trade liberalization, and been consolidated by its entry into the GATT in 1986. The US had always been Mexico's main trading partner, but in the 1990s, Mexico moved up to become the third partner of the US. It was also making the agreements already mentioned with the Group of Three and bilaterally with Chile, and had tried to negotiate an agreement with the EU. For Mexico, therefore, NAFTA was part of a series of new linkages into the international system.[1]

Initially, there were expectations that NAFTA would be expanded to other Latin American countries, individually, probably with Chile as the first. There is an accession clause, and negotiations with Chile opened formally in 1995 (OAS, Compendium 1996). Discussions over the FTAA (see below) seem to have overtaken this, while US interest in the non-North American countries has fallen.

FTAA

The US proposed hemispheric economic cooperation in 1990 and a Free Trade Area of the Americas in 1994; working groups were set up in 1996. There are disagreements over whether it should start with conventional trade liberalization or look first at other obstacles to trade and trading practices (as in APEC). It is forcing the Latin American regions to clarify their positions on how they negotiate with third countries (discussed in Chapter 11), thus affecting the existing regions, even before it exists. Formally, it is supported by all the Latin American and Caribbean countries, but tensions are emerging. MERCOSUR wants to be more fully integrated within itself before it joins another organization. This may include expanding to cover most of South America, to strengthen its bargaining position, as well as completing the current programme of integration, and possibly extending it. The FTAA has a target date of 2005, but this is now accepted as the target to begin, not to complete, implementation.

SACU

SACU dates from the colonial period, with the first agreements signed not by the countries, but by colonial officials. After two earlier agreements, SACU was signed in 1910, and revised in 1969. As each of the member countries became independent, it semi-automatically rejoined the union. It provides an almost complete customs union (there are a few product exceptions), with pooled tariff revenue, allocated now on a basis only tenuously connected with trade shares. The tariffs and trade policy are effectively set by South Africa, which administers the union. Both the distribution of revenue and the decision-making structure are under discussion. The gains and losses of the individual members are now discussed in terms of trade and tariff gains, but in the past there has been a strong political and security motive, in particular for South Africa in maintaining ties during the apartheid period. The current renegotiations (which began before the change in South Africa's government) are probably the first real examination of the case for continuing or ending SACU. The nature of the choice is different here, whether to break up, not whether to join. The difficulties of putting on barriers and de-integrating economic sectors require modifying the point of view taken in Chapter 2. SACU is also exceptional as the only group, other than the EU, with inter-country transfers (and these are a much higher proportion of government revenue for the smaller members than they are within the EU), so that these are a major element of the choice.

SADC

SADC replaced SADCC (Southern African Development Coordination Conference) in 1992. SADCC was founded in 1980, with all the present members except South Africa (1994), Mauritius (1995) and the Congo and Seychelles (1997). It was to provide political and economic protection for its members against South Africa, and included provisions for infrastructure assistance and coordination of other policies. South Africa was admitted after the change of government. In 1996, a proposal for a free trade area was adopted, but it has not yet been ratified by all the members, and no programme has been established. The motives for SADCC were clear, but SADC is more nebulous. The need for regional infrastructure and cooperation on other joint activities remains. The motives for the trade protocol were less clear, except as a step towards liberalization (for South Africa), and to reach the South African market (for the others). The SACU countries and several others, however, already have trading agreements with South Africa, so, as in NAFTA, there is an element of consolidation of existing agreements. There is perhaps an assumption that a full trade agreement is the next step for countries with a variety of bilateral trade and other linkages. There have not been studies of the economic gains.

AEC

In principle, all the African countries have had a goal, since 1994, of eventual full free trade. The African Economic Community has no current working groups or institutional structure, except within the Organization for African Unity, so African integration is further in the future than Latin American or Asian.

ASEAN

ASEAN was founded in 1967, and adopted the goal of a preference area in 1977, and of a free trade area, AFTA, in 1992, with a transition period until 2003 for the least sensitive goods, and to 2008 for normal goods. The most sensitive will remain excluded. The original members were joined by Vietnam in 1995 (with a longer transition period), and Burma and Laos in 1997; Cambodia remains an applicant. The motives for ASEAN were political, to form a bargaining group in the area, excluding non-Asian countries, and a 'common political fear.... It was also external threat that had held ASEAN together right through the years'

(Tan, 1992, p. 1). Tan emphasizes, however, that economic progress between 1967 and 1992 was on a purely country basis, with no ASEAN economic link. The preferences covered few goods, excluding those with high tariffs. The economic crises of 1997 led to renewed interest and an agreement to encourage intra-regional trade at the expense of extra-regional imports 'to save foreign exchange'. If this leads to an increase in total exports by the members, i.e. trade diversion, it may only reduce real incomes because of higher costs; the limited intra-regional tariff preferences may avoid the usual welfare damage of lower tariffs. If it diverts exports by ASEAN from outside the region to the region, it will reduce income and not save foreign exchange.

For Singapore, the motive for the FTA was to gain access to the other countries, which are all relatively closed, while it is already open. Indonesia had opposed an FTA until 1992. For the others, it was perhaps to strengthen the links when the need for political or security unity had diminished (Tan, 1992, p. 13). A regional group was also seen as necessary to counteract the *de facto* weakening of regional links as barriers to the rest of the world declined (p. 14). But this argument is circular; it leaves the question of why avoiding a weakening of links was necessary, if the original motive had disappeared or diminished. Here, as in some of the Latin American groups, it seems that the history of a link itself provides the motive for continuing it. The assumption has become that the members must have common interests, and it is necessary to find these, not to analyse whether or not they still exist. Suggesting that ASEAN acts as a constraint requiring the economies to deregulate internally (Mangkusuwondo, 1992, p. 9), again presupposes that some link among the countries is now so important that a commitment to them has serious political weight. The fact that the scheme has no apparent economic rationale suggests a strong political, regional solidarity motive. The 1992 date also, of course, corresponds with the revival of integration in Europe and the negotiation of NAFTA, so that the ASEAN countries were feeling left out of other regions.

ASEAN has a framework agreement on services, but no preferences have been negotiated so far.

SAARC

The South Asian countries adopted a plan for a preferential trading area, SAPTA, not a full free trade area, in 1992, and the effects so far are small. The members include countries which are still in military conflict (India and Pakistan), as well as with serious political differences

(India with Bangladesh and Sri Lanka). The limited preferences, but continued meetings, suggest a more political than economic motive at present, although the existence of extensive unofficial border trade suggests scope for a FTA.

ANZCERTA

Formal cooperation between Australia and New Zealand dates from 1965, but the present free trade area dates from 1988. It is almost complete. Some agricultural goods are excluded by Australia. Although the two countries clearly have common political interests, and differences from the other Asian and Pacific countries among which they are located, it seems to be a combination of a few specific economic interests and an assumption of more general common economic interests that motivated the agreement.

APEC

APEC falls between the FTAA and the AEC in substance. Conferences among the Pacific countries date from the 1960s. Then cooperation between Japan and Australia, after 1967, led to broadening in the 1970s. From 1978, the US was interested (and ASEAN was becoming more active as a group) (Soesastro, in Garnaut and Drysdale, 1994). APEC itself was founded in 1989 but it was the Bogor declaration of 1994 which established trade goals (free trade for the developed members by 2010 and the developing by 2020). There are no proposals, or working groups, beyond the annual report and summit to implement these targets, and there is disagreement (the targets are too vague to require formal commitments and therefore explicit explanation) over whether the target means free trade among the APEC countries, and perhaps some like-minded partners, or with the world, through regionally simultaneous MFN changes. The original understanding of the group proposing it seems to have been the world; the interpretation of more reciprocity-minded trade negotiators is to confine liberalization within APEC. The APEC group includes countries with security conflicts and strong political differences: China, Taiwan, and the United States; and countries with differences on economic policy: Japan, the US and South-East Asia. Like the FTAA, it also includes members in existing sub-regions: all members of NAFTA, ASEAN, and ANZCERTA are members. In 1997, Russia, Vietnam and Peru were admitted, but membership was then closed for ten years. The criterion is to be that countries must be on the

Pacific Ocean, and also have close relations with existing members and accept the goal of trade liberalization by 2020. The group has thus become much more formal in its structure. Colombia, Ecuador, and Panama, however, meet these criteria, so it is clear that a *de facto* criterion of choice by the existing members is now also in force. The group was explicitly completing its Asian membership in the context of the Asian financial crisis. In spite of its size and diversity, it has proved resistant to new members; it has opposed admitting the South Asian countries. This suggests that there is some underlying concept of who is and is not wanted. It is similar to the OECD, which has a strong sense of identity and of who should be a member, but which has avoided moving beyond a consultative and research agency. The NAFTA members would also be members of the FTAA, so there is potential overlap. APEC is different from the other politically motivated groups, except perhaps SAARC, in having strong economic interests actively opposed to moving to an FTA, as well as continuing, not past, political conflicts.

A note on security

A minimum level of peace and military trust among members of regions was suggested in Chapter 2. The slightly different argument was that it is precisely former enemies which may want to institutionalize the end of conflict.

The role of security is obvious in the original post-war founding of the EEC, including those from both sides of World War II. The East European countries could not have been considered for membership before 1989, while encouraging them to join has now become a priority. This fits both arguments.

The question of military conflict has not been important for the NAFTA members for at least 75 years, so any security consideration is more indirect. Mexico has taken an independent stance, relative to the US, on hemispheric security politics, for example with relation to Cuba, although not as strongly as actions like Brazil's nuclear initiative. There seems to be no obvious change in this relationship associated with NAFTA.

The Andean countries include several continuing conflicts, with Chile (originally a member) in border conflict with Peru and Bolivia, Peru in dispute with Ecuador, and Colombia's internal unrest being a potential threat to all its neighbours. The Andean arrangements appear to have continued alongside these conflicts, with neither a motive nor an effect of trying to counteract them. The Central American countries' position is similar.

There are no obvious security motives in CARICOM or the Group of Three. Argentina and Brazil and Argentina and Chile have long histories of conflict and rivalry, with military presence on the Argentine–Brazilian borders important until recently, and Chile opposing Argentina as recently as the Falklands war in 1981. The founding of the Argentina–Brazil relationship followed the end of military government in the two countries. They now undertake joint military manoeuvres (with massive publicity and emphasis), and these are beginning between Argentina and Chile. Brazil has moved its principal defence forces from the Argentine border (to the Colombian). Here, as in the EU, there is a clear parallel in policy between economic and military integration.

SAARC is closer to the Andean or CACM model, with several traditional conflicts and rivalries continuing and little impact or association with the trade integration. ASEAN may have been more of a defensive mechanism. 'ASEAN was founded ... in response to the threat of communism in Indochina', with economic motives initially secondary (Akrasanee and Stiftel, in Imada and Naya 1992, p. 27). It had a predecessor in the deliberately military South-East Asia Treaty Organization (SEATO). The security motive appears to remain strong, in spite of the changes in the position of communism in the region and the world. Weibe (1997) has argued that 'solidarity on security issues' remains a motive for the group not to divide on economic questions, for example the environment, in spite of the strong interests which member countries display in other, non-ASEAN, organizations. ANZCERTA includes military allies, not former enemies.

In Africa, SADCC in its original form had an explicit security function, to help the members protect themselves from disruption by South Africa and eventually to promote democracy there. The members openly or covertly supported military action against the then South African government, a similar situation to ASEAN. Its present form, as SADC with South Africa as a member, is not a precise case of bringing enemies together because of the change of regime in South Africa, but there is clearly a security motive binding the region.

Conclusions

The revival of interest in regions is clear in these histories, with a range of new and revived organizations starting around 1985–6 and continuing through the 1990s, to reach a peak of implementation in 1994. Since then, negotiations have continued within the groups, and for the foundation of the FTAA. The fact that countries have not normally done detailed calculations of trade and investment gains and costs suggests either that other motives are sufficiently important to outweigh any likely economic effect or that the regions are seen as only a step towards full liberalization, and countries have confidence that the eventual effects from this will be positive. The frequent citing of investment gains even if there are no potential trade gains, which can only come if there is a confidence effect entirely independent of economics, also supports the idea that these regional groups have primarily non-economic motivations. Investment can substitute for potential trade gains, but production-inspired investment must be derived from the increases in demand from trade effects.

Table 3.2 summarizes the discussion of this chapter. It is the customs unions and more integrated FTAs which have shown ability to adapt to new members and new responsibilities. They are also those with the longest list of motives for integration. SADC also scores highly on both adaptability and motives, so it may have potential for deeper integration.

In counting the motives for groups, recent military conflict is counted as positive because preventing future conflict is among the most commonly present motives or pre-existing conditions for the regions, along with political cohesion, trade access, and pre-existing economic integration. Political cohesion's role is self-evident, as forming a region is a political decision; what is surprising is that fewer than half the regions had a history of political cooperation in the past. The trade motive is consistent with the prevalent background of economic integration. One explanation for the large number with recent military conflict is clearly that both wars and regional integration tend to happen among neighbours, but the evidence from this chapter shows that for many of the regions, including the EU, MERCOSUR, CACM, ASEAN, and SADC, reconciling enemies and preventing future wars were explicit objectives. Those where there is evidence of this in declarations of purpose are included in the military and security classification, which covers seven countries. Investment access was present as a motive in slightly under half the regions, a perhaps surprisingly low score. None of the other motives was important in more than half the regions, or consistently important in the more integrated regions. While several regions are involved in sectoral planning (discussed further in Chapter10), this now tends to cover matters of obvious regional cooperation, such as infrastructure or energy, while more traditional industrial policy or planned development has diminished as a regional activity. The importance of outsiders, whether in encouraging regions directly or in stimulating them to form as a reaction, is small.

Notes

1 One reason given for this is that the EU lost interest in Mexico, and Latin America, when Eastern Europe underwent its political changes in the late 1980s, and this impelled Mexico into NAFTA. What is certainly clear is that both Mexico and the US were seeking new linkages at a time when Europe was not available.

4
What do Members of Regions have in Common?

The generalization that regions need some common interest to hold the members together needs to be broken down. This chapter will look for any attributes which seem universal among members of the most successful regions. Secondly, the political analysis which suggested that the level of common interests was a constraint on regions (see Chapter 2) means that we want to ask how much more diverse regions are than countries and how much less than the world. Given the diversity within countries, this is not a straightforward question, and the approach will be impressionistic. For regions which have existed for some time, it is useful to ask whether there has been a convergence of economies or common interests. Regions can be founded either to build interdependence or to administer and institutionalize existing interdependence. Over time, the two motives merge and interact. A comparison at any point cannot reflect this process.

Geography

Geographical closeness or contiguity can be expected to make any economic exchanges easier and cheaper, but it may also imply at least some common economic characteristics, of resources, climate, etc. Most regions are predominantly situated in one geographical unit. Many, however, have at least some parts separated, by another country or by water, so that a region which is not contiguous cannot be considered unusual.

It has been argued that not having geographical unity makes administering a region more complex. Viner argued that 'the existence between them [members of a customs union] of "high seas" is sufficient

Table 4.1 Geographical and other non-quantifiable indicators

	EU	SACU	MERC-OSUR	CARI-COM	Andean	CACM	NAFTA	G3	ANZC	ASEAN	SAARC	SADC	LAIA	FTAA	APEC	AEC
Geography																
common borders	no	yes	yes	yes	yes	yes	no	yes	no	yes	yes	no	yes	yes	no	yes
transport links	yes	yes	no	yes	no	yes	yes	yes	yes	yes	yes	no	no	no	no	no
size	large	middle	large	small	middle	small	middle	large	large	large	large	middle	large	large	large	large
Population																
size	large	middle	large	small	middle	middle	middle	middle	middle	large	large	middle	middle	large	v.large	large
range	large	large	large	large	middle	middle	middle	large	middle	large	large	large	large	large	large	large
GDP Size	large	small	middle	small	small	small	middle	large	middle	middle	middle	small	large	large	large	middle
Range of income																
PPP income per capita	middle	middle	middle	large	middle	middle	small	small	small	large	middle	large	large	large	large	large
Human Development Index	small	large	large	large	large	large	small	small	small	large	large	large	large	large	large	large
Level of income per capita	high	middle	middle	middle	middle	low	high	middle	high	low	low	low	middle	high	middle	low
Is a there a dominant power?	no	yes	semi	no	no	no	yes	semi	semi	no	semi	yes	yes	no	no	no
Political and social integration	yes	no	yes	yes	yes	yes	partial	yes	yes	some	some	some	some	some	yes	no
Responsive elite	yes	yes	yes	yes	yes	yes	yes	yes	yes	yes	yes	some	some	some	yes	no
Business support	yes	no	yes	yes	limited	limited	partial	no	yes	limited	no	partial	no	no	partial	no
Popular support	yes	no	yes	some	no	some	no	no	yes	yes	no	yes	no	no	yes	no
Authority of governments	yes	some	increas-ing	yes	limited	yes	some	no	yes	some	no	partial	no	no	limited	no
Interest group interaction																
Is there a regional identity?	yes	no	yes	yes	no	yes	no	no	yes	yes	no	yes	yes	no	no	no
Permanent status	yes	no	yes	yes	no	no	no	no	yes	no	no	no	no	no	no	no

to cut down, perhaps drastically, the administrative economies of customs union[s]' (Viner, 1950, p. 60). This may seem an appealing argument at first sight, but clearly it is not a complete obstacle. Even countries are divided by seas or other countries, and the colonial empires, which were among the first customs unions, were all geographically disperse. While some difficulty in enforcing controls may exist, it is not normal to consider this an insuperable problem of national administration.

In fact, because shipping has traditionally been among the cheapest forms of transport, customs unions or FTAs around (and named for) seas are among the oldest and most common examples, dating from at least the Ionian League, through the Mediterranean, to APEC. On the other hand, it is not difficult to find examples of neighbouring countries where the border is not in practice open for trade, because of mountains or other obstacles.[1] Again, trade within countries has sometimes taken place not across the apparent land connection, but by sea routes which connect around a barrier, and perhaps also around other countries (an obvious example is the US East and West coasts in the nineteenth century). If the correct specification of 'geographically near' for the purposes of analysing a region is convenient or low-cost transport, not kilometres between borders,[2] then it becomes difficult to rule out any grouping among coastal countries. Changes in transport systems, as suggested in Chapter 2, will change the practical regions. The WTO is itself the most prominent exception to a rule that only geographically concentrated countries have a common interest in trade liberalization and regulation.

Most of the members of the regions considered here are geographically contiguous (Table 4.1), taking that to include 'near' sea crossings for CARICOM, but exceptions include the EU, APEC, ANZCERTA, the Group of Three and SADC. Even if we define 'near' to mean nearer than other groups, Australia would be nearer to Indonesia, an ASEAN member, than to New Zealand.

In most of the regions, geographical nearness is associated with ease of transport and travel within the region (relative to outsiders), but there are important exceptions. In the Andean Pact, lack of good land links has been a permanent obstacle, and it is one also for the two new associates of MERCOSUR – Bolivia and Chile. For the original MERCOSUR, centred on the valley of the River Plate, there is a tradition of strong trading links, although these do not extend to northern Brazil and southern Argentina. The Group of Three, the Central Americans, and CARICOM all depend on the Caribbean, while NAFTA has both land and sea links.

SADC includes one country, Mauritius, separated from the others by both sea and a non-member country, Madagascar, and transport links tend to divide this region into sub-regions. SACU is a self-contained region. In Asia, both ASEAN and SAARC are (accepting short sea crossings) contiguous regions, while APEC stretching from the west coast of Burma (or the west border of Tibet) to the east coast of the US, the long way around, is as spread out as the WTO.

The regions vary tremendously in geographic size, so that it is clear that there is no minimum size that they are trying to reach, to obtain transport or other economies of scale, nor any maximum which constrains what can be treated as a unit.

But although almost all the regions pass a test of geography, this does not identify which countries should be in a region. For all the groups, it would be possible to imagine alliances among those on one border with partners across that border, without the members on the opposite 'side'. The most recent example of a change in perceptions of a region is the change from considering the border of Europe to fall between East and West Germany, to including all the former East European countries as potential members of the EU. Geography is at best an indicator.

Size of population

Population is a characteristic differentiating regions and their administration from countries. In countries national subdivisions normally take account of population distribution, although there are examples of traditional sub-divisions with a clear identity, which are independent of population weight (the revival of separate interests in Scotland or Catalonia, or the virtually immutable division of the US and Germany into states and Länder, for example). Therefore population is an important characteristic in looking at regions as long as the members need to find ways of balancing and reconciling different interests, with different weights.

All the regions studied here (except Central America, the Andean Pact and the Group of Three) have wide variations in size, defining this as a ratio of more than 5 to 1 between the largest and smallest (see data in Table 4.A1). This dispersion is important for the interactions of power within the region. In a few regions, there is one country which is clearly dominant in size: the US in NAFTA, South Africa in SADC and SACU, India in SAARC, Brazil in MERCOSUR. In other regions, notably the EU, Andean Pact, ASEAN and APEC, the largest country is balanced by other middle-sized ones. These differences suggest very different forms of region but need to be supplemented by income differences (discussed below).

The total size of the population of the region is also an important characteristic, because the size of a political unit influences the type of structures which it must have, and perhaps its viability and permanence. It is clearly important for its weight and role relative to other countries and *de facto* with the multilateral institutions. APEC (2 billion) and SAARC (1 billion) are massive; several are the size of what are considered large, but not unwieldy, countries, at around 200–400 million: EU, NAFTA, MERCOSUR and ASEAN, followed by SADC, the Group of Three and the Andean Group. ANZCERTA, CACM and SACU are the size of average-size countries, while CARICOM in total is only 5.7 million.

Economic size

Comparing GDP produces similar wide variations, within and among regions, but the variations in income per capita are rather less. Using the 5 to 1 definition of large difference, this is found only in CARICOM, ASEAN and SADC, while in the Group of Three and ANZCERTA, the highest income is less than twice the lowest. The variations in HDI (Human Development, taking account of life expectancy and education as well as income) are harder to define as 'large' or 'small'. Taking a variation greater than 0.2 as high, and less than 0.1 as low, almost all the groups have 'large' differences, with only the EU, Group of Three and ANZCERTA small, and NAFTA moderate. The variation among the regions in total output, like that for population, is very large. The EU, NAFTA, and APEC are large (more than US$8,000 billion), while MERCOSUR is $1bn, and ANZCERTA, Group of Three, ASEAN, and SAARC are about $0.5bn; SACU, CARICOM, the Andean Pact, CACM, and SADC are small.

To measure the importance of the region to the world economy and to its members, it is necessary to look at both population and output measures. It is also relevant to look at the size relative to the countries: even if the region is 'small', is it so much larger than its members that acting collectively means a significant increase in their power? Is there is a minimum size below which neither a region nor a country has a significant weight? It is difficult to accept this. Singapore, for example, would be very small on either the population or the output rankings used here. Only regions like CARICOM (for population and income) or CACM (for output) are made up of countries that need to be in a region to reach any size.

The regions which are large in both population and output are the EU, NAFTA, and APEC, while CACM and CARICOM are small on both measures. Most of the others are larger on the population than the output measure, while the Group of Three and ANZCERTA are average on both. On output and population, there are a few regions where one country accounts for more than half the region. These are South Africa in both SACU and SADC, Brazil in MERCOSUR, the US in NAFTA, Mexico in the Group of Three, Australia in ANZCERTA, and India in SAARC. The US and South Africa are also much higher in income than the average for their region, which could further increase their potential dominance (the 'dominant power' line of Table 4.1).

A direct consequence of differences in size will be the resulting differences in the share of trade in the economy, and probably also a different importance of tariffs in government revenue. These influence attitudes to the region: its importance to each member country, but also the fiscal costs of forming a region. Large differences in size can also have the effect of causing concern to both the large members, which do not want to accept decisions in which they do not have the major weight, and the small, which fear being overwhelmed, both economically and in decision-making.

In terms of average regional income level, there are wide differences among the regions, from the poorest in SAARC, SADC, CACM and ASEAN to the EU, NAFTA and ANZCERTA. The discussion in Chapter 2 suggested advantages for more developed regions in terms of the likelihood that interests would remain the same. The oldest surviving region, SACU, almost at low-income level, does not confirm this, but the fluctuations in the fortunes of the Latin American regions, for example the Andean Pact, CARICOM, and the CACM since the 1960s, do suggest difficulties for countries developing at different rates and with different policies.

Economic sophistication

Another difference related to level of development has been suggested by economists in MERCOSUR. There was little preparatory analysis and calculation of effects before the region was formed, and this is contrasted with the extensive literature on the EU, while ANZCERTA has also attracted considerable study. This comparison, however, is misleading. Analysis before the first European moves was equally limited, while the MERCOSUR literature is now catching up. ASEAN has been studied and, unlike Argentina and Brazil, Chile, at a similar level of income, is analysing the implications of MERCOSUR in detail. There are differences: the African groups have in general been analysed by outside consult-ants, and rarely in the context of how regions are studied elsewhere, and pre-NAFTA studies largely ignored the methods developed to study the EU.

The widely differing analyses of NAFTA and the lack of consensus on how to analyse even the direct trade effects of a region suggests that uncertainty about the results of the analysis may make it of relatively little use. There is certainly a correlation between the level of develop-ment and the preparedness of negotiators, but this is observed in all external negotiations, and it is not clear what conclusion should be drawn specifically for regions. There is no reason to believe that the dis-advantage will be greater in regional than in multilateral negotiations or than in domestic policy, but it may make unsuccessful negotiations or mistakes, leading to unsuccessful regions, more likely, and thus be an additional explanation for the failure of some past developing regions. It could influence the outcome in negotiations between countries at very different levels of development, as are found in NAFTA or APEC.

But there may be a more important conclusion. That trade gain and loss analysis has tended to follow, rather than precede, signing regional agreements strongly suggests that the decisions were not based on trade or other economic motives.

Political congruence

At a minimum, only countries with some belief in the usefulness of trade policy and the administrative competence to implement it are likely to form regions. These are not sufficient conditions, as the coun-try's belief may be in liberalization or the use of multilateral mecha-nisms. During periods of import-substituting policies, regions would have little appeal for 'large' countries (the size of 'large' depending on the nature of production). Brazil and the US showed little interest in regions until recently, and Japan, South Korea, China, and Taiwan have joined only the least substantial, APEC.

There is also a need, parallel to that in economic policy, for some degree of expected stability. Frequent changes of policy, past or expected, will not give either the government or its potential partners confidence to make institutional links. It is argued for some regions that the link itself gives a political 'anchor' to policy, but this is an essentially circu-lar argument. It is only if the government has a strong commitment to a policy that it will institutionalize it by regional commitments, and only if regional partners have confidence in the commitment that the region will have institutional strength.

A different argument, suggested in Chapter 2, is that countries need domestic support, whether through democratic or other means, which gives legitimacy and permanence for a regional link. The criteria given there were: support from the political elite, the economic decision-makers, and popular opinion; authority of the member governments; cross-border interaction among interest groups. These are difficult to measure and compare, but Table 4.1 suggests some characteristics, developed in detail in Zormelo, 1995. The first three are obvious preconditions, defining support within the member countries from the political elite, the economic decision-makers, and popular opinion. The need for authority of the member governments has two elements. It is needed for practical implementation, but it can also be argued that governments need confidence in their own authority before being willing to share or delegate it to a regional administration.

The EU (with some reservations at some times in some countries, but no more than normal within a country) meets all these, and this is probably also true for ANZCERTA. MERCOSUR and CARICOM probably meet most of the criteria. NAFTA and APEC probably have less broad-based support, and the variety of governments in the APEC region makes it difficult to assume that all are committed. Popular support may not be essential or ascertainable in ASEAN, but that region meets the other criteria. SAARC has less support, and some of the governments have important problems within their countries which reduce their interest in the region. SADC suffers additional weakness from domestic uncertainties and because its largest member, South Africa, is also trying to establish new ties outside the region with the EU. 'Group interaction' within the regions is impossible to measure, except impressionistically; some evidence is given in Chapter 10. There are clear examples in the EU, ASEAN, MERCOSUR, CARICOM and NAFTA of increasingly regular contact by interest groups, economic and non-economic, and there is a long history for Australia/New Zealand. It is possibly also true of Central America, COMESA and SADC and perhaps the Andean Group. It probably exists on a very limited scale for APEC as a whole, and only for business.

On these political integration criteria, the most integrated are the EU, MERCOSUR, and ANZCERTA, with no other groups satisfying all the criteria, even in part. The groups which meet three of the criteria are APEC, CACM and CARICOM. Only business support is present in all the regions. In NAFTA, there are some interest groups that go across all three members, and those in the US and Canada are encouraging and providing examples for those in Mexico.

The stage of development of political institutions may be an additional factor. Institutions for regulating trade, choosing policies, and settling disputes at the regional level implicitly assume that mechanisms exist at the country level, to implement the regional decisions and also to provide the precedent and example for those acting at regional level. This is not true for all countries which are members of regions. Even in MERCOSUR, legal systems to regulate economic decisions are not fully developed. Political systems are also weak, so that the questions of participation in executive decisions and control of administrative decisions are still being settled.[3] As will be discussed in Chapter 10 on linkages going beyond trade, the interest groups do not yet exist at the national level. The other regions face similar problems. This suggests that the institutional development of regions among developing countries may be different from that among developed, moving in parallel with, and occasionally leading, domestic institutions, rather than being built on them. This provides additional strains for regions in surviving. On the other hand, it could give regions a greater legitimacy in developing countries, if they provide examples for domestic institutions.

Common background or sense of community

If regions are a move to building a larger form of country, in economics and institutions, is there a regional analogue to a sense of national identity, and is it a prerequisite or a result of the region? If this is an important part of the explanation for 'which regions', then it must be balanced against the perception that there is also a growing global cultural similarity, which has been cited as contributing to global integration: 'An increase in world-wide cultural uniformity is probably one of the most important preconditions for a greater degree of global economic integration and interdependence' (Panić, 1988, p. 7). This could be interpreted, in terms of the description of Chapter 2, as a reduction in the differences which are a constraint on the size of regions.

Differences remain even within old groups like the EU, but there is a common sense of what is Europe (and of what is not: the opposition to Turkey's joining the EU is not purely its different level of development or questions about its commitment to democracy and human rights). There is a long history of the area which roughly corresponds to the present EU having common interests, similar institutions, and strong contacts among the populations. A similar sense of common interests can be found in Latin America, but the period is much shorter and the contacts much more limited. Until recently, the ties to the former colonial powers and to the US and France, the two traditional models (economic and political/cultural respectively), were strong, and only some historical nostalgia bound the countries together. Within Latin America, the difference between the Portuguese and the Hispanic legacies was a barrier. Even greater was that between both and the Caribbean, with its Anglo-French background and closer ties to the US. A Latin American identity can weakly explain Latin America as a group, but not the subregional groups. It is hard to see a special sub-regional identity, greater than the common Latin American, except possibly for the Central Americans. While it is true that the Andean countries roughly corresponded to the old Spanish division of the Americas, this seems a rather distant link for an industrial development region of the 1970s.

CARICOM, in contrast, represents a clear group with a sense of common interests. The common colonial heritage has been preserved not only in similar national institutions but in common institutions, including some more usually found for a single country (or even sub-division of a country): a university, sports teams, etc.

For both MERCOSUR and ASEAN, it has been argued that a sense of common interests was created, perhaps deliberately, before economic integration was attempted. Hurrell (1996, p. 1) argues that for MERCOSUR the 1970–85 period was when 'the essential political/security foundations for future economic cooperation are prepared', while Ariff suggests that within ASEAN, it has been argued that the ASEAN experience before introducing preferential trade has helped: 'Hindsight tells us that it was wise of ASEAN to have spent its early years just laying the political foundations as a prelude to regional economic co-operation' (Ariff in Imada and Naya, 1992, p. 48). This is different from the security or military argument. The argument is that while it was military interests which brought the countries together in the first instance (as perhaps also in the EEC), the habit of cooperation then helped to create a common identity. It may be too soon to reach such a conclusion.

NAFTA would be difficult to explain in terms of a cultural history. The US and Canada might fit this, but Mexico fits only if NAFTA is seen as a deliberate attempt to change its culture: 'The Mexicans clearly now seek an American future rather than with their southern neighbours.'

(Bhagwati in de Melo and Panagariya, 1995, p. 30). This, however, does not fit the model of similarity leading to a region; instead it suggests that some other interest is requiring the adjustment of 'culture'. It also does not fit the simultaneous entry by Mexico into the Group of Three. The two may suggest that Mexico is preserving its ties in both directions.

The SACU countries in Africa have a joint colonial history, but they are growing apart. The historical links among the SADC countries are less firm. They represent three strands of colonial history and a large variety of African heritages. They do, however, have recent common interests, represented by SADCC, and now the South African wish to establish an African identity.

Australia and New Zealand have common backgrounds, perhaps reinforced by the differences from their nearest neighbours. SAARC represents groups which chose to separate when their colonial history ended, and to stress their different cultures and religions. This is an unusual background for a region.

A different aspect of the importance of cultural factors is the idea that regions can grow out of linkages within a common cultural group, even if it is a minority within countries. The example is that of the Chinese in Asia. They are not important, however, in all the ASEAN countries (the Philippines, for example), and they are important in countries which are not in ASEAN (China, Taiwan). The linkage is potentially an important one, but of a different type from the general common history discussed here.

Summary

On geography, the exceptions include some of those which appear to be most integrated on other measures – the EU and ANZCERTA. On the economic and political measures, the regions show a variety of characteristics, and it is difficult to find any common pattern, except wide variation within regions. A few are dominating groups at the world level, but these include only two of the relatively integrated groups. In a few, a single member dominates, but this is the exception. On the political criteria, the EU, MERCOSUR and ANZCERTA are the most integrated, while the EU, CARICOM, possibly some of the Latin American sub-regions, ANZCERTA, SADC and ASEAN could claim a regional identity. Table 4.1 summarizes these results. The disparate indicators in this chapter cannot be summarized. No region meets all the suggested criteria for success; only the EU and ANZCERTA could meet the development requirement.

Notes

1 There is still only one road considered to be 'permanently' open between Argentina and Chile, and that was closed for 25 days during June–July 1997.
2 Some gravity models use distance between political capitals. This is even more misleading because they are often not the economic centres.
3 In MERCOSUR, 'the national parliamentarians and their party organisations had only a passive role ... The only country which displayed politicization before its participation in the process was Uruguay' (Hirst, 1992, p. 145).

Table 4.A1   Economic Indicators

		Pop (million) 1995	HDI[a] 1994	GDP (US$m) 1996	GDP per capita (PPP$)[b] 1994
EU					
	Austria	8.05	0.932	233,350	20,667
	Belgium	10.14	0.932	269,199	20,985
	Denmark	5.23	0.927	174,237	21,341
	Finland	5.11	0.940	124,975	17,417
	France	58.14	0.946	1,539,087	20,510
	Germany	81.64	0.924	2,352,472	19,675
	Greece	10.45	0.923	122,870	11,265
	Ireland	3.60	0.929	67,392	16,061
	Italy	57.29	0.921	1,214,272	19,363
	Netherlands	15.45	0.940	392,550	19,238
	Portugal	9.92	0.890	107,133	12,326
	Spain	39.21	0.934	581,565	14,324
	Sweden	8.83	0.936	230,609	18,540
	United Kingdom	58.61	0.931	1,159,250	18,620
	EU	**371.67**		**8,568,960**	**18,564**
SACU					
	Botswana	1.46	0.673	5,278	5,367
	Lesotho	2.03	0.457	778	1,109
	Namibia	1.54	0.570	3,107	4,027
	South Africa	41.24	0.716	133,923	4,291
	Swaziland	0.91	0.582	1,147	2,821
	SACU	**47.18**		**144,233**	**4,150**

Table 4.A1   Continued

		Pop (million) 1995	HDI[a] 1994	GDP (US$m) 1996	GDP per capita (PPP$)[b] 1994
MERCOSUR					
	Argentina	34.77	0.884	297,460	8,937
	Bolivia	7.41	0.589	6,972	2,598
	Brazil	155.82	0.783	564,818	5,362
	Chile	14.20	0.891	71,906	9,129
	Paraguay	4.83	0.706	8,879	3,531
	Uruguay	3.19	0.883	18,963	6,752
	MERCOSUR	**220.22**		**968,998**	**6,056**
CARICOM					
	Antigua and Barbuda	0.07	0.892	1,047	8,977
	Bahamas	0.28	0.894		15,875
	Barbados	0.26	0.907	1,872	11,051
	Belize	0.22	0.806	609	5,590
	Dominica	0.07	0.873	221	6,118
	Grenada	0.09	0.843	260	5,137
	Guyana	0.83	0.649	540	2,729
	Jamaica	2.53	0.737	4,243	3,816
	Montserrat	0.01			
	San Cristobal				
	St. Kitts and Nevis	0.04	0.853	207	9,436
	St. Lucia	0.14	0.838	509	6,182
	St. Vincent and the Grenadines	0.11	0.836	260	5,660
	Trinidad and Tobago	1.29	0.88	5,166	9,124
	CARICOM	**5.94**		**14,935**	**5,997**
ANDEAN					
	Bolivia	7.41	0.589	6,972	2,598
	Colombia	35.10	0.848	98,073	6,107
	Ecuador	11.46	0.775	19,040	4,626
	Peru	23.53	0.717	60,938	3,645
	Venezuela	21.64	0.861	67,311	8,120
	ANDEAN	**99.14**		**252,335**	**5,529**
CACM					
	Costa Rica	3.33	0.889	9,016	5,919
	El Salvador	5.66	0.592	9,503	2,417
	Guatemala	10.62	0.572	15,723	3,208
	Honduras	5.95	0.575	4,011	2,050
	Nicaragua	4.54	0.530	1,888	1,580
	CACM	**30.1**		**40,141**	**2,885**

NAFTA				
	Canada	29.61	0.960	585,105	21,459
	Mexico	90.49	0.853	334,792	7,384
	USA	263.17	0.942	7,636,000	26,397
	NAFTA	**383.27**		**8,555,896**	**21,527**
Group of 3				
	Colombia	35.10	0.848	98,073	6,107
	Mexico	90.49	0.853	334,791	7,384
	Venezuela	21.64	0.861	67,311	8,120
	Group of 3	**147.23**		**500,176**	**7,188**
ANZCERTA				
	Australia	18.05	0.931	392,679	19,285
	New Zealand	3.54	0.937	64,161	16,851
	ANZCERTA	**21.59**		**456,840**	**18,886**
ASEAN				
	Brunei	0.29	0.882		30,447
	Indonesia	193.75	0.668	236,872	3,740
	Malaysia	20.69	0.832	84,049	8,865
	Philippines	70.27	0.672	83,789	2,681
	Singapore	2.99	0.900	94,063	20,987
	Thailand	59.40	0.833	167,489	7,104
	Vietnam	73.79	0.557		1,208
	ASEAN	**421.18**		**666,263**	**3,987**
SAARC				
	Bangladesh	118.23	0.368	29,055	1,331
	Bhutan	1.64	0.338		1,289
	India	929.00	0.446	310,044	1,348
	Maldives	0.25			
	Nepal	21.46	0.347	4,408	1,137
	Pakistan	130.25	0.445	60,282	
	Sri Lanka	18.11	0.711	11,976	3,277
	SAARC	**1218.94**		**415,764**	**1,227**
SADC				
	Angola	10.82	0.335		1,600
	Botswana	1.46	0.673	5,278	5,367
	Lesotho	2.03	0.457	778	1,109
	Malawi	9.79	0.32	1,470	694
	Mauritius	1.09	0.831	3,953	13,172
	Mozambique	17.42	0.281	1,499	986
	Namibia	1.54	0.57	3,107	4,027
	South Africa	41.24	0.716	133,923	4,291
	Swaziland	0.91	0.582	1,147	2,821
	Tanzania	30.34	0.357	5,255	656
	Zambia	9.37	0.369	3,297	962

Table 4.A1   Continued

	Pop (million) 1995	HDI[a] 1994	GDP (US$m) 1996	GDP per capita (PPP$)[b] 1994
Zimbabwe	11.53	0.513	6,171	2,196
SADC	**137.54**		**165,879**	**2,223**

Notes :   Regional GDP per capita is the weighted average of the member states' GDP per capita, weighted by the population.
[a] Human Development Index
[b] Purchasing Power Parity
Source: IMF, *International Financial Statistics*; UNDP, *Human Development Report, 1997*

5
Regulation and Obligations of Regions

Countries forming regions face a variety of legal obligations already in force which affect the scope and the form of their agreements. These include their own domestic constitutional rules, but there are also international obligations. These include those to the multilateral institutions, principally the WTO, IMF, and the World Bank; those to other countries with which they already have bilateral agreements; and, because of the overlapping among regions, or between a continental group and the regions within it, obligations to regions of which they are already members (Table 5.1, p. 89).

WTO regulation of regions

The international regulation of trade regions dates formally from the founding of the GATT, the General Agreement on Tariffs and Trade, in 1948, but Viner (1950, p. 4) traces it back to the 'widespread existence of contractual obligations not to resort to tariff discrimination, and the general acceptance of customs unions as a derogation from such obligations'. In doing so, he brings out what has remained a dual aspect of regulation. It regulates the coverage and the form of existing agreements, but it also encourages a particular type of agreement to emerge. These agreements 'tended to restrict the field for special tariff arrangements between independent countries to agreements of a type which could plausibly be held to meet the criteria of a "customs union"'.

Under the system of bilateral arrangements which governed most trade among advanced countries from the nineteenth century to the foundation of the GATT, countries normally bound themselves to offer each trading partner 'Most Favoured Nation' treatment. Even though the analysis of trade diversion and creation had not been formally developed until Viner's 1950 publication, it was obvious that countries outside paying higher tariffs for entry into a market than other suppliers suffered damage to their interests, even if the damaging effect of trade diversion on the region itself was not understood. GATT carried forward this interest in ensuring that no countries were treated differently from their competitors. Against this was the perception that trade liberalization was good for an individual country and regional liberalization could be seen as a step towards general liberalization. Even the trade creation and diversion arguments suggested that the world as a whole could gain more than it lost from a regional group if creation exceeded diversion, and therefore regions with compensation could be beneficial if they compensated the losers. There was also the problem of the existence of a variety of imperial preferences. These could not be forbidden because they merely extended the geographical limits of countries, within which free trade, and thus discrimination against the rest of the world, was accepted. If the economic ideal is free trade, choosing among any other systems, whether country- or region-based, is a choice among second-best solutions.

Under what circumstances should countries be able to treat each other differently from 'normal', and is it desirable or feasible to have a range of degrees of special treatment? The second question is a practical one. The first is more difficult because it requires the international system to judge the legitimacy of the preferences of different countries in their international relations. Including such judgements was a major innovation when GATT was founded. Unlike other international institutions such as the World Bank or IMF, the essential element of GATT (now the WTO) has been that it is based on regulations and legal processes for defining, implementing and enforcing them. The others rely on consent or implementation through countries' own legal systems. Discretion to respond to members' changes in preferences or the organization's own changes in perceptions about appropriate economic policy (as in the IMF or World Bank) would not be consistent with this, but the assessment of what type of relationship between countries is closer than normal is inevitably political. Any GATT definition had to be in terms of outcomes, not intentions or motives.

The answers to when countries can discriminate under GATT and the WTO have followed two potentially contradictory strands. One takes the country as the standard. Special treatment was allowed if there was a special relationship, like that between a country and its colonies

(Viner, 1950, p. 16) and if it was as extensive as in a country, i.e. virtually without exceptions. Regions fall under these provisions. The second strand dates from the major revision of the GATT in 1971 to provide a special section on developing countries. Initially, the allowance was for all 'developing countries', but the Uruguay Round introduced a distinction between least developed and other developing, with different degrees of special treatment. This has been extended in the agreement reached on Least Developed countries in 1997 under which not only do they receive improved access to developed countries, but some middle-income developing countries have started to offer them preferences. Thus, in contrast to the rules for regions, there is a range of intermediate positions between country and MFN.

The concept of preferential treatment for regions requires an agreed definition and acceptance of what 'normal' treatment is. On those subjects where countries have a variety of different arrangements with different partners, and there is no international standard, for example for cooperation on infrastructure or external pollution effects, or, until recently at least, on rules to regulate investment flows, the word 'region' is unlikely to be used, because there is no perception that having a special relationship is unusual or needs an identifying name. The definition of regions has moved in parallel with the growing coverage and legal rigour within GATT and the WTO, and, as will be seen, the type of agreements which constitute a 'region' has extended. These two trends have brought in not only different types of economic activity (the extension to services, investment, etc.) but different institutions, including dispute settlement procedures, standard setting, etc. This is repeating what happened on trade. It was the growth of the concept of MFN in the nineteenth century which forced the development of the customs union exception agreement.[1] Given that one of the principal objectives of establishing the GATT was to introduce certainty and international sanctions against arbitrary changes in trading arrangements, the exceptions to the MFN principle had to be further defined and limits set.

GATT permitted regional groups which became, as far as trade was concerned, effectively the same as countries. The explanation given in the GATT agreement was 'the desirability of increasing freedom of trade by the development, through voluntary agreements, of closer integration between the economies of the countries parties to such agreements.... The purpose of a customs union or of a free-trade area should be to facilitate trade between the constituent territories and not to raise barriers to the trade of other contracting parties with such territories.' (GATT, 1986, Article XXIV).[2] As GATT was designed to regulate and have as members 'customs territories' rather than 'countries', a customs union could be viewed simply as the substitution of one customs territory for a number of pre-existing ones, although this has not been carried to the logical outcome of having only the customs union as a member. For customs unions, the requirement was that the new common tariff was 'not on the whole' higher or more restrictive than those of the countries forming the region (GATT, 1986, Article XXIV). For a free trade area, which does not fit the customs territory model, the requirement was that tariffs be eliminated on 'substantially all the trade' within the area. For both, 'regulations of commerce' were also not to be raised above the pre-agreement level, but these were not defined.

The rationale was that without the obligation to go 'almost' all the way to free trade, regional groups would free the products where group members were competing with non-members (and thus divert trade from them) and keep restrictions where they were competing with each other (and thus hinder trade creation). The rule does not prevent non-member countries from being damaged from trade diversion. But it tries to limit the damage first by limiting the number of regions to those where the members are willing to accept the full obligations of Article XXIV and then by not allowing them to increase tariffs. Because diversion depends on the relationship between the difference between regional and other prices and the tariff, there can be no rule (other than 0 tariffs) which can guarantee that there will be no damage to outsiders, and the fact that production patterns and costs will change within the region and outside it means that any solution can only be approximate and based on information available at the time the region is formed. Where there is production using inputs from in and outside the region, the rules about what goods are treated as coming from the region, the rules of origin, become an essential part of the regulation of the region, and of its effect on the rest of the world. The effects of these are also unpredictable over time.

In the 1960s, most colonies became independent and ceased to be covered by the provisions for extended customs areas under imperial preferences. At the same time analysis of how countries develop led to a set of beliefs: that they should have the right to assistance and special treatment; that they needed to be able to use trade policy, including import protection and export promotion, as part of a development strategy; and that they might need a larger market area than that of an individual country to provide a start for new industries. These arguments were pressed particularly by the Latin American countries, partly because their economists had participated in the theoretical analysis, but also because they did not have the preferential access available under special schemes for former colonies. As a result, in 1971, Part 4 was added to the GATT agreement, allowing developing countries 'special and differential treatment'. This included exemption from the MFN rules for special preferences by developed countries for the developing countries and greater freedom for the developing to alter their own tariffs. In 1979, this was supplemented by the 'Enabling Clause on Differential and More Favourable Treatment, Reciprocity and Fuller Participation of Developing Countries' which allowed regions among developing countries to be notified to the Committee on Trade and Development. This gave them the freedom to form 'regional groups' without meeting the full requirements of Article XXIV.

In practice, even for developed countries, control has been effectively non-existent. Most groups were, as required, notified to the GATT, and thus the controls at least have ensured transparency. Then each was reviewed by an *ad hoc* committee, but the reviews never rejected a proposed agreement. Decision (as in the GATT dispute process) could only be adopted by consensus, and thus the members of the group themselves would have had to agree. The use of *ad hoc* committees meant that no general patterns of examination or precedents for what was permitted were developed. The most significant new region of the 1950s, the European Economic Community, was welcomed for political and security reasons by the country which might have been most economically damaged by trade diversion, the US, and therefore not challenged. Other groups did not include countries large enough to have a major impact on world trade. Later, as the EC expanded and the original conditions which ensured support for it changed, the emphasis in the review was on calculating the possible trade diversion effects, and negotiating compensating changes in tariffs, not judging whether the expansion should be allowed. Implicitly, it was assumed that the formation of regions was a decision properly left in the hands of the countries involved.

Events in the 1980s led to changes in this process. The EC's moves to integrate more closely into the Single European Market and to extend itself to, first, southern Europe in the 1980s, then northern Europe in the 1990s, and potentially eastern Europe in the 2000s, combined with the formation of NAFTA and the developing country regions, ended the assumption of limited effect on the rest of the world. Regions were no longer special cases, to be treated individually, but a major trend affecting the nature of the world economic system. Larger countries were joining regions, so more had direct trade effects, but even small ones could have a systemic effect.

The adoption of the WTO brought two changes in the legal regulation of regions. An Understanding on Article XXIV re-emphasized the need to cover 'substantially' all trade, and, although there is still no formal definition, the principal trading countries and a newly active WTO secretariat have tried to build a consensus around a belief that no major sector can be entirely excluded.[3] (This would be consistent with the services provisions, as described below.) The provisions had always allowed transition periods, but as these gave additional 'flexibility' to the requirement for substantial coverage, the new Understanding limited transition to ten years. It tightened the rules about not increasing barriers from not 'on the whole higher' to an 'assessment of weighted average tariff rates and of customs duties collected', with detailed requirements for the calculation. Effectively this only gave legal force to what had become the practice. It did not attempt to clarify the provisions on other 'regulations of commerce', although it had become clear that rules of origin were being used, particularly in free trade areas, as an essential element of protection. The Understanding also introduced periodic reviews of regions in formation, and the WTO later substituted a single Committee on Regions for the old working group system.

For developing countries, there was an additional modification, although more by association. The negotiations put more emphasis on reciprocal obligations (except for the least developed), and although some special provisions for smaller concessions or longer periods of adjustment were built into the settlement, in general the old presumption that special and differential treatment was the rule was shaken. Formally, this meant that even regions of developing countries started to be examined under the normal Article XXIV provisions, rather than the more flexible ones for Part 4 treatment; informally, it meant that the presumption that developing countries should be able to use trading rules relatively freely was weakened, so any examination would be more rigorous.[4]

The second innovation of the Uruguay Round was to extend the regulation of regions beyond trade in goods. For subjects not covered by the GATT, there had been no requirement of MFN treatment. The Uruguay Round extended the responsibilities of the new WTO to services, regulations and standards like intellectual property and the use of health standards as a barrier to trade, and implicitly to some aspects of investment. In parallel, the General Agreement on Services included (as Article V) a provision that countries could liberalize trade in services within a group, provided the agreement had 'substantial sectoral coverage' and was part of 'a wider process of economic integration or trade liberalization among the countries concerned' (GATT, Uruguay Round, GATS, Article V).

Significantly, the phrase 'substantial sectoral coverage' was to be 'understood in terms of number of sectors, value of trade affected and modes of supply'. As most existing regions, especially those in Latin America, took the opportunity of their initial services offers to specify their regional partners as exceptions to the MFN rule (as was allowed at that point), this provision may take some time to be tested.

Another significant change in treatment of regions in the WTO was the admission of the EU as a member, although additional to, not instead of, its member states. This marked the logical outcome of treating it as the customs jurisdiction which is making commitments to other members of the WTO, since trade in goods is a matter of EU, not member state, competence. The EU, not the individual members, had already been the unit which was reviewed as part of the WTO's regular Trade Policy Review assessment process. This step is in part a return to the past, when imperial powers were recognized as the members with responsibilities for applying GATT rules to theirs colonies. The other customs unions have not been admitted, and are still treated as separate countries, including in the trade reviews.

No new region has yet completed a process of review under the new WTO Article XXIV or GATS Article V rules, so it cannot be certain that the process will in practice be more restrictive than in the past. But the fact that regions have been put through the full process, even if they are made up of developing countries, and statements of support for more rigorous enforcement of WTO rules, even by regions like the EU, suggest stronger enforcement. The new rigour may be reflected not only in the criticism or rejection of regions in the review process, but in the way in which regions are negotiated in the first place. The agreements which the EU has signed with the East European countries all included provisions for eventual free trade, explicitly to meet these new requirements. There have been agreements signed, however, since the adoption of the new rules which clearly violate them.

The assumption that regions should cover 'everything', first all goods, now services and some new areas as well, may have provided an impulse to them to go further than before. If the ten-year rule is enforced, then this will be a major difference from past regions, which have had longer planned periods of transition, and where the nature of the final opening may not have even been included in the initial treaty. This progressive approach may not be allowable if the ten-year rule means that the details of the ten years need to be established before the first notification to the WTO. (But Canada and Chile signed a free trade agreement in 1997 with a 17-year transition period.)

Examining notifications shows how limited and concentrated the spread of regions was under GATT. Of the 98 agreements notified to the GATT under Article XXIV procedure, 25 were agreements of the EEC, including those with new and potential members, and 23 were its association agreements with developing countries before and under Lomé; thus almost half were from the EEC, with a further 10 involving the EFTA countries. Of the rest, 22 involved agreements with eastern European countries, which were not in the GATT and where formal bilateral agreements were needed. In contrast, only three included the US, with Israel in 1986, then the US–Canada agreement of 1989, and NAFTA in 1994. Only six are in Latin America or the Caribbean, with four each in Africa and the Pacific and one in the Middle East. If we add those under the enabling clause, this increased the Latin American total to nine, with four in Asia, four in the Middle East, and five in the Pacific.

The first stage of CARICOM was notified as CARIFTA in 1968, being superseded by CARICOM in 1973. CARIFTA and CARICOM enjoy the distinction of being two of the six regions ever to be formally accepted by the GATT, and CARICOM is one of the two surviving accepted regions (the other is that between the Czech and Slovak Republics) (WTO, *Regionalism*, 1995).

The Central American Common Market was notified, although of its members, only Nicaragua was in the GATT in 1959.

The LAIA was notified in 1981 under the Enabling Clause (LAFTA had been notified under the general procedures). Most other agreements among Latin American countries have been notified only as subdivisions of this. This procedure has continued under the new WTO regime for regions, with the Group of Three being officially notified to LAIA, and then by LAIA to the WTO. This suggests that, for some groups among developing countries, the new enforcement regime can be little different from that under GATT. MERCOSUR, however, was initially notified to LAIA, but then directly to GATT, although still under the Enabling Clause. Because of concern among some developed countries (in particular the US), however, an Article XXIV working group was set up, and in February 1996 its examination was transferred to the new Committee on Regions, and the formal gathering of information was completed by May 1997 (IDB, INTAL, 1997, p. 47).

In contrast, NAFTA was notified under the normal procedures; it could not fall under LAIA because it included two non-members, or under the Enabling Clause because only Mexico is 'developing'. It was notified under GATT, not WTO, rules. It was initially examined by a

Table 5.1 External legal constraints on regions

	EU	SACU	MERCOSUR	CARICOM	Andean	CACM	NAFTA	G3	ANZC	ASEAN	SAARC	SADC	LAIA	FTAA	APEC	AEC
Notification under GATT/WTO	notified	grandfather	notified enabling	approved	notified enabling	notified	notified	notified enabling	notified	notified enabling	notified	not yet	notified enabling	not enabling yet	no	no
Need authorization to join other agreements	yes	yes	yes	yes	no	yes	no	no	no	no	no	no	yes	no	no	
Allowed to join other agreements	no	yes	no	yes	yes	yes	yes	yes	yes	yes	yes	yes	yes	Yes		
Restricted by obligations to other agreements	no	yes, EU	yes, LAIA	yes, EU	yes, LAIA	no	yes, LAIA	yes, LAIA	no	no	no	yes, EU	no	yes, various		

working group, but is now also being examined by the Committee on Regions.

The Andean Pact was not notified originally, but in its revised 1987 form it was notified under the Enabling Clause. The FTAA does not yet have trading agreements to be notified.

SACU has not been officially notified because it predated the GATT, and although the membership has formally changed, with the independence of Botswana and later of Namibia, the actual coverage of the customs area has not. As it covers all trade in goods, it would probably be accepted. The other African areas, SADC and the AEC, do not yet have formal trade agreements to be notified.

The Australia–New Zealand agreement was notified, in its original form in 1966 and later in 1983 when the initial agreement was replaced by ANZCERTA.

The original preferential ASEAN was notified under the enabling Clause in 1978. SAARC was not notified until 1997, and APEC has not been notified because it has no substantive trade content.

Restrictions from other international organizations

The World Bank and the IMF have normally supported unilateral and non-discriminatory reductions in tariffs, and questioned special arrangements within regions, especially regional obligations to maintain a particular level of tariffs (for example in Central America in the 1980s). Unusually, in southern Africa, they have supported regional groups, especially since South Africa's change of regime.

There has been a *de facto* restriction on what regions can cover with special rules because of the increasing number of multinational agreements, for example on the environment and CFCs, on intellectual property, on sanitary and phytosanitary standards, and on shipping and air services. All of these restrict the scope for countries, and therefore regions, to differ from 'what is normal'. The regional development banks have tended to promote regionalism among their members. They implicitly embody a perception that their regions have interests that are sufficiently common, and sufficiently different from other areas, to give regional credit a role. The Inter-American Bank 'was created in 1959 with the specific mandate to promote regional integration and economic and social development in Latin America and the Caribbean.' (Iglesias, 1997, p. 6). The African Development Bank has urged integration since the early 1990s, on the traditional grounds of promoting development and economies of scale.

Restrictions from other regions

An essential division among regions is in their rules on whether their members can participate in other regions. The customs unions require their members to obtain the region's consent to make agreements with others, as this would affect the common relationship with the rest of the world. None of the FTAs has restrictions, although the resulting need for rules of origin means that there is a potentially serious effect from increasing effective barriers within the region if countries have a variety of bilateral arrangements.

The EU does not allow membership in other regions with overlapping competences. It also restricts membership in regional groups by the countries to which it gives trade preferences, by means of a legal obligation to offer to the EU any access which they give to any other country outside the preference regime. The members of SACU, all of which, except South Africa, receive preferences from the EU, have secured a derogation from this; other regions among its associated countries have not included non-members. This has become an issue in the case of Caribbean attempts to acquire rights in the US market parallel to Mexico's access under NAFTA. If the Caribbean countries joined NAFTA, Lomé would require them to offer an FTA to the EU. The Australia–New Zealand arrangements with the developing Pacific islands have similar rules.

The rules of the LAIA required any sub-region of its members to be open to all members of LAIA, and further that any agreement with a non-member should be open to any member. Such a rule assumes that the purpose and preconditions of regions are embodied entirely in their trade arrangements, with no element of a special political relationship. Alternatively, it is a view that all Latin American countries share the common interests which could provide the additional motives for a region. The rules of the Group of Three and the common tariff of the Central American Common Market have in practice kept out other members, but they are in principle open to other Latin American countries. NAFTA and MERCOSUR clearly broke the rules, and have had to negotiate alternative agreements in compensation. NAFTA included two non-members, but Mexico has not opened it to the rest of the LAIA. MERCOSUR included a provision forbidding all countries which were members of another group to join in the first five years. In Latin America, this meant all countries except Chile. This restriction expired on 1 January 1997, and it is now open to other countries, but subject to negotiations. The members cannot join other regions without consultation with each other. Neither NAFTA nor the Canadian–US agreement which preceded it regulates members' relations with other regions. When the US began negotiations with Mexico, Canada was initially excluded, but asked to join. Since the signing of NAFTA, Mexico has joined the Group of Three, Canada has signed a free trade agreement with Chile (in July 1997), and all three are active members of APEC. The negotiations of the three in FTAA are coordinated, but not joint, so there is no necessary presumption that all would need to take the same positions, or even that all would join or stay out. Similarly, the Group of Three and the Andean Pact allow their members to join other groups; Colombia and Venezuela have joined the Group of Three, while Bolivia has joined MERCOSUR.

Except for SACU, the African arrangements (including those not discussed here) do not restrict membership in other groups. This can be attributed to their still preliminary stage of integration. In the future, overlapping membership among SADC, COMESA, any revival of East African cooperation, and the Indian Ocean Commission could bring conflicting obligations. Members of SACU must have the prior agreement of the other members to join another agreement. In fact, there have been a variety of bilateral agreements of individual members (discussed in Chapter 11), as well as membership in Lomé by the members other than South Africa. Until recently, these were not questioned, but the negotiations of South Africa with the EU have been subject to investigation and comment by the other members (although South Africa has not fully accepted that they could have a veto power, as specified in the SACU Agreement), and a negotiation between Namibia and Zambia was broadened to include all of SACU.

The Asian groups have no restrictions on membership in other groups, but in practice there is almost no overlap as there are fewer groups and no tradition of bilateral arrangements. Only APEC, which includes all of NAFTA, ASEAN, and ANZCERTA, and an associate of MERCOSUR (Chile) could face a problem of conflicting obligations.

Summary

The growing number and importance of regional organizations have led to more concern and therefore more careful studies of regions' effects on excluded countries. At the same time the increase in other obligations, at the multilateral level and to overlapping regions, tightens the legal restraints on countries making regional arrangements (see Table 5.1). Only LAIA has attempted to provide standard rules and procedures to reconcile different arrangements within its region. The EU and MERCOSUR are the most constrained by their obligations to themselves, and MERCOSUR also by LAIA. The other customs unions, full or partial, are also limited, but have some freedom to make outside arrangements: SACU, CARICOM, and CACM. LAIA is some constraint on the other Latin American countries (although Mexico's joining NAF-TA has weakened this). The other groups have not accepted any constraints.

It is too early to say whether the increase in the number of regions has reached a point where the obligations will delay or prevent new regions, although it is tempting to draw parallels with the complexity of overlapping MFN arrangements and then discriminatory tariffs, before the founding of the GATT helped to simplify the system.

Notes

1 The first complaint by an excluded country that a customs union was not complete and therefore violated its MFN rights was by Sardinia against Austria and Modena in 1857 (Viner, 1950, p. 7).
2 'Voluntary agreements' seems an odd description of contractual arrangements.
3 'If agricultural restrictions are prohibitive, then agricultural trade is by definition not substantial' (Sampson AER, 1996 p. 90). Although writing unofficially Sampson was a WTO official.
4 The WTO review of Mexico (WTO, Mexico 1997, p. xvii) included a recommendation that 'there is scope for Mexico to bring together its regional and multilateral efforts for example, by binding its regional commitments under the WTO; this would also confirm internationally the major shift that Mexico has made, over several years, away from its earlier protectionist policies'. It is not clear what this means. The individual regions of which it is a member are notified and may be approved by the WTO, but this does not constitute binding in the sense that MFN tariffs are bound. The WTO has not found a way of 'binding' the extra commitments for least developed countries which have been negotiated under its auspices in 1997. The idea that the WTO should acquire an overall enforcement function for regions seems difficult to implement, given the different procedures and rules of the groups.

Part II
Trade and Investment

6
Formal Arrangements on Trade in Regional Groups

The degree of formal integration varies much more widely among the various groups than the formal distinction between free trade areas and customs unions might imply. After describing the EU, which has integrated all forms of trade, this chapter looks at the other groups, first those with the least formal integration. Then some common elements are discussed: rules of origin, the use of mechanisms like safeguards and anti-dumping, and the allocation of tariff revenue among the members of customs unions. Table 6.1 summarizes the objectives of the groups.

The EU

The EU demonstrates that even free trade among a region's members, normally considered the minimum form of integration, will vary in its characteristics according to how far the region has gone on other linkages. The EU has eliminated all tariff and non-tariff barriers among its members, moving towards full elimination of formal border controls. This represents an exceptionally deep integration because it required consensus, or in controversial cases formal agreement, on what goods could circulate within each country. This had two types of precondition. The one traditionally included in regional analysis was common controls on goods entering the EU via any member country. This had to include not only tariffs, but non-tariff barriers and health and safety standards; in other words not merely a customs union on tariffs, but on all other border regulations. The second was agreement on common standards for goods produced or consumed within any country of the region. Thus, full free trade, that is, the ability for goods to circulate not merely

Table 6.1 Proposed and actual trade liberalization

	EU	SACU	MERCOSUR	CARICOM	Andean	CACM	NAFTA	G3	ANZC	ASEAN	SAARC	SADC	LAIA	FTAA	APEC	AEC
Full customs union																
Actual	x	x	x	x	x	x										
Planned	x	x	x	x	x	x										x
Full free trade																
Actual	x	x	x	x	x	x	x	x							x	x
Planned	x	x	x	x	x	x			x						x	x
Partial free trade (all planned)								x	x	x	x	x		x		
Manufactures									x	x						
Sensitive excluded							x	x	x	x	x	x				
Agriculture excluded									x	x						
Special regime	x		x				partial				x	x				
No progress yet														x	x	x
Include NTBs?	x	x	x			x	x	x				x				
Still use safeguards?	no	no	no	yes	yes	yes	yes	yes	no	yes	yes	yes	yes	yes	yes	yes
Rules of origin																
Common	yes	no	not yet	no	no	yes	no	no	no	no	no	planned	yes	yes	yes	yes
Complex	yes	no	no	no	no	no	yes	yes	no	no	no	no	yes	yes	yes	

without paying a tariff but without controls, effectively requires that a region goes well beyond even the formal requirements of a customs union.

The common external regime includes a common MFN tariff structure: it is the EU which notifies tariffs and binds them in the WTO, and it is the EU's trade policy, not that of its individual members, which is examined under the WTO's trade policy review mechanism. This is the traditional pre-GATT and GATT concept of a 'customs area', the technical basis for GATT membership. At a practical level, this meant the development of common customs forms and procedures. It also has common preference arrangements. In the case of the EU, this means a wide range of agreements with the selected developing countries in the Lomé Agreements, those in other special groups like the Mediterranean, Andean, Central American countries, Least Developed countries, all developing countries, and various classes of the East European and other formerly centrally planned economies. Most of these date from after the formation of the European Community, but those with the developing countries, especially the former colonies of individual member countries, had to be harmonized over the course of the EC's development. This was an unusually complex process because some members had special arrangements with individual groups of countries or on particular products. It led to the external regime including special protocols for sugar, beef, bananas, and rum. Even after the foundation of the EC, the individual member countries established separate quota regimes for clothing and textiles under the Multifibre Arrangement, and on an industrial basis for cars and some other commodities. Only with the final removal of controls at the border in 1993 were what originally had been country quotas transformed into European quotas.

All negotiations on goods with other countries or at the multilateral level are joint; as a corollary, trade dispute procedures such as complaints about dumping or subsidies in other countries are handled at European level. As the common external regime means that importers cannot bring goods through a member country with low barriers into one with higher, there is no need to determine at internal borders the 'origin' of a good: whether it was produced within Europe or transshipped from outside; rules of origin within the region are no longer necessary. The rules for external trade (required because of the wide variety of different preference regimes) are set for the EU as a whole.

The moves to common standards at the border and within the region, were affected by the progress on multilateral regulation. While increasing integration means a constant need to harmonize regional standards, as individual countries set new standards or change those which exist, there is also a tendency for the need for regional standards to be eroded, as the multilateral setting continues. This is an important lesson for regional analysis, that what a region 'needs' to include to provide free trade within itself, and also a common regime with the rest of the world, is not a fixed menu; it both increases and decreases.

In some developing country agreements examined here, however, in particular those with a declared objective not going beyond free trade, there appears to be an implicit assumption that this is a fixed goal. This can be true only for the limited concept of no tariffs, and even for that it risks being overtaken by multilateral liberalization.

AEC, APEC, and FTAA

The AEC remains purely an objective, of free trade and eventually customs union and full economic union by 2028 (a transition period of 34 years from the signing in 1994). There are no actual initiatives or working groups yet in place.

APEC has adopted slightly more detailed objectives, of free trade by the more advanced countries by 2010 and by all by 2020, but there remains disagreement over the means to do this. It could be tariff cuts on an MFN basis, with APEC providing coordination of the timing and perhaps the commodities and extent of the cuts, but applying them to all. Alternatively it could be on a reciprocal basis, either within the region only or with provision for agreed arrangements with non-member countries. Clearly the last would break WTO rules on MFN and would violate the 10-year transition rule. Until it is agreed which is the objective, it is not possible to challenge it, or examine APEC under WTO procedures. At the 1996 meeting, the members produced individual plans (which together constitute the Manila Action Plan) to eliminate tariffs by the target dates, with staged cuts during the transition period for some, but not all, countries. There are also proposals for common action to liberalize some sectors at an early stage of the process. In 1996, tariffs on information technology products were eliminated (this was later extended to all countries in the WTO agreement). In 1997, APEC agreed to eliminate tariffs on 15 sectors, and individual countries made further announcements of planned tariff cuts. All cuts agreed up to now would be MFN, not limited to the region. One probable reason for the indistinct objectives and lack of formal progress so far is that the work on integration was initially led by non-governmental groups of businessmen and academics. There is discussion of 'trade facilitation' (see Chapter 10), but the only practical objective is simplifying or harmonizing customs forms and procedures from 2000. There are also proposals on standards for some products from 2000.

The FTAA has moved to the establishment of a negotiating framework, with sectoral official-level working parties on tariff and non-tariff questions, and formal procedures for monitoring and reporting on these. There is, however, no agreed sequence on how to move towards the objective of free trade within the region, with a conflict between those (led by the US) which want to make progress specifically on tariffs and those (led by Brazil) which emphasize procedures and other barriers. As both are important elements of all existing agreements, this suggests a lack of commitment to the objective of a free trade area, and instead greater concern for particular national advantages in other markets within the region.

All three continental programmes recognize that there will be progress by regional groups within them, and do not expect to replace these.

SADC

SADC is the only other agreement included which has still not passed the stage of planning and working groups. There are a variety of bilateral agreements among its members (and a customs union, SACU, among five of them). It is possible that part of the programme will be to harmonize and extend these. In 1996, a Trade Protocol was signed (although by 1998 ratified by only three members, Botswana, Mauritius and Tanzania) which set a programme for negotiating staged intra-regional reductions in tariffs, with a completion target of eight years, 2004. The 1997 negotiation decided that countries should reduce their tariffs on a linear basis, therefore according to their own existing tariff structures, and not to meet particular levels by particular dates in the transition. Countries were to submit proposals under it by December 1997, but little progress was made. The framework envisaged the possibility of excluding some sensitive products and reimposing barriers. In particular, there are proposals for sugar to be subject to quotas within the region.

SAARC

The objective is free trade by 2005. In 1996, tariff reductions on about a quarter of products traded were agreed. There remain prohibitions on trading some products (notably Pakistan has a permitted list of products that can be imported from India), and Pakistan has still not given India even MFN status. The effective coverage is therefore little more than MFN.

ASEAN

The objective is internal free trade, with continuing exceptions for the most sensitive products. The outcome of the present programme, the Common External Preferential Tariff (CEPT), would be only preferential access and only for some products. There were no formal criteria to determine sensitivity. Other products were divided into 'fast track' and 'normal' classes, with the fast track to see intra-ASEAN tariffs lowered to 0.5 per cent within seven to ten years (by 2002), and the normal given targets of ten to fifteen years. Agricultural goods will wait until at least 2010, or 2020 if the Indonesian and Philippine position prevails. The initial cuts actually occurred in 1995, not 1993. The fast track list included about 40 per cent of intra-ASEAN trade (although only 6–7 per cent of total ASEAN trade), and excluded agricultural goods and cars. NTBs are not included, but customs surcharges were eliminated at the end of 1996 for goods on the CEPT list.

ANZCERTA

Almost all intra-regional trade (there remain a few excepted products) is free of tariffs and NTBs (the agreement was initially signed in 1983, and completed in 1990). There has been harmonization of customs procedures and some progress on other business standards affecting trade.

The Group of Three

This is the first of the two Latin American groups where the objective is limited free trade. For Colombia and Venezuela, trade was liberalized in 1992; Mexico signed in 1994, with a transition period, starting in 1995, and with reductions of 10 per cent a year in tariffs to completion in 2005. The agreement includes non-tariff barriers. There are some exceptions. Colombia excluded 0.8 per cent of its imports from Mexico, and Mexico 1.8 per cent of its imports from Colombia (Echavarria in Lipsey and Meller, 1996, p. 146). These were mainly in agricultural and processed foods; 20 per cent of agricultural goods are permanently excluded, and 81 per cent of foods (and 0.2 per cent of chemicals). These are the only permanent exclusions. Textiles and clothing were temporarily excluded in Mexico–Venezuela trade, but were expected to be included by 2005, and cars and car parts were subject to 12-year transition periods. There was asymmetry in the liberalization between the existing Colombia and Venezuela agreement and Mexico, with more goods achieving free entry into Mexico immediately. Most NTBs were eliminated (with the exceptions of oil and used clothes, and national security and health), but safeguard action is still allowed.

NAFTA

The NAFTA agreement provides for staged tariff reduction over 15 years from 1994, with agreed national schedules. By the end of the period, there will be no exceptions. About 60 per cent of trade was included from 1994; much of Mexican trade had entered the US duty-free under the GSP or as primary goods before the establishment of NAFTA. The principal remaining tariffs for the US are in some foods, clothing and footwear, and for Mexico in foods, oils, light manufactures including plastics, leather, wood, clothing and some metal and electrical manufactures (US Government, 1997 p. 32). Mexico exempted imports from NAFTA when it raised some tariffs back to its WTO-bound limit (a rise from a 20 per cent applied level to 35 per cent) after the 1994 peso crisis. The reductions in telecommunications agreed in NAFTA have already been overtaken by the WTO agreement of end-1996. NAFTA provides for the removal of NTBs, including the phasing out over 10 years of Mexican restrictions on local content in cars. There are still some exceptions permitting subsidizing agricultural trade (OAS, Compendium 1996), if third countries' trade is involved, and members can still take safeguard action against each other, including that related to MFA or GSP provisions (ibid).

CACM

The remaining groups considered here have the objective of a common external tariff, and perhaps other common external policies, as well as intra-regional free trade. In Central America most manufactures were liberalized by the 1970s, excluding cars, but agricultural goods remain under some restrictions, with coffee, sugar, wheat, cigarettes, and also some petroleum products excluded (UN ECLAC, *Centroamérica*, 1997, p. 9). The process has been completed for El Salvador, Guatemala, Honduras, and Nicaragua, with Costa Rica in transition, although there are still some surcharges within the region. A common external tariff of

5–20 per cent was adopted in 1993, lowered to a ceiling of 15 per cent in 1996; it now covers most tariff lines, although estimates vary from 80 to 95 per cent (UN ECLAC, 1996; UN ECLAC, *Centroamérica*, 1997, p. 7; Garay and Estevadeordal, 1996, p. 7), with a further stage in the process by 1999. Safeguards are still allowed.

Andean Group

The Andean group has been simultaneously negotiating agreements for subsets of its members, Colombia, Venezuela, and Ecuador and for some members with new members, Colombia and Venezuela with Mexico, and Bolivia with MERCOSUR, plus deeper integration moving to a common external tariff. Peru has not participated in any of these. Apart from Peru, there was free trade in manufactures, excluding capital goods, by 1993. Agriculture was excluded. The common external tariff, covering 95 per cent of tariff lines (UN ECLAC, *Desenvoluimiente*, 1997, p. 4) was agreed in 1994, and came into force in 1995. It is applied by Colombia and Venezuela, with a few exceptions, and Ecuador, with major exceptions, but not by Bolivia, which retained a lower tariff (of 5–10 per cent). The rates are from 5 to 20 per cent. The tariffs were set by negotiation at the outset, and the regime has not been revised since then. Members can still take safeguard action against each other.

CARICOM

There is free trade within the region, but with some exceptions on oils and fats. A common external tariff of 0 to 35 per cent was established in 1993, to be reduced to 24 per cent by 1998, although there are still exceptions for individual countries. Quotas and licences are also being removed, but again not yet uniformly across countries (Nogueira, 1997, p. 13), and countries may not take safeguard actions against each other.

MERCOSUR

There is substantial free trade within the region, although the countries maintain lists of exceptions, with transition periods to 1999 for Argentina and Brazil and to 2000 for Paraguay and Uruguay. Argentina had 223 exceptions, mainly in steel, textiles, paper and shoes; Brazil had 29 in wool and food products; Paraguay had 272 in textiles, food, shoes, and steel; Uruguay had 1018 in textiles, chemicals, steel, machinery, plastics, and food.

Cars and sugar are excluded from the free trade arrangements and treated separately. For cars, Argentina had requirements of local content, and Brazil high tariffs. The agreement provided for a period of transition to 2000 during which Argentina could continue to require balancing exports, but with Brazil being given an advantageous position in this. On sugar, Argentina wanted to continue to protect marginal producers from the Brazilian industry, while Brazil imposes an export tax to promote local processing. Wheat is included in regional free trade, but not in the CET; Brazil has a minimum price regime (OAS, Compendium 1996). The free trade area has been further limited by two cases where countries raised barriers. In 1992, Argentina raised its 'statistical levy' from 3 to 10 per cent. This was reduced back to 3 per cent, but declared contrary to WTO rules in November 1997. In March 1997, Brazil restricted the use of import credits, requiring cash payment instead of financing at up to twelve months. In both cases, the countries appear to have taken the measures in reaction to external problems, without considering the possibility that these might violate the spirit, if not the rules, of MERCOSUR. In both cases, some concessions to the region were subsequently made, but the possibility of such action may be an important constraint on whether traders can expect the security normal in a free trade area. In November 1997, MERCOSUR made a joint 3-point increase in the external tariff. This was proposed (and imposed) by Brazil. For Argentina, it came when it had just had to remove its statistical tax of 3 per cent, so it accepted the increase. Paraguay and Uruguay were compelled to follow suit.

There is a common external tariff of 0 to 20 per cent. On this, the exceptions cover 12 per cent of tariff lines, with differences to be eliminated by 2001 for Argentina and Brazil and 2006 for the others. There is still no common tariff on capital and high technology products; Brazil had local industries behind high barriers, while Argentina had a 0 tariff which it wanted to retain. (It had reduced this tariff during the period of the Argentina–Brazil agreement, contrary to the treaty.) A provisional agreement would have allowed Argentina to keep its 0 tariff, and Brazilian producers to receive subsidies. The target for an agreement is 2001 for capital goods and 2006 for telecommunications.

The external tariff represented a substantial reduction on the previous tariff level for Argentina and Brazil, In 1990 the average tariff was 17 per cent (already down from 45 per cent in 1987). Following the emergency rise of November 1997, the CET was 15 per cent. For Brazil, the 1990 tariff had been over 30 per cent, and over 100 per cent in 1980, coming down to 14 per cent by 1994.

The agreements with Chile and Bolivia provide for transition periods, of ten years for Bolivia (which had had a tariff of 5–10 per cent), but for up to 18 years for the most sensitive goods, sugar and wheat, for Chile. Chile has a uniform tariff, which was 11 per cent, since reduced to around 9 per cent. 56 per cent of trade is covered during the first eight years, with an initial reduction of 40 per cent in tariffs; a further 41 per cent have a ten-year period, most of the rest with cuts in the tenth to fifteenth year.

From 1995, members could no longer take safeguard action against each other.

SACU

Almost all trade within SACU is covered by the free trade area. There is still the possibility for the smaller countries to put quotas on the export of some agricultural products. There are only limited controls at the borders.

All aspects of the external regime are set by South Africa, with the other members required by the SACU agreement to adopt the same tariffs and other external rules. There was provision in the agreement for individual members to impose special external tariffs for infant industry protection, but the requirement that any protected industry be able to provide 80 per cent of the SACU market has meant that this has not been used by the smaller countries, while South Africa has imposed a tariff at SACU level. There are, however, some bilateral arrangements. All members except South Africa receive preferences under the EU's Lomé arrangements, which gives them duty-free access to the EU market for all manufactures and most agricultural products. In addition, Swaziland receives a quota under the sugar protocol and Botswana and Namibia receive quotas for beef. The EU therefore requires the administration of customs checks to permit verification of origin to avoid South African goods entering under the special regimes. There are also (as will be discussed in Chapter 11 on relations with the rest of the world) bilateral agreements between South Africa and Zimbabwe, Malawi, and Mozambique, and between Botswana and Zimbabwe. In principle, these could give rise to trade flows evading the SACU tariff into other countries, but this has not been an issue in the past. Namibia, however, was stopped from signing an agreement with Zambia, which was moved to the SACU level, so that there may be more concern now.

Summary

Some of the groups described here are too new or too limited to expect a direct effect from tariff reductions on trade (creation or diversion). These include the three continental regions, SAARC, SADC and perhaps ASEAN. The EU and SACU, and probably the Caribbean, as well as ANZCERTA, are too old to identify new results in the last few years. The groups where it is sensible to look at recent figures for trade to indicate the potential or the results of regions are therefore the Group of Three, NAFTA, CACM, the Andean countries, and MERCOSUR.

Rules of origin

For a country with no regional arrangements, no intra-country discrimination, and MFN treatment for all other countries, it is only necessary to identify all goods crossing its border as 'foreign'. While this is the perfectly compliant WTO standard, no country follows it, and therefore all countries need more defined rules for determining origin. Even countries with MFN for all other countries need rules if they discriminate internally, for example in public procurement policies. Countries with different preferential regimes for developing countries, perhaps at more than one level, or ex-colonies need rules to avoid goods from less preferred regions gaining more favourable access by entering through more preferred countries. A free trade area which is not a customs union is the extreme case of this: as long as the members operate different external regimes for non-members, they need to identify goods crossing from another member as either 'regional' or 'external', and, if external, whether they are entitled to a preferential regime. The rules for identifying 'regional' products must be the same. (This may mean applying different rules to different trading partners, or for different purposes.) Even in a full customs union, rules are necessary unless there is not only a CET but also common preferences, common NTBs and common regimes for health and safety and all other standards governing goods within the customs union, and common rules of origin. This means that some form of control or inspection remains necessary at the internal borders of FTAs and all but the most complete customs unions.

Although Viner (1950, p. 60) recognized the possibility that administering an incomplete customs union could have costs because of different border regimes, this has not been sufficiently recognized in analysis of the costs and benefits of regional groups. It is only recently that empirical work has suggested that the administration of rules of origin can be a serious limitation on the functioning of a free trade area. If the rules are drawn particularly tightly or if the production conditions or characteristics of a product mean that they are difficult to meet, then they can constitute a border barrier within a free trade area. If rules adopted at the outset by a region effectively define as foreign (non-regional) any goods which were previously produced using foreign imports, it is arguable that this constitutes an increase in impediments to trade outside the region. As it is capable of producing trade diversion, it might be suitable for international regulation. But even if there is not an increase in protection at the outset, the fact that production conditions change means that the rules of origin could become a barrier in the future.

Even within an MFN system, there can be exceptions, for example provision for temporary import or imports of raw materials for processing and export, or for reimporting processed goods where individual goods are treated differently according to their purpose. These products, however, tend to remain within one firm or within a recognized chain of production, and are not for final consumption. The administrative system, therefore, is not normally a problem. Similarly, rules of origin can work efficiently for goods which are traded frequently, by a limited number of major traders, who become familiar with the requirements. The more complex production patterns become, however, the more firms are involved and, if imports are close substitutes for domestic goods or for imports from different trading partners, and if there is a high share of exports in production, the more difficult it becomes to administer them. As with any regulation, it is also possible to use oppressively detailed or onerous verification and enforcement as an additional barrier.

There is no internationally agreed standard for rules of origin. It was first proposed that there should be common rules, or at least common procedures, for rules of origin in 1973, and this was revived in GATT in 1981 (Palmeter in IDB and UN ECLAC, 1995, p. 201). Following the Uruguay Round, there is a now a WTO commitment to try to establish a common regime for MFN rules of origin. This would at least ensure that statistics by country of origin were compatible. There is no agreement that preference regimes or FTAs should follow the same rules, and these are now a major part of regional negotiations.

There are three commonly used bases for rules of origin, but these give rise to a very large number of possible rules. Goods grown or entirely produced with local inputs within a country have that origin. Where non-national inputs are used, the rule can look either at the share of local value added or at whether the processing was sufficient to change a customs heading. But any percentage or any level of customs heading can be used, with variations among commodities even within the rules of single countries and different more specific regimes for particular goods.

Rules of origin are no longer needed within the EU, but remained in force and a barrier to trade in a few commodities on which there were country quotas or special regimes until 1992. The EU has a variety of different rules for its external agreements and preferential arrangements. They are based on tariff heading (usually at 4-digit level, but occasionally requiring more substantial transformation), but supplemented by percentage requirements for processed goods, and in some cases (clothing and textiles, for example) requirements specific to the industry. The extensive use by the EU of preference arrangements has encouraged the development of the 'technology' of rules of origin, with industrial variations.

Of the continental regions, only the FTAA has started to consider the type of rules of origin to apply; this is with the working groups. It would be likely to follow one of the existing western hemisphere models, and the fact that Canada has used NAFTA rules of origin in bilateral arrangements like that with Chile, and Mexico used them in the Group of Three, suggests that the NAFTA countries will try to extend those rules to the FTAA.

The SADC Trade Protocol outlines the types of rules of origin to be adopted. They are based on local content or change of tariff heading (40 per cent local materials or 35 per cent value added or a change of heading; the level of heading has not yet been specified). This flexibility provides both relative openness and simplicity. The only industry with special rules is fishing, and that requires only that production be local in one of: country of registration, nationality of crew, or nationality of ownership, to give national origin. (The EU requirement for Lomé fish requires all three, plus area of catch.) A possible complication will be the existence of different rules of origin in the various bilateral regimes within SADC. The SADC regime would allow exporting countries to certify origin, without verification by importers.

ASEAN requires that 40 per cent of the value be ASEAN content, but with additional rules for textiles and clothing since 1996.

The US had a variety of rules of origin for its preferential agreements before the agreements with Canada and Mexico, and the NAFTA rules are different again. There were 1498 rules in the US–Canada agreement, and Palmeter (IDB and UN ECLAC, 1995, p. 193) estimated that there were 11 000 in NAFTA, and that the cost of record-keeping would add 3 per cent to the costs of importing (all records must be kept for five years; both exporters and importers must submit certificates; and the importing country can verify the certificates). The rules include change of heading, share of value added (normally 50–60 per cent depending on the form of the calculation), and for some industries specific processing requirements. These are particularly important for cars, dairy products, electronics, textiles, tools, and energy, but also apply to a range including food processing. There is one form of simplification, where imports and domestic products are used as substitutes in production, in which 'inventory management' rules, rather than explicit identification of each input, are allowed. The industries with special provisions include many of those where production using imports from a variety of countries, in substitution, is most frequent, particularly cars, electronics, and textiles. These mean that the rules are likely to be a barrier to trade, and were intended to be. The textile rules in general follow the most restrictive form, of requiring that clothing be made from locally made textiles from locally made yarn ('yarn forward'). The regime for cars gives detailed regulations for different parts and factories. As indicated above, the Group of Three follows the NAFTA rules.

The Central American Common Market requires a change of heading or 25 per cent local content. For fish, it requires territorial water sourcing or national registration or ownership. In 1996, it introduced more detailed rules, excluding processes considered insufficient to give origin.

The Andean group uses customs heading or 50 per cent value added, the standard level set by LAIA, but with only 40 per cent required for the less developed, namely Bolivia and Ecuador, with some special industrial requirements.

CARICOM and SAARC do not appear to have rules of origin.

MERCOSUR, like the Andean Pact, has different rules for the larger and smaller countries. Goods not yet under the CET are subject to a requirement of a change of heading or 60 per cent local content for Argentina and Brazil, but 50 per cent for Paraguay and for some products for Uruguay. The rules also apply for cars and sugar because of the special regimes. The administration of rules of origin in MERCOSUR is more like that of an FTA than a customs union because goods are still controlled and pay tariffs at intra-regional borders.[1] The MERCOSUR rules for clothing are less liberal than the previous Argentine rules for imports from Chile, so that there has been an increase in barriers.

In SACU, there have been no rules of origin, but recent attempts to set up a car assembly plant in Botswana for exports to South Africa has caused negotiations to restrict this type of processing.

Safeguards, anti-dumping, balance of payments tariffs, etc.

These are trade mechanisms used as substitutes for tariffs which impose duties (anti-dumping or countervailing), and therefore which seem to be in conflict with a free trade arrangement. They are no longer permitted within the EU, SACU, ANZCERTA, or CARICOM (although there are provisions for duties put on at Community level for an individual country). They are allowed to a limited extent in the Group of Three, only using tariffs. The Andean group allows safeguard clauses for balance of payments reasons. CACM allows anti-dumping measures. NAFTA allows both bilateral measures and application within the region of any general measures that are taken (although, as seen above, Mexico did not apply its general increase in tariffs to the other members in 1994). MERCOSUR has had emergency tariffs. SADC has not yet regulated these measures, and ASEAN and SAARC allow them.

Allocation of customs revenues

If a customs union collects tariffs at the regional border, it needs a way of allocating these among the member countries. For nation states, distribution according to the general principles of its taxation is normally accepted as fair, with no allowance (except perhaps for customs or port costs) for the location of the border or the destination of the good. For a customs union, this need not hold. For the EU, border taxes are now treated as EU revenue. The other regions do not have a central 'government' with a need for revenue, and must allocate what is collected among the members. For SACU, there is a formula based on the destination of the goods (by including imports from other SACU countries),[2] but adjusted for what are considered to be the costs to the smaller members of being in the union (loss of control over the level of tariffs and the price-raising effect of the tariff). In practice, this is not used. An alternative formula, based on allowing the smaller countries a minimum ratio to their imports and consumption, is binding. This effectively gives the smaller countries more than they would get on the basis of their actual share in total SACU imports. The formula is under renegotiation because South Africa wants to increase its share. The existence of such a formula implied a common interest in the customs union, not simply a way of distributing what is collected according to where it is ultimately consumed. The interest in revising this is a move away from such an assumption. Any move to base the distribution more closely on actual movements of goods would require more rigorous controls at the borders and probably the application of some type of criterion of origin. Because the MERCOSUR countries still collect tariffs at the borders, and provide for cross-shipment in bond where necessary, the distribution problem does not arise.

Notes

1 'Almost two years after the customs union was launched, most member countries continued to demand origin requirements for all products entering from another member country, thereby impeding the free flow of goods. One reason for this procedure is that there is still not available a final consolidated list including the products subject to the MERCOSUR rules of origin and the requirements applicable to each of them' (IDB, Intal, 1996, p. 19).
2 This follows the British colonial tradition of allocating by place of consumption (Viner, 1950, p. 79).

7
Trade in Regions

Measuring trade in regions

The question we examine in this chapter is whether trade within a region is greater than 'normal'. This can be used for potential groups as a measure of whether the countries are suitable candidates to form a region, and, for actual groups, to measure whether there has been an increase in intra-regional trade following the formation of a region. The concept used, which will also be used for investment in Chapter 9, and other linkages in Chapter 10, is 'intensity'. This is used instead of complementarity because it allows us to look at the changes in a region's trade over time.

An examination of trade structures for complementarity, to find the potential trade creation advantages for the proposed area, normally looks at the existing trade structure, allowing for how this will change, given what is known now about present production and resources, if barriers are removed or altered. Complementarity is a limited measure even for industrial countries, because it is static. It is more inappropriate for developing countries where the economic structure changes more rapidly and more fundamentally than in industrial countries; and is indeed a target of government policy. This applies to sectors and technology, but also to macroeconomic variables like trade, as well as fiscal and other balances, rates of exchange, and monetary policy, and often to perceptions of the proper role of government. In practice, complementarity measures tend to produce higher numbers for trade groups among industrial countries or between industrial and developing than for purely developing country groups. Unlike developed groups where the economic objective of forming a region is assumed to be increasing static efficiency, the declared objective of some developing groups has been to achieve economies of scale either through coordinating development, or through the market effects of a larger group.

The most satisfactory way of identifying the effects of a region might be through 'gravity' modelling. This attempts to explain a country's trade by modelling each of its bilateral flows based on the characteristics of the two countries, size, distance, policy barriers, and complementarities. In principle, each of these should be specified in absolute terms, to explain total flows, and also in relative terms to take account of other trading partners. If this could be done satisfactorily, the effect of changing trade barriers with one (or a set of) countries could then be measured directly and used to judge which potential partners would be most likely to have major effects.

Alternatively, it would permit direct estimation of the effect of barriers to trade, and therefore the effects of removing some of those barriers on the formation of a region. It would, of course, need re-estimation over time, as production and technical possibilities changed. In practice, understanding of the non-policy influences on trade is not sufficient to provide a convincing policy-free base-case on which to estimate the effects of policy. The economic size of a country is difficult to measure; giving appropriate weight to different types of wealth, and distance, even for simple transport costs, depends on technical conditions. For more complex effects, 'distance' in the sense of different ways of doing business, even language differences, is not measurable. It is the cost of transactions, not of transport, that is needed. Barriers other than size and distance can also arise for non-trade policy reasons, including differences in other policies or constraints on doing business. The normal gravity model method of taking literal distances between countries cannot capture this. Finally, data constraints would be likely to make it impossible to adjust for changes in the economic conditions. Neither the data nor such models are available for the developing country regions considered here.

The alternative used here is to assume that the influences which would be identified in a complete model are operating on all the trading patterns of a country, before and after the formation of a region. In the absence of a region, these determine the shares of other potential members in each country's trade. If a region is formed, its effects will be reflected in changes in these shares. But the simple changes in share are not a sufficient measure. Other factors may be influencing a country's total trade performance, and therefore increasing or decreasing its share in all its trading partners. To correct for this, we calculate 'intensity' – the ratio of the share of intra-regional trade for a country or for the region as a whole to the share of the region in total trade. Thus it assumes that general economic variables and general policies influence all trade; both policy and some particular economic variables influence the share of individual partners' trade within this; changes in policy towards those partners (in this case forming a region) determine changes in share.

Clearly, this cannot be used uncritically to measure whether the region has had an impact on trade. Production patterns, general trade policies, other policies by the members, policies of third countries, etc. all can have effects on specific trade flows, causing intra-regional trade to increase or decrease independently of the direct 'regional' effects. Some of the other influences can be identified in particular cases: for a few regions, models have been built which will allow a more precise approach to the question.

Dividing by a country's share in world trade corrects for the effect of size, as well as for other changes affecting aggregate trade, but it is insufficient. Almost all the small regions have higher intensity ratios than the larger (Table 7.1). Arithmetically, this is not surprising. The intra-regional trade share can be interpreted alternatively as the ratio of actual intensity to the maximum achievable if all trade were intra-regional, so that while a region with about 40 per cent of world trade (for example, the EU) has a maximum feasible intensity of 2.5, one with less than 1 per cent of world trade (CARICOM) has a maximum of over 100. If countries tend to have a certain share of their trade with close neighbours, then the smaller the region, the larger the measured intensity will be. For this reason, comparisons between regions of roughly the same size are more valid than those of different sizes. In most cases, we are interested in changes in the intensity, which will not be affected by this bias.

The level of the simple measure, the share of the region in regional trade or that of one of its members, is nevertheless also an important statistic. It is a direct measure of the importance of the group, to all its members or to each member. Changes in it permit direct comparison between the effects of regionalization on the economy and those of all other external transactions.

The ambiguities of share and intensity measures can be seen by looking at the GATT and WTO. The expansion of membership means that, if we include current applicants, effectively all trade is now intra-WTO, giving a share and an intensity of 1. The share would have been lower, but the intensity higher before this expansion because there was less trade with the non-members, mainly centrally planned or poor African countries.

In terms of trade creation and diversion, if transport costs were 0 or constant, and all countries were competitive in all commodities, then any intensity greater than 1 would measure trade diversion. Alternatively, if we assume (correctly for many of the regions considered here) that there was no diversion before the region was created because all imports were treated approximately the same, without preferences, then, under the unrealistic assumption that demand for a region's products is constant, or changing equally, in and outside the region, so that there are no production or trade reasons for shares to change, an increase in intensity because of an increase in trade within the region, and a fall in the region's share in total trade, would be indicative evidence of trade diversion. If the share in total trade does not fall or rise, and the intensity rises because intra-regional trade rises (or rises more), then there may have been trade creation.

Intra-regional trade and intensity must be used together. They must be computed not only for the region as a whole, but for individual countries, as long as it appears that decisions are still being made primarily from a country, not a regional, perspective. Such calculations implicitly assume that countries still see themselves as having a choice, of being in or outside the region. Countries or regions do not move along a monotonic progression from country to regional identification; regions (and countries) go through periods of greater and lesser integration. Looking at individual countries is also important in regions which are considering expansion. The effect will be different on different existing members, and therefore this raises the possibility that the question 'which countries' are a region will depend in part on the sequence in which the region was formed. Including the new member might have been an improvement at the beginning, relative to the position of no region, but if it competes with existing members (if it reduces trade diversion), it may not be welcome as a new member.

The measures used in the standard tables in this chapter compare the region's share in a country's or region's exports (or imports) with the country or region's imports (or exports) in total world trade. This is to compare sales with markets.[1] It is arguable that some types of trade, broadly natural resource-based, are too driven by supply and fixed technologies to be useful in attempting to measure the real integration of a region. This might suggest using a measure of intensity of trade restricted to manufactures. As seen in Chapter 6, agriculture is often excluded from FTAs, especially in their early stages. It would be wrong, however, to look only at manufactures, if agriculture is included in the FTA. Because of the normally relatively high degree of protection of conventional agricultural products, and their relative lack of differentiation, trade creation would be expected to be particularly high in such a region. If protection remains against outside suppliers, trade diversion would also be high. Unfortunately, data are poor for many of the regions, and it is difficult to find a satisfactory definition of non-competing products. This may be particularly true in geographical regions where products may be 'specialized' relative to the rest of the world, but are in fact produced and traded extensively within the region. Comparisons of the importance of the region and of different products are possible for some areas, and it is important to use these, both to compare included and excluded products and to analyse the nature of the regional integration.

Table 7.1 gives the shares and intensities for all the regions examined here except SACU.[2] It indicates the difficulties of making comparisons across regions where the small ones tend to have higher intensities. It also shows the large changes which can occur from year to year, again especially in the smaller countries where a small shift can greatly alter the ratio. Data on trade for the less developed countries tend to be published with long delays, so that the data for the last two years are often only estimates; as a result, total world trade is also an estimate, and revisions can have a significant effect. Finally, direction of trade data are often uncertain in small or land-locked countries where there is substantial indirect trade and also in more important countries which use, or are, entrepots with ports serving other countries. One advantage of regions with important trade preferences is that the division of data between trade within the region and outside it may be accurate because the distinction is important for tariff collection, but the corollary of this is that where there is completely free trade and lack of customs control within a customs union, data may be poor because there is no revenue reason to collect the data. Intra-EU trade data are now compiled from VAT returns, not from customs returns, and therefore exclude non-VAT firms (especially small companies). The changes recorded in flows at the transition from customs to VAT data strongly suggest that there is now significant 'missing' trade. Intra-SACU data in principle have a revenue purpose, in allocation of the total revenues, but in practice controls are informal or lacking.

A final reservation about looking for direct effects from a trade group can be noted from the USITC (1997) analysis of the effects of NAFTA. It noted that, as well as the direct effects from changes in trade barriers, the moment of entry into an FTA may see a one-off adjustment effect: 'New treaty partners and new trade partners tend to go out of their way

Table 7.1 Summary, intensities (%)

	Exports							Imports						
	1990	1991	1992	1993	1994	1995	1996	1990	1991	1992	1993	1994	1995	1996
EU 12														
Share of intra-region trade	60.50	61.74	61.79	56.42	54.39	55.23	54.01	58.39	58.38	60.06	54.29	53.09	54.28	54.11
Share in world markets	41.50	41.21	40.56	35.10	34.93	35.09	34.48	39.53	38.00	37.52	35.16	34.75	36.37	35.76
Intensity	1.46	1.50	1.52	1.61	1.56	1.57	1.57	1.48	1.54	1.60	1.54	1.53	1.49	1.51
EU 15														
Share of intra-region trade	66.26	67.26	67.10	62.04	59.71	60.61	59.61	64.28	64.02	65.72	60.44	59.37	60.16	60.03
Share in world markets	45.37	44.72	43.90	38.00	37.99	38.20	37.59	43.15	41.31	40.75	38.14	37.90	39.81	38.92
Intensity	1.46	1.50	1.53	1.63	1.57	1.59	1.59	1.49	1.55	1.61	1.59	1.57	1.51	1.54
MERCOSUR 4														
Share of intra-region trade	8.89	11.11	14.32	18.43	19.45	20.48	22.75	13.85	15.21	16.28	16.77	19.20	19.39	20.49
Share in world markets	0.88	0.98	1.22	1.51	1.46	1.48	1.66	1.34	1.27	1.31	1.42	1.44	1.37	1.40
Intensity	10.15	11.33	11.70	12.20	13.28	13.81	13.73	10.34	11.95	12.47	11.78	13.37	13.43	14.62
MERCOSUR 6														
Share of intra-region trade	11.49	14.07	17.42	21.57	22.14	22.97	25.12	17.08	18.43	19.13	18.90	21.43	20.36	21.62
Share in world markets	1.12	1.24	1.52	1.84	1.77	1.82	2.02	1.61	1.54	1.58	1.68	1.73	1.70	1.71
Intensity	10.23	11.34	11.44	11.73	12.51	12.61	12.41	10.63	11.93	12.09	11.22	12.40	11.94	12.65
CARICOM														
Share of intra-region trade	7.75	7.91	7.69	8.09	7.75	7.12	7.18	5.39	4.97	4.88	4.97	3.91	3.63	3.27
Share in world markets	0.21	0.21	0.20	0.23	0.18	0.17	0.20	0.14	0.13	0.13	0.13	0.12	0.11	0.12
Intensity	37.59	37.81	38.76	34.43	43.08	42.40	36.42	38.58	37.02	36.77	37.04	33.43	31.96	28.16
ANDEAN														
Share of intra-region trade	4.21	6.01	7.80	9.99	10.28	12.01	11.10	6.24	7.17	7.78	9.06	10.77	12.68	13.49
Share in world markets	0.52	0.62	0.72	0.77	0.72	0.74	0.69	0.90	0.82	0.73	0.76	0.79	0.77	0.81
Intensity	8.07	9.63	10.91	12.94	14.31	16.16	16.11	6.95	8.79	10.62	11.90	13.67	16.49	16.73

CACM

Share of intra-region trade	14.83	16.96	19.56	17.71	16.40	15.78	17.73	9.08	10.79	11.74	12.39	12.12	12.82	13.48
Share in world markets	0.19	0.20	0.23	0.27	0.26	0.26	0.26	0.13	0.12	0.12	0.17	0.15	0.18	0.19
Intensity	76.93	86.94	82.32	71.30	64.91	66.68	75.24	72.25	87.43	95.22	79.95	75.81	79.38	83.94

NAFTA

Share of intra-region trade	41.26	42.17	43.53	45.56	47.69	46.03	47.37	33.20	35.21	35.42	40.33	37.23	37.55	39.00
Share in world markets	19.76	19.54	19.87	21.56	21.66	19.81	20.49	15.82	16.40	16.29	17.42	17.13	16.63	17.18
Intensity	2.09	2.16	2.19	2.11	2.20	2.32	2.31	2.10	2.15	2.18	2.32	2.17	2.26	2.27

Group of Three

Share of intra-region trade	2.03	1.82	2.63	3.26	3.09	3.05	2.48	1.98	1.61	1.94	2.48	2.43	3.31	2.88
Share in world markets	1.25	1.93	2.25	2.40	2.43	1.97	2.22	1.48	1.80	1.74	1.94	1.98	2.11	2.37
Intensity	1.62	0.94	1.17	1.36	1.27	1.54	1.12	1.33	0.89	1.11	1.28	1.23	1.57	1.21

ANZCERTA

Share of intra-region trade	7.48	7.41	7.52	8.56	9.51	9.96	9.70	7.53	7.67	7.65	7.93	8.16	7.92	8.46
Share in world markets	1.43	1.35	1.33	1.39	1.45	1.40	1.44	1.42	1.43	1.36	1.40	1.38	1.29	1.40
Intensity	5.22	5.50	5.65	6.16	6.56	7.12	6.73	5.30	5.38	5.61	5.66	5.89	6.14	6.06

ASEAN (ex Singapore)

Share of intra-region trade	4.66	4.60	4.91	5.12	6.07	6.34	7.14	4.49	4.60	5.00	4.89	5.49	5.96	6.42
Share in world markets	3.00	3.33	3.43	3.88	4.16	4.56	4.68	2.62	2.92	3.17	3.61	3.79	3.91	3.98
Intensity	1.55	1.38	1.43	1.32	1.46	1.39	1.52	1.71	1.57	1.58	1.35	1.45	1.53	1.61

ASEAN

Share of intra-region trade	17.09	18.34	18.24	19.57	21.14	21.79	21.43	15.09	16.51	16.96	17.38	16.35	16.25	16.38
Share in world markets	4.81	5.23	5.36	6.15	6.57	7.00	7.17	4.14	4.56	4.81	5.56	6.03	6.21	6.31
Intensity	3.56	3.50	3.40	3.18	3.22	3.11	2.99	3.64	3.62	3.52	3.13	2.71	2.62	2.66

Table 7.1 Continued

	Exports							Imports						
	1990	1991	1992	1993	1994	1995	1996	1990	1991	1992	1993	1994	1995	1996
SAARC														
Share of intra-region trade	3.13	3.59	3.88	3.54	3.71	4.38	3.50	1.91	2.48	2.99	3.07	3.25	3.82	4.09
Share in world markets	1.12	1.03	1.09	1.09	1.08	1.15	1.19	0.79	0.78	0.82	0.89	0.90	0.90	0.94
Intensity	2.79	3.49	3.56	3.24	3.44	3.81	2.93	2.40	3.17	3.64	3.46	3.62	4.26	4.37
SADC														
Share of intra-region trade	2.95	4.48	7.08	7.11	8.01	10.46	11.39	5.06	5.57	7.72	8.46	8.62	10.21	11.82
Share in world markets	0.77	0.76	0.77	0.71	0.71	0.74	0.72	0.92	0.86	0.81	0.83	0.77	0.72	0.75
Intensity	3.84	5.90	9.15	10.04	11.22	14.18	15.78	5.52	6.43	9.48	10.15	11.12	14.19	15.81
Latin America and Caribbean														
Share of intra-region trade	13.48	14.18	16.80	18.46	19.14	18.84	19.10	16.05	14.84	15.04	15.32	15.78	16.85	16.96
Share in world markets	3.06	3.91	4.55	5.08	5.00	4.77	5.37	3.58	3.83	3.78	4.14	4.22	4.36	4.67
Intensity	4.41	3.63	3.70	3.63	3.83	3.95	3.56	4.48	3.88	3.97	3.70	3.74	3.86	3.63

FTAA

Share of intra-region trade	45.19	46.82	49.18	51.58	53.53	52.07	53.53	40.17	41.73	41.64	41.06	43.53	43.99	45.74
Share in world markets	21.93	21.94	22.68	24.81	24.71	23.09	24.09	18.62	19.04	18.88	20.19	19.93	19.44	20.06
Intensity	2.06	2.13	2.17	2.08	2.17	2.26	2.22	2.16	2.19	2.21	2.03	2.18	2.26	2.28

APEC

Share of intra-region trade	68.77	69.14	69.85	72.02	73.90	73.77	73.95	67.15	69.80	70.46	70.32	71.74	72.22	71.38
Share in world markets	40.88	42.00	42.60	46.59	47.35	46.09	47.19	37.88	40.18	40.91	44.50	44.73	43.92	43.59
Intensity	1.68	1.65	1.64	1.55	1.56	1.60	1.57	1.77	1.74	1.72	1.58	1.60	1.64	1.64

AEC

Share of intra-region trade	7.27	7.66	8.12	8.29	8.93	10.16	10.33	7.51	7.14	7.52	7.79	8.41	9.44	10.04
Share in world markets	2.64	2.44	2.64	2.50	2.31	2.25	2.35	2.41	2.22	2.18	2.12	1.95	1.85	2.04
Intensity	2.76	3.14	3.08	3.32	3.87	4.61	4.39	3.12	3.24	3.45	3.68	4.31	5.12	4.91

Source: IMF, *Direction of Trade Statistics Yearbook*

to do business with each other' (p. 2). This suggests that the early observations after a trade group is formed should not be assumed to be directly correlated with the size of tariff cuts. Later observations suffer because they are more likely to be affected by other events and policy changes.

The table shows that while the share of intra-regional trade has increased in most of the regions, it has not done so in some, including two of the oldest, the EU and CARICOM. The picture for intensity shows falls in the ASEAN countries and APEC, but increases in some of the Latin American regions. There is evidently not a simple pattern of increasing regional trade.

The EU

The share of EU intra-trade, taking the current membership of 15 countries, was about two-thirds in 1990, but had fallen by 1996 to about 60 per cent. This is greater than the shares of any of the other regions, with only the continental, APEC and FTAA, being comparable. But it is high partly because the share of the members in world trade is high, at around 40 per cent. This has been falling, so that the intensity has risen, with the rise mainly occurring in 1992–3. The average level is about 1.5 to 1.6. The pattern is similar if the 12 member figures are calculated, so that the addition of three new small members does not seem to be the explanation. This pattern of falling share and rising intensity would be consistent with an increase in trade diversion; and it almost coincides with the final reduction in internal barriers following the completion of the internal market in January 1993.

If we look at the data for individual countries (Table 7.A1), the share of intra-regional trade is always above 50 per cent, and intensity around 1.5; the region is important to all the members. The shares are lower for some of the more peripheral countries, including Finland for exports and Ireland for imports, and also for the larger, including Germany and the UK, for which there is the one fall below a half, in the 1996 figure for imports.[3]

The intensity for manufactures is less than for agricultural products, probably the result of the protection for intra-EU trade in food under the Common Agricultural Policy: high tariffs mean that trade within the region is disproportionate to trade outside the region.

MERCOSUR

As Chile and Bolivia became associate members in 1997, the data show trade among the original four members and with six members. This region shows the most marked increase in the share of intra-regional trade, with a doubling of exports for the original members, from under 10 per cent to over 20 per cent, and an increase of imports from about 14 to 20 per cent. The share of imports in world markets has almost doubled, so that there is a smaller increase in intensity, The share of exports in world trade has also increased, although more modestly. The figures therefore do not suggest trade diversion on the criteria given above. The recent performance of MERCOSUR is different from the increase in intensity observed for the EU, because there it accompanied a fall in share in world trade.

MERCOSUR is early enough in its integration for it to be still possible to compare trade before and after its formation. From 1985 to 1990, when Argentina and Brazil were starting an FTA but the others were not members, intra-MERCOSUR exports had risen from 6 to 9 per cent, and imports from 10 per cent to 15 per cent, principally because of exports from Argentina to Brazil. But this represented a recovery from unusually low levels; the early 1980s figure was 12 per cent.

Taking the six countries, the changes are smaller, not surprisingly as Bolivia and Chile would have had no effects from membership before 1997. It is noticeable that they have a depressing effect on the regional intensity level, suggesting lower intra-regional trade between them and the rest of MERCOSUR, at least until regional effects appear.

Paraguay, the smallest trader in the original four, had the largest increase in its regional imports and exports (from 30 to 45 per cent and from 40 to 58 per cent) respectively (Table 7.A2). Although the increases are large, that for exports is not as great as the increase in MERCOSUR imports as a share of world trade, so even this rise may not indicate that there has been trade creation: intensity has fallen. There had already been an increase from 27 to 30 per cent between 1985 and 1990, before Paraguay entered the FTA with the others. The 1990s increase, therefore, may not be explained by MERCOSUR. For imports, the increase does suggest creation and perhaps diversion, although Paraguay's free trade zones and role as a centre of unrecorded trade could mean that the increase is more in the recording of trade than in trade itself. A large fall in share from 1985 to 1990, however, from 54 to 30 per cent, suggests that the flows are highly variable. For exports, MERCOSUR is now as important to Paraguay as the EU is to its members on average, although the ratio is closer to those of the larger members than the smaller, while for imports it is approaching 50 per cent. Uruguay, the next smallest trader, shows a similar pattern, but with small increases, and the region still accounts for under half its trade. As in Paraguay, there has been a fall in intensity for exports, but little change for imports.

Of the larger countries, Argentina has about an average change in its intra-regional exports; a doubling of share gives a small increase in intensity, but the share of intra-regional imports has risen only slightly because its imports as a share of world imports have increased by almost 300 per cent, from very depressed levels in 1990. Therefore, during this time, intra-regional exports became more important than imports, a sharp contrast to the pre-MERCOSUR years. Argentina's exports to the region had already almost doubled, from 8 to 15 per cent between 1985 and 1990, during the period when it was implementing the free trade agreement with Brazil. Its exports to Brazil rose from 6 to 12 per cent. In that period, there was a much smaller change in its regional imports, from 18 to 21 per cent (Zormelo, 1995, pp. 39–43).

Brazil is the only country to see large increases in its intra-regional imports and exports, with corresponding increases in intensity. For exports, this was accompanied by a fall in its share of world exports, suggesting some diversion, but there was a rise in share for imports. In the years from 1985 to 1990, its exports to the region had not increased, remaining at about 4 per cent, although it had had an increase in imports, from 5 to 10 per cent. Exports may therefore have caught up with the previous increase in imports.

For Argentina and Brazil, MERCOSUR is substantially less important than the EU is to its members, with intra-regional trade at about a third for exports and a quarter for imports for Argentina, and both under a sixth for Brazil. (Preliminary figures for 1997 do not alter this picture, IDB INTAL, 1997, p. 11.) These are much lower shares than for the smaller MERCOSUR members, suggesting a significant asymmetry in the importance of the region to the members for trade. If we look at the intra-regional trade including the new members, the ratio for imports rises to over 40 per cent, but both ratios are still below 20 per cent for Brazil. Chile is particularly important for Argentina.

For Bolivia and Chile, before their FTAs came into effect, the region was substantially less important than for the original four. For Bolivia, a small country, intra-regional trade was about 20 per cent, and had been falling sharply in the period 1990–6; for Chile, the share had been rising for exports in the 1990s, after stagnating between 1985 and 1990, and it remained at around 15 per cent for imports, little changed from its level in the 1980s.

One clear picture which emerges is of rapidly growing imports from all areas; the increase within MERCOSUR must be seen as a part of this.

As noted in Chapter 6, average tariffs had fallen sharply, and the CET is lower than preceding tariffs, so a rapid increase in imports would be expected. Disaggregating imports into different categories finds that more have shifted from MERCOSUR to non-MERCOSUR sources than the reverse (Devlin, 1996, in IDB newsletter). One analysis that did find substantial trade diversion (Yeats, 1997) did not take full account of the changes in tariffs and ignored the rapid increase in total imports.

Table 7.2 allows us to examine the shares by broad economic category. For exports, intra-regional trade is highest for fuels and transport equipment, and both show significant growth since 1991. This is true for both Argentina and Brazil, although the growth for cars and car parts is more spectacular for Brazil. It is low for food and raw materials, and has been falling, and about average for both consumer and capital goods. For Paraguay, the importance of MERCOSUR for fuel and other primary products means that it has become less important for manufactured goods than it is in total. Imports show a different pattern, with transport still important, but food also high. Both cars and some foods are under special arrangements (see Chapter 6).

For Argentina, MERCOSUR is the major market for cars and other manufactures, as well as fuels, while for Brazil it is only over 50 per cent for cars; it is low for other transport and for all other goods. There has, however, been growth for almost all commodities for both countries. In contrast, for Paraguay and Uruguay, MERCOSUR is important in almost all goods, and again there have been increases in most goods. On the import side, it is important to Argentina for some foods, and for specialised products within fuels and transport parts, and for Brazil, only for foods.

The most rapid growth, by sector, has been in fuels, for all four countries (Izam, 1997, p. 12), and in some sectors which were very restricted at the beginning of the integration, notably in cars for Argentina, while individual foods have also grown rapidly. For Brazil, cars and car parts, food, and clothing are important. For Paraguay, food, clothing and simple manufactures have grown; for Uruguay, food clothing and cars (ibid., 1997, pp. 13–20). For Chile, MERCOSUR is important in exports mainly for manufactures, again including transport equipment, but for food in imports. For Bolivia, it is most important for exports for car parts, and this is the only sector in which it is a major market. On imports, it is again only important for petrol. These results show that MERCOSUR is important in only a limited range of sectors.

Looking at shares of commodities in intra-MERCOSUR trade, rather than MERCOSUR shares relative to other shares, suggests a concentrated

Table 7.2 MERCOSUR: Regional trade as a share of world trade by broad economic categories, 1995 (%)

				Exports			
	MERCOSUR 4	Argentina	Brazil	Paraguay	Uruguay	Chile	Bolivia
Food and Beverages	18.41	29.48	5.88	57.07	49.83	10.73	9.20
Primary, for industry	22.24	38.74	4.26	52.03	88.41	35.64	5.22
Primary, for consumption	24.02	28.46	10.80	83.54	38.18	10.41	2.60
Processed, for industry	9.43	14.01	3.12	88.06	94.66	13.08	1.29
Processed, for consumption	19.35	30.08	8.39	46.36	34.92	10.48	34.51
Industrial Supplies, nes	13.72	18.28	10.49	56.10	32.45	8.70	2.22
Primary	10.03	16.65	4.04	64.32	10.63	8.15	2.03
Processed	14.58	18.66	12.01	44.34	35.86	8.91	2.40
Fuels and Lubricants	41.66	43.65	27.47	96.80	94.66	55.23	68.50
Primary	41.95	43.39	0.40	0	0	99.90	68.20
Motor spirits	38.31	40.04	32.39	100.00	95.90	52.13	100.00
Other	60.19	62.13	12.89	91.00	48.70	51.74	0
Capital Goods	24.77	42.67	21.32	92.50	77.44	30.75	12.71
Capital goods	26.36	53.37	22.31	92.40	76.65	33.93	12.79
Parts and accessories	21.80	30.44	19.45	100.00	81.26	23.34	0
Transport Equipment	44.64	84.91	29.85	100.00	95.94	38.41	89.59
Passenger motor cars	72.13	96.61	55.36	100.00	99.30	13.69	0
Industrial	41.63	82.36	22.30	100.00	43.35	48.43	0
Non-industrial	39.98	66.20	27.48	0	97.32	45.33	0
Parts and accessories	40.82	83.35	28.75	100.00	95.94	32.99	89.59

Consumer Goods, nes	26.15	48.56	18.33	55.02	59.17	47.68	3.93
Durable	24.64	68.95	16.08	8.60	96.04	21.41	0.90
Semi-durable	14.57	24.28	9.63	65.25	48.59	31.21	1.32
Non-durable	50.39	69.18	40.54	47.58	82.81	64.42	26.63
Other, nes	20.93	19.88	21.62	0	0	6.77	0
Total	20.57	32.31	13.40	56.68	47.41	10.81	12.54

Imports

Food and Beverages		42.71	55.86	66.07	48.52	14.64
Primary, for industry		72.60	63.42	74.86	36.45	9.26
Primary, for consumption		19.01	45.01	66.43	25.37	12.24
Processed, for industry		55.75	54.67	72.25	64.52	6.99
Processed, for consumption		39.93	58.12	63.20	53.68	22.10
Industrial Supplies, nes		30.48	10.35	57.32	22.02	29.17
Primary		49.58	23.98	67.25	16.68	17.30
Processed		29.28	8.57	56.11	22.61	30.41
Fuels and Lubricants		16.00	14.62	48.32	38.27	82.15
Primary		0.05	19.01	41.74	45.69	0
Motor spirits		13.03	9.18	55.58	2.07	82.50
Other		80.37	6.08	82.99	28.43	63.11
Capital Goods		10.29	1.71	24.39	8.30	19.54
Capital goods		9.68	1.90	22.67	8.91	20.57
Parts and accessories		11.71	1.44	29.63	6.55	16.08

Table 7.2 Continued

			Imports				
MERCOSUR 4	Argentina	Brazil	Paraguay	Uruguay	Chile	Bolivia
Transport Equipment	36.55	18.17		47.85	13.69	8.29
Passenger motor cars	23.17	7.36		41.81	4.37	2.80
Industrial	23.98	37.10		61.06	17.60	9.78
Non-industrial	5.99	4.44		21.12	1.32	4.83
Parts and accessories	51.56	23.51		55.63	21.76	13.16
Consumer Goods, nes	17.70	11.62		35.44	8.55	20.32
Durable	15.24	16.09		22.44	3.35	11.94
Semi-durable	18.54	10.60		36.07	8.99	12.60
Non-durable	18.62	9.79		47.29	13.91	26.24
Others, nes	4.94	9.06		36.29	4.77	4.22
Total	23.96	14.00		46.37	18.20	21.72

Source: OAS, Foreign Trade Information System

composition even more strongly. For Argentine exports to Brazil, 100 customs lines account for 90 per cent of the total, a much more concentrated pattern than for total Argentine exports. Oil and wheat alone are almost a third, with maize at 4 per cent, and other foods another 11.5 per cent; cars are 4.5 per cent, but other car parts add a total of 7 per cent (1994 data). These products alone thus explain more than half (Fernando Porta in Chudnovsky, 1996, pp. 203–4). Trade is still also concentrated in relatively few, and large, companies. There is so far little evidence that new companies are moving into the market.

Trade within MERCOSUR is important in relatively few sectors, not across the whole range of production. There have been some very rapid increases, but these have in general been in the traditional traded sectors. Surveys of industry and officials suggest that in most industries the region has not yet become an important element of industrial planning. The most important changes in the structure of an industry have perhaps been in cars (discussed in Chapter 10 as a sectoral phenomenon). The products where regional opening might have brought either trade creation or substantial diversion because they were heavily protected before MERCOSUR (sugar and cars) are still excluded, so that there is little effect. These limited results are consistent with the history which suggested that MERCOSUR was intended initially principally for political reasons, with economic links coming later.

CARICOM

As the share of CARICOM in world trade is 0.1 to 0.2 per cent, giving large swings for small changes, and data for some of the countries are missing or only estimated for recent years, the calculations for this region are much more uncertain than for MERCOSUR. The share of the region in total trade is falling, but intra-regional trade is falling even faster, giving a decline in intensity for both imports and exports. The high numbers for intensity suggest a strong regional influence, whether from CARICOM or other factors. The shares of CARICOM for individual countries are high for its size, but still low compared with those of larger regions, and therefore suggest caution in assessing its importance in the members' external policy (Table 7.A3). The highest shares for intra-regional trade are found in the smallest or most central countries, including over 20 per cent for Barbados, Dominica, Grenada (although Grenada is falling) and St Vincent; other countries are much lower, with Belize, Guyana, and Trinidad and Tobago falling sharply to 5 per cent or lower, and Jamaica more stable, but at only 3 per cent. Barbardos,

Dominica, Grenada, and St Vincent all have intensities well over 100. Data by commodity are not available.

As CARICOM is a long-standing region, the changes will represent changes in economic relations with other countries, more than changes within the community itself. The region has been increasing its links with Latin American countries, as well as preserving access to the US and the EU (discussed further in Chapter 11).

ANDEAN GROUP

Although the Andean group is one of the oldest, intra-regional trade was still low in 1990; it has increased greatly since then. As there has been little change in the region's share in total world trade, the result is a sharp rise in intensity. Before then, intra-regional trade had changed little from the early 1980s, at around 4–5 per cent, although this represented an increase on its early years – 1960: 1 per cent; 1970: 2 per cent. The share of the region is now about 11 per cent for exports and 13 per cent for imports, lower than MERCOSUR, but with about the same intensity, given the smaller size. On exports, there were large increases for all the countries except Ecuador and Peru (Table 7.A4). The countries whose regional integration increased (see Chapter 6) were Venezuela and Colombia, with some participation by Ecuador; Bolivia (with an increase from 6 to 22 per cent) was negotiating entry into a different group; Peru was on the side lines. These differences do not therefore correspond to differences in institutional integration. On imports, all saw major increases in share. As in MERCOSUR, the members were cutting their MFN tariffs during this period, so that preferences for Andean members were correspondingly reduced.

For Bolivia, the Andean Group accounted for about the same share of exports as its new group, MERCOSUR (Tables 7.A2 and 7.A4), but the share to the Andean countries had been increasing and that to MERCOSUR falling. On imports, however, MERCOSUR is much more important. Except for Bolivia and Ecuador, the Andean shares for all the countries were below 20 per cent.

For Bolivia, the Andean countries were important especially for food exports and for a few manufactures, and not a major supplier for any imports. For Colombia the Andean market was important for manufactures, especially cars, while it mainly imported primary goods. Venezuela had no important trade flows. The Andean market was the principal market for manufactures only for Ecuador, which is not primarily an exporter of manufactures, but it was more important for manufactures than for other commodities for Venezuela and Ecuador. If we look at the changes in exports over the 1990–5 period, manufactured exports to the Andean market rose faster than to the rest of the world for all five countries. It had always been a more important market for manufactures and other non-traditional exports than other areas.

The Andean countries thus show the traditional Latin American pattern of relatively high exports of manufactured goods to the regional market. In spite of the general reduction in tariffs, tariffs on these are still high.

Central American Common Market

This is similar in size to CARICOM, but intra-regional trade shares are much greater, with a regional figure of about 18 per cent for exports and 13 per cent for imports. These very high figures, higher than those of the much larger Andean Group and only slightly below those of MERCOSUR, give the highest levels for the intensity measure of any group considered here. Although both shares and intensities have been rising in recent years, they remain much lower than in the early 1980s. Shares then were around 20 per cent, falling to 11 per cent in 1986. The increase came between 1960 (7 per cent) and 1970 (25 per cent). The highest intra-regional trade figures are for exports for El Salvador and Guatemala and for imports for Nicaragua, at 30 per cent and over. Although lower, the figures for other countries are also high for the size of the region, and increasing (Table 7.A5). For exports, as the share of the region in world trade has been increasing, there has been little change in the intensity, while for imports there has been an increase in intensity. CACM, even more than CARICOM, raises the question of how important regional influences other than tariffs are in leading to high regional trade.

NAFTA

The share of intra-regional trade in NAFTA has been growing, and as there has been no change in the area's share in world trade, this has led to an increase in intensity for both imports and exports. As in MERCOSUR, the recent period corresponds to the time of the group's formation, so that there is a possibility that this implies trade diversion (Table 7.1). The share of intra-regional trade for NAFTA as a whole is important (47 per cent for exports; 39 per cent for imports), but not as large as for the EU. The more important difference between the two regions is the contrast in NAFTA between the smaller members and the large, the US. For Canada and Mexico, intra-regional trade is more than 80 per cent for exports, and around 70 per cent for imports. For the US both shares are about 30 per cent (Table 7.A6). Thus, the region's importance is greater for Canada and Mexico than for most of the smaller EU countries, while the US has a much lower share than for the larger EU countries, similar to that of Argentina in MERCOSUR, although higher than that of Brazil, the largest member. NAFTA's smaller share in world trade means that the intensity for the US is comparable with that for the larger members of the EU. For all three NAFTA countries, the intensity has been increasing, although Mexico has also seen an important increase in its share in world trade.

As in the other Latin American regions, NAFTA's liberalization has been combined with a major general liberalization, undertaken by Mexico in the 1990s. Against this, Mexico underwent a large devaluation in 1995 because of its exchange crisis of end-1994, the first year of NAFTA, which reduced all its imports in 1995 by 9 per cent. Its imports from the other NAFTA countries, however, fell by only 5.5 per cent.

The share of exports and imports to NAFTA is high for Mexico (above 50 per cent) in all sectors, with little difference by commodity except for the low number for chemicals. NAFTA is important to Canadian exports for all products, with little difference between manufactures and primary products (Table 7.3). The highest share is for cars and car parts, and that has been true since before the establishment of NAFTA because of the US–Canada car agreement of the 1960s. For the US, cars are again important mainly because of their importance in trade with Canada: this is the only good for which NAFTA accounts for more than half of US exports. The pattern for imports is similar, except that there is no good for which NAFTA accounts for more than half of imports for the US; cars are again the most important.

In 1997, the US Government published two analyses of the changes in trade following the establishment of NAFTA. There have also been other attempts to use gravity or other models to analyse the effects. The USITC (1997) report gave a detailed sectoral analysis of trade flows and employment in the US two years after NAFTA. Its emphasis was on the sectoral results because it 'found no effects of NAFTA on either GDP levels or growth rates in the United States in large part due to the limited time period in which NAFTA has been in effect and the size of the US economy compared to Mexico and Canada. Aggregate domestic

Table 7.3 NAFTA: Regional trade by major SITC sector and by country, as a share of world trade (%)

	Exports NAFTA		Imports NAFTA	
	1990	1994	1990	1994
NAFTA				
Fuels, lubricants, etc.	55.9	68.9	24.5	31.3
Machines, transport equip	45.9	51.6	37.3	39.2
Manufactured goods	58.1	64.0	38.1	41.1
Chemicals, reltd. prod.nes	28.9	35.3	38.3	40.8
Misc manufactured articles	33.2	43.3	15.4	21.4
Cars and car parts	84.9	82.0	47.0	53.7
Other primary	27.5	34.3	43.8	48.8
Manufactures	44.0	50.3	33.1	36.0
All commodities	41.7	48.4	33.4	37.4
CANADA				
Fuels, lubricants, etc.	84.1	90.1	29.5	25.2
Machines, transport equip	89.6	91.2	73.1	75.4
Manufactured goods	80.8	84.2	65.5	69.3
Chemicals, reltd. prod.nes	68.4	78.8	75.5	77.9
Misc manufactured articles	83.1	84.7	52.5	61.2
Cars and car parts	98.0	96.6	77.8	86.0
Other primary	45.8	56.8	62.3	63.8
Manufactures	85.2	88.1	69.1	72.7
All commodities	75.4	82.2	65.9	69.8
MEXICO				
Fuels, lubricants, etc.	58.5	75.2	83.5	78.7
Machines, transport equip	88.3	94.1	67.6	69.9
Manufactured goods	73.3	79.1	68.7	72.5
Chemicals, reltd. prod.nes	45.9	53.9	67.0	69.4
Misc manufactured articles	66.0	93.5	65.6	71.5
Cars and car parts	91.9	90.2	70.3	79.1
Other primary	85.3	84.8	69.4	77.7
Manufactures	76.9	89.9	67.5	70.6
All commodities	71.0	87.7	68.5	71.2
USA				
Fuels, lubricants, etc.	24.5	25.4	23.0	30.7
Machines, transport equip	32.3	34.2	25.7	27.3
Manufactured goods	42.0	49.4	29.8	29.8
Chemicals, reltd. prod.nes	21.4	26.7	22.4	22.8
Misc manufactured articles	26.5	31.1	7.9	11.2
Cars and car parts	73.2	68.6	36.3	43.0
Other primary	16.0	20.5	36.0	40.3
Manufactures	31.1	34.4	22.2	23.9
All commodities	28.2	31.7	24.1	26.5

Source: ITC, *PC/TAS International Trade Statistics 1995*

employment effects of NAFTA were also not discernible, which was not an unexpected result considering the state of almost full employment prevailing in the United States.' (p. 5). It found effects in only a few industries. Two types of sectoral examination were carried out. It used trade equations (with monthly data) from five years before NAFTA to 1996, expressing trade as a function of relative prices, incomes, and exchange rates, with dummies for the three post-NAFTA years. It identified an effect as 'a threshold of three statistically significant annual changes (of the same direction)', i.e. where all dummies had the same sign. This may not have fully allowed for correlation among the dummies, and cannot remove the effect of any other change which may have occurred in 1994 and had a continuing effect. Using this criterion, it found significant effects on US imports from and exports to Mexico for: wood products, printing products, plastics, machinery, electrical lights, radios and TVs, and medical instruments, and on imports alone for: clothing, soft drinks, metals, and car parts; and increased exports alone of: textiles, paper products, and chemicals. Two industries were expected to show significant effects from trade diversion, because of the level of protection and strict rules of origin: cars and textiles and clothing. The statistical tests tend to support this.

The second approach by the USITC used industry data on 68 sectors, and showed that in motor vehicles, textiles and clothing, US imports from non-NAFTA countries increased much less than those from NAFTA – motor vehicles: 10.9 per cent compared with 26 per cent; textiles: 5 per cent compared with 18 per cent, and clothing 15 per cent compared with 21 per cent. The USITC (1997, p. 5.9) concludes that 'evidence of trade diversion is best illustrated in the analysis of apparel products, where there has been a significant increase in US imports from NAFTA partners and a commensurate decrease in imports from Asian and Caribbean Basin countries between 1993 and 1996'. There were also increases in imports of fruit and vegetables from Mexico relative to those from the rest of the world. There was an increase in imports of fish, but as there was no tariff on Mexican imports before NAFTA, it does not consider this a NAFTA effect. The fish effect, along with some increases observed in 1994 that were not maintained in 1995 and 1996, may support the 'new partner' (or publicity) effect of a new FTA.

On the export side, it found increased exports of cotton and textiles, for processing industries in Mexico to meet the rules of origin for textiles and apparel exports to the US, and, in some cases, the establishment of new factories in Mexico; this suggests an effect from the strict rules of origin in this sector. By raising the costs of producing NAFTA-qualifying clothing in Mexico, and thus reducing the effective preference for Mexican goods over those from the rest of the world, the rules of origin could reduce the trade diversion (Kelegama, 1997, p. 236). US exports of cattle and beef were displacing imports from Australia and New Zealand, because Mexico's MFN tariff was 15–25 per cent. On appliances, it found that there was a shift of assembly plants from Asia to Mexico to meet the rules of origin requirements.

Most of these observations suggest trade diversion as well as creation, supporting the indication from the growth in intensity. Data on US imports of yarn, textiles, and clothing by country show where the changes were occurring. Between 1995 and 1996, imports from Mexico and Canada rose. The other areas showing a rise were the Caribbean and China, but Taiwan, Hong Kong, and South Korea all had small falls, while ASEAN was little changed. For all non-NAFTA countries, there was a small rise.

Gould (1998) uses a gravity model, with additional variables to take account of Mexico's liberalization and the pre-existing Canada–US free trade agreement. He found a significant effect from NAFTA on US exports to Mexico and almost equally large but slightly less significant effects on its imports from Mexico. Trade diversion effects gave a small negative effect on US exports to Canada, so that overall there was a slight negative effect for the US and also for Mexico (because of the direct US–Mexico effects), with a small positive effect for Canada. All these net effects, however, were around 0.5 to 1 per cent of the countries' total trade, and only for Mexico were even the two gross effects important. He concludes that the important effects are the sectoral ones: 'freer trade does not determine the number of jobs available in a country, but it does determine the types of jobs available'. Longer-term dynamic simulations of NAFTA can give much greater welfare gains for the participants (for example, Kouparitsas, 1997).

The detailed data and analysis available for NAFTA give a fuller picture of the types of effects which can be seen only in outline using the more limited data available for the developing country regions. But the conclusions are not very different. This detailed sectoral analysis suggests that aggregate measures that show only small effects can be misleading, In NAFTA, as seems to be the case also in MERCOSUR, the effects tend to be concentrated in a few sectors, where they may be large. This does not necessarily imply that effects will be as concentrated over the medium or longer term. Both NAFTA and MERCOSUR are new.

As production changes over time, in a situation where the FTA would be part of the background, other sectors may respond. The problem is that, beyond a few years, comparisons with the pre-FTA situation will become increasingly difficult.

Group of Three

There has been a small increase in intra-regional imports in the Group of Three, but only fluctuations in the share for exports. For both the shares are very small, at 2–3 per cent, although the region itself is substantially larger than the Andean Pact, where the share was 16 per cent. This gives very low (and falling) intensities; the ratio of about 1 indicates no regional effect at all even from proximity and other non-institutional effects. It is Mexico which accounts for these very low shares (Table 7.A7). Colombia and Venezuela (also linked by the Andean Group) have significant, although still small, shares of trade, and intensities well above 1. These are much smaller than their Andean Group shares because both Peru and Ecuador are more important trading partners for them than Mexico. For Mexico the share of intra-regional trade is under 1 per cent, and the intensity is much less than 1, that is, it trades less with the region than would be expected simply from the region's share in world trade. There is no commodity group for which the G3 is important, for either imports or exports. For Venezuela, the group is important for its manufactured exports, taking more than half its exports of cars, but it is also important for primary goods other than fuels; this means that Colombia is an important importer for all Venezuela's non-traditional exports. These low trade flows raise the question of why the Group of Three was negotiated. It clearly was not for trading reasons.

ANZCERTA

ANZCERTA is included here because it forms part of APEC, but also because it offers a developed country example of a very small region. The share of intra-regional trade is growing, but remains under 10 per cent for the region as a whole, although its share in world trade is larger than that of the Andean Group, and only slightly lower than MERCOSUR. The intensity is therefore lower than in most of the Latin American regions or CARICOM. This suggests that the high intensities found in Latin America are not simply because they are small regions, separated by large distances from other trading partners.

There is some asymmetry between the two members, especially on imports, where intra-trade is 5 per cent for Australia and 24 per cent for New Zealand (Table 7.A8). Even New Zealand, however, is not as dependent on the region as the US is on NAFTA; the region is thus only about as important in economic terms to the more affected member as MERCOSUR is to its least integrated member. For both, the share of regional trade for manufactured exports is about twice as high as for all commodities, although there is little difference between manufactures and other commodities for imports. This conforms to the simple model proposed at the beginning of this chapter, that manufactures are more differentiated; it also reflects the fact that agriculture is not protected heavily in ANZCERTA.

ASEAN

The data for ASEAN suffer from the problem that much trade goes through the port of Singapore, and therefore data for intra-regional trade may include some trans-shipped goods. For this reason, the shares were calculated with and without Singapore. In addition, Singapore does not report trade with Indonesia: these figures have used Indonesia's reported trade with Singapore (Table 7.A9).

Including Singapore, intra-regional trade is about 21 per cent for exports and 16 per cent for imports. Although this share has been rising, especially for exports, the share of the region in total world trade has risen more so that intensity has been falling. The same pattern holds for the region excluding Singapore. The share of the region in world trade is substantially higher than for any of the other regions considered here, except the EU and NAFTA, so the low regional shares give a low level for the intensity measure, of 2–3.

The region is most important for Brunei, especially for its imports; for Singapore itself, at about 25–30 per cent; and for Malaysia, at about 28 per cent for exports and 18 per cent for imports. But for all, this is because of the share of trade coming through Singapore. For Thailand, the shares are under 20 per cent, and for Vietnam low for exports, but over 20 per cent for imports. The share is lowest for Indonesia, at about 10 per cent. If Singapore is excluded, however, all the country ratios fall below 10 per cent, and the intensity is only 1.5. Clearly the correct numbers fall between these extremes. Even on the higher numbers, the shares are well below those of MERCO-SUR. ASEAN is not of major trading importance to any of its members.

Table 7.4 Commodity structure of ASEAN trade, 1990, 1993 (%)

Country		Year	Total value (US$ m)	Food items	Agricultural raw material	Fuels	Ores & metals	Manufactured goods	Chemical products	Other manufactured goods	Machinery	Unallocated
Brunei	Exports	1990	2,212	0	0	86.4	0.2	12.6	0	11.5	1.0	0.8
		1992[a]	2,366	0.6	0	96.9	0.1	2.4	0.1	1.0	1.3	0
	Imports	1990	1,000	19.2	0.4	0.9	1.3	77.9	6.9	36.5	34.5	0.3
		1992[a]	2,607	15.7	0.4	0.6	1.1	81.8	6.3	37.2	38.2	0.5
Indonesia	Exports	1990	25,681	11.2	5.0	44.0	4.4	35.5	2.4	31.6	1.4	0
		1993	36,843	10.8	4.2	28.4	3.5	53.1	2.2	45.9	4.9	0
	Imports	1990	22,008	5.1	4.7	8.9	4.3	76.9	16.1	18.2	42.5	0.2
		1993	28,333	6.5	5.2	7.7	4.0	76.3	14.4	19.6	42.4	0.3
Malaysia	Exports	1990	29,420	11.7	13.8	17.8	2.1	54.2	1.7	16.4	36.1	0.4
		1993	47,128	9.4	8.7	10.3	1.2	69.7	2.1	23.3	44.2	0.6
	Imports	1990	29,170	7.3	1.4	5.3	3.6	82.2	8.8	21.6	51.7	0.2
		1993	45,616	6.1	1.2	3.7	3.5	83.9	7.5	21.1	55.4	1.5
Philippines	Exports	1990	8,194	24.9	4.8	4.9	6.1	39.0	3.4	22.1	13.5	20.4
		1993	11,271	15.6	1.5	2.0	4.5	41.6	2.3	20.7	18.7	34.8
	Imports	1990	12,993	10.3	2.4	14.9	3.4	53.2	11.4	15.8	26.0	15.8
		1993	17,638	7.8	2.3	11.5	2.9	59.6	9.6	17.5	32.4	16.0

			Value									
Singapore	Exports	1990	52,753	5.2	2.6	17.9	1.6	71.7	6.6	17.6	47.5	1.1
		1993	74,071	5.0	1.4	12.2	1.5	78.5	6.4	17.3	54.8	1.5
	Imports	1990	60,954	6.1	1.7	15.9	2.1	73.2	7.6	23.3	42.4	1.1
		1993	85,041	5.9	0.9	10.9	2.2	79.0	6.9	23.2	49.0	1.1
Thailand	Exports	1990	23,072	28.7	5.1	0.8	1.0	63.1	20.0	41.4	19.8	1.2
		1993	37,158	21.9	4.0	1.1	0.5	71.1	2.8	40.6	27.7	1.5
	Imports	1990	33,048	5.0	4.7	9.3	3.6	75.0	10.4	24.0	40.6	2.4
		1993	46,065	4.7	4.2	7.5	3.2	77.9	10.1	23.2	44.5	2.5
ASEAN	Exports	1990	141,332	12.5	5.9	20.2	2.4	57.3	3.8	23.9	29.5	1.9
		1993	208,837	10.6	4.0	13.1	1.8	67.9	3.8	27.8	36.2	2.8
	Imports	1990	159,533	6.4	2.7	11.4	3.1	74.1	9.9	21.9	42.4	2.3
		1993	225,300	6.0	2.3	8.3	2.9	77.9	8.8	22.0	47.1	2.5

Notes: [a] values refer to 1993 values although the structure is for 1992

Food items refer to SITC 0 + 1 + 22 + 4

Agricultural raw materials refer to SITC 2 less (22 + 27 + 28)

Fuels refer to SITC 3

Ores and metals to SITC 27 + 28 + 68

Manufactured goods refer to SITC 5 to 8 less 68 of which: chemical products refer to SITC 5; other manufactured goods refer to SITC (6 +8) less 68; and machinery and transport equipment refer to SITC 7

Source: *ASEAN Economic Bulletin*, November 1996, using data from UNCTAD, *Handbook of International Trade and Development Statistics* (1995)

For Brunei, most of its exports to ASEAN are fuels (Table 7.4), while it imports manufactures. Indonesia has been moving to a more balanced pattern, from a high share, almost a half, of fuels to mainly manufactured goods. Again, manufactures make up the majority of imports. For all the other countries, trade is mainly in manufactures. Foods are not large for any of the flows (over 20 per cent only for the Philippines and Thailand). This reflects the lack of progress on lowering barriers on agricultural goods.

For all members except Singapore, ASEAN is a major supplier of fuels, reflecting the role of Singapore in the oil trade. ASEAN is a significant market for Malaysia in most sectors, but again this is mainly the role of Singapore; it is also a major market for manufactures for Indonesia and the Philippines. ASEAN is an important market for cars for Singapore, Malaysia , the Philippines and Thailand, but the low level of exports of cars from all of these means that they are not in fact major commodities in intra-ASEAN trade. What is important is manufactures generally. Their role, however, reflects the general pattern of ASEAN trade, not a greater specialization for regional markets, as in Latin America; manufactures are the major part of ASEAN exports to all destinations, and the ASEAN share is never significantly higher for exports of manufactures than the average. It is slightly higher for Indonesia and Thailand, about the same for Malaysia, and lower for the Philippines and in most years for Singapore (because of the role of oil). As intra-ASEAN tariff reductions apply only to manufactures, this small difference between manufactures and other products suggests little effect for ASEAN.

The region does not, therefore, seem as integrated for its size as the Latin American regions.

SAARC

Intra-regional trade in SAARC is slightly lower than in ASEAN excluding Singapore, at about 3–4 per cent, but the share of the region in world trade is much lower, so that intensities are higher similar to those for ASEAN including Singapore for exports, and higher for imports. The shares and intensity are rising for imports. For India, the largest member, the share is very low for imports, at under 1 per cent, but it is similar to the average for exports (Table 7.A10). For Pakistan, the two shares are similar, at about 2.5 per cent, but this represents a fall for exports and a rise for imports in the last six years. Bangladesh and Sri Lanka also have had a falling share for exports, but the share of their imports from India has surged, giving a rise in share for the region from 7 to 17 per cent for Bangladesh, and from 7 to 12 per cent for Sri Lanka. The smaller countries, the Maldives and Nepal, have large shares, for both exports and imports, of more than a quarter. This gives a very unbalanced distribution of interest in the region, with India important for two of the other members, although it does not itself have a high share of intra-regional trade. But even the highest shares do not represent serious dependence on the region, although the figures for Bangladesh and Sri Lanka imply a stronger commitment than those for most ASEAN countries.

For Sri Lanka, SAARC has been increasingly important as a supplier of manufactures, because of its high share for cars, but even this is only about 20 per cent. This is reflected in the export figures for India.

As the SAARC intra-regional liberalization has been very limited, it is difficult to attribute these changes to it. India has been liberalizing its imports more generally, as well as in SAARC; the increase in SAARC trade has affected its exports.

SADC

In relation to world trade SADC is comparable to the Andean group, at just under 1 per cent. The share of intra-regional trade is also similar, and has risen since 1990, giving it high intensity. But although there are a variety of bilateral arrangements among the members, as well as SACU for five of them, none of these has changed, and SADC itself is still has only at the stage of proposals for trade integration. Therefore, any increase in intra-regional trade cannot be the result of changes in trade policy. Some of the rise could reflect increased trade (or increased recording of trade) with South Africa following the change of government there in 1994, but the rise began before this. For SADC (and perhaps also the Andean countries), the distance from major trading partners means that the lower within-region transport costs are themselves a form of implicit preferential arrangement.

The share of intra-regional trade has risen from 3 to 11 per cent (Table 7.1). South Africa has become the dominant member, accounting for about two-thirds of other members' imports from the region (Table 7.A11). Its exports to the region increased from 1.7 per cent of its total trade in 1990 to 12 per cent in 1996, but for imports SADC remains of very limited importance, increasing only from 0.4 to 1.7 per cent. Excluding the SACU countries, however, its principal markets in SADC are Mozambique and Zimbabwe, for which its ports provide access to the rest of the world. As in the case of Singapore in ASEAN, there is a possibility that some of this is trans-shipment, rather than trade. For Malawi, Mozambique, Zambia and Zimbabwe, SADC is a major source of imports, at over 50 per cent (again some may be trans-shipment), but it is above 20 per cent for exports only for Mozambique and Zimbabwe. These figures suggest a significant imbalance in the region, comparable to the differences observed in other regions dominated by a single country. Zimbabwe, the second country in the region, is the most dependent on South Africa for its imports and exports.

For Zimbabwe's imports, SADC is slightly more important in manufactures than primary commodities. For exports it is a major, and growing, market for Zimbabwe's manufactures. Most of South Africa's imports from SADC are raw materials or semi-processed items; even among manufactures, textiles and clothing (which account for a quarter of the total), are also relatively simple items (Cassim, 1995). Its exports to SADC are mainly manufactures, and of a more specialized nature. For both Zimbabwe and South Africa, SADC is important in providing a market for goods which are more advanced than their exports to other areas (mainly developed countries). This follows the pattern of Latin America, rather than of Asia. The pattern of South African trade, however, with imports of raw materials and exports of advanced manufactures, suggests a pattern of exporting to less developed countries, rather than the exchanges among equal, even if equally uncompetitive, countries found in Latin America. Among the SADC countries, only South Africa, Zimbabwe, and perhaps Zambia have a share of manufacturing in total output (around a quarter) sufficiently important and varied in composition to make benefiting from the region's effects on manufactures a significant contribution to development.

Latin America and Caribbean

As described in Chapter 6, so far none of the continental groupings offers any tariff or other trade preferences, so any above normal regional trade flows must be explained by other factors. Although there are no formal proposals to revive the LAIA or combine it with the Caribbean and CACM into a Latin American and Caribbean free trade area, this is the possible outcome of the various MERCOSUR alliances – the proposed MERCOSUR-Andean Pact link, Colombia and Venezuela's ties to CARICOM, CARICOM and CACM's arrangements, and the Group of Three – or alternatively of the US being unable to join an FTAA because of domestic opposition to trade groups. It is therefore useful to look at the trade of this potential region, as well as that of the FTAA (in the next section). It would account for about 5 per cent of world trade, and this share has been growing (Table 7.1). Intra-regional trade has also been growing, but less rapidly, to only 18–19 per cent, giving a slightly falling intensity. As was seen in several of the Latin American regions, intra-regional trade was high at the beginning of the 1980s, at about 16 per cent, falling to 11 per cent in the mid-1980s, and then recovering, so that it is not clear if the 1990s rise is because of the growing number of integration agreements or simply a recovery of the region and its imports from the depression of the 1980s.

For most of the Caribbean countries, the Latin American countries are not important trading partners (Table 7.A12). The exceptions are Belize, for which a Latin American and Caribbean group would supply about 20 per cent of imports, because of its trade with Mexico, although the share of exports is small, and Trinidad and Tobago, with broadly based trade. For the Central Americans, it would add little to the CACM. A Latin America and Caribbean region would account for more than half the trade of Paraguay and Uruguay (but only because of their trade with MERCOSUR) and a high share also for Argentina, Bolivia, Ecuador and Peru (for imports), Panama and Venezuela. Such a region, however, would cover only a quarter of trade for Brazil, Chile, Colombia, and 5 per cent for exports and 2 per cent for imports for Mexico. For Argentina and Brazil, most of the advantage in regional trade is explained by MERCOSUR. There seems, therefore, on the basis of present trade flows to be little advantage from such a region. Flows could increase with a removal of barriers, but the small current base of trade does not indicate large potential effects. For some of these, however (for example Chile), the region is more important for manufactures than for all trade. In addition, the average figures ignore the possible gains for some of the countries on the borders of regions, with high trade for example between Brazil and its northern neighbours, as well as between Belize and Mexico. A simulation by UN ECLAC (Baumann and Carvalho, 1997, p. 6) found that most of the effect of an FTAA on Brazilian exports of manufactures would come from liberalization within South America, not from the membership of the NAFTA countries; Brazil would be an important market for the rest of the region.

FTAA

The FTAA gives very much higher figures. About half the region's trade is intra-regional, and with the region accounting for about a fifth of world trade, this gives a high intensity. All three have been increasing

Table 7.5 FTAA: Regional trade as a share of world trade by broad economic categories, 1995 (%)

	Exports												
	MERC-OSUR	Argentina	Brazil	Paraguay	Uruguay	Chile	Bolivia	Costa Rica	El Salvador	Guatemala	Nicaragua	Colombia	Peru
Food and Beverages	33.30	48.40	18.50	61.90	60.70	49.90	80.00	48.90	46.20	59.30	59.20	34.60	35.60
Primary, for industry	33.00	48.00	17.30	53.20	92.00	79.20	67.80	27.40	21.90	46.60	16.20	25.90	38.20
Primary, for consumption	44.40	37.40	60.70	88.40	44.40	60.50	40.00	51.80	90.40	72.80	91.60	43.60	46.60
Processed, for industry	24.30	47.00	10.30	95.30	98.50	25.80	99.00	70.10	93.00	55.80	73.60	57.10	33.60
Processed, for consumption	35.90	54.00	19.50	65.20	49.60	41.60	95.60	74.00	98.60	98.90	91.60	56.20	28.00
Industrial Supplies, nes	37.90	39.40	36.30	71.10	47.10	25.60	41.90	84.20	97.70	92.80	78.10	67.80	23.20
Primary	24.00	32.20	17.50	77.40	26.70	18.60	26.70	48.50	72.70	77.50	79.80	38.80	29.20
Processed	41.20	41.10	40.70	62.10	50.30	28.20	54.60	91.50	99.20	97.90	77.80	69.50	21.30
Fuels and Lubricants	86.80	91.70	58.70	96.80	96.00	86.30	100.00	74.00	95.40	100.00	97.60	76.10	72.40
Primary	92.80	96.00	0.40	0	0	100.0	100.00	0	100.00	100.00	100.00	75.70	86.0057
Motor spirits	74.10	76.70	69.20	100.00	95.90	0	100.00	73.90	91.40	100.00	97.50	79.00	.40
Other	84.90	86.90	36.00	91.00	100.00	81.20 / 93.40	83.30	100.00	100.00	100.00	100.00	71.70	85.50
Capital Goods	73.50	82.70	71.80	100.00	88.50	89.40	90.80	87.90	97.30	97.60	62.90	89.90	73.90
Capital goods	75.30	88.50	73.40	100.00	87.90	87.90	90.70	95.90	96.60	97.70	93.50	91.90	82.20
Parts and accessories	70.10	76.10	68.50	100.00	91.20	93.00	100.00	81.10	99.30	97.00	58.90	85.40	64.80
Transport Equipment	77.10	92.80	71.40	100.00	97.50	84.60	94.80	100.00	99.90	99.60	85.40	98.90	83.20
Passenger motor cars	92.00	99.70	86.90	100.00	99.40	99.20	0	0	100.00	76.90	63.70	100.00	94.40
Industrial	67.80	90.70	56.90	100.00	60.8	70.70	0	100.00	100.00	98.90	99.90	99.70	98.10
Non-industrial	78.70	98.80	70.10	0	98.8	88.70	0	100.00	100.00	100.00	100.00	82.40	49.50
Parts and accessories	77.90	92.00	73.90	100.00	98.2	94.00	94.80	100.00	99.90	99.80	83.20	98.10	74.10
Consumer Goods, nes	74.70	84.90	71.60	91.10	82.30	94.80	95.80	83.40	98.50	96.30	85.50	89.10	65.20
Durable	75.80	89.90	73.10	8.60	98.70	89.20	99.60	99.30	100.00	99.70	99.10	94.60	80.60
Semi-durable	73.60	72.70	73.50	91.00	78.00	91.00	82.80	93.40	97.60	97.90	73.50	87.90	60.50
Non-durable	76.00	97.30	65.60	96.70	91.30	98.50	82.70	76.00	98.80	95.60	88.80	89.30	57.60
Other, nes	57.50	84.60	41.50	0	100.00	12.70	0	0	100.00	0	100.00	71.40	82.20
Total	47.50	55.90	42.80	67.80	60.40	33.90	62.40	61.30	71.20	72.20	64.30	64.20	30.60

					Imports					
	Argentina	Brazil	Uruguay	Chile	Bolivia	El Salvador	Guatemala	Nicaragua	Colombia	Venezuela
Food and Beverages	76.40	76.20	83.00	82.80	89.80	85.30	82.60	90.10	90.30	74.70
Primary, for industry	94.90	88.70	84.40	98.50	99.60	100.00	99.60	99.90	95.40	97.20
Primary, for consumption	86.80	68.40	94.50	85.70	95.60	95.60	90.20	95.00	89.00	93.50
Processed, for industry	85.90	68.60	84.80	82.30	83.20	84.60	66.60	94.00	92.90	85.20
Processed, for consumption	67.90	77.80	76.70	75.60	83.70	80.40	78.80	84.50	85.50	44.00
Industrial Supplies, nes	61.70	50.00	72.10	64.40	80.80	82.60	79.00	80.90	69.90	74.80
Primary	72.80	60.40	79.30	79.80	94.00	90.90	96.20	86.10	80.70	85.40
Processed	61.00	48.70	71.20	62.80	79.40	81.70	77.90	80.50	68.90	73.30
Fuels and Lubricants	47.20	40.60	60.40	69.20	99.10	90.50	73.70	97.90	90.50	7.80
Primary	50.90	43.20	50.90	68.40	71.40	100.00	100.00	100.00	100.00	88.50
Motor spirits	36.80	43.50	74.60	66.70	99.40	83.50	58.00	90.30	91.60	89.10
Other	89.40	16.30	84.00	82.90	87.90	90.10	99.50	99.90	64.10	47.50
Capital Goods	50.20	34.20	50.70	52.20	60.70	70.40	77.70	62.00	53.10	67.30
Capital goods	52.90	35.10	51.40	51.80	59.80	68.20	77.90	63.50	52.90	68.30
Parts and accessories	44.20	32.70	48.50	53.70	63.80	76.50	77.10	57.50	53.90	65.50
Transport Equipment	54.80	37.30	56.90	46.40	25.50	60.90	71.30	40.90	63.00	69.40
Passenger motor cars	38.30	21.10	48.50	30.80	13.60	57.10	77.80	23.10	57.10	60.10
Industrial	57.10	65.90	73.30	55.70	24.50	64.30	80.10	32.30	77.00	83.90
Non-industrial	41.30	48.30	32.30	47.30	21.10	58.90	35.60	27.90	35.50	43.70
Parts and accessories	63.50	43.70	66.30	51.20	48.40	59.50	47.00	68.30	54.40	75.80
Consumer Goods, nes	46.70	36.30	54.10	34.20	70.80	86.30	80.50	80.50	57.50	74.70
Durable	37.90	35.60	42.50	26.80	60.00	90.80	86.20	74.50	53.00	79.60
Semi-durable	47.30	27.90	55.40	31.10	60.00	80.20	73.10	69.30	58.10	72.50
Non-durable	52.30	44.50	63.90	47.00	78.80	87.30	81.50	85.10	59.40	73.70
Other, nes	17.90	39.40	84.40	24.10	38.70	80.40	41.20	98.60	49.70	54.70
Total	55.60	44.30	63.00	56.00	62.60	79.00	77.30	78.70	65.20	72.20

Source: OAS, Foreign Trade Information System

during the 1990s, although the change in share in world trade has been smallest; there has therefore been a large rise in intensity, reflecting the increases in intensity, and perhaps therefore trade diversion, in regions such as MERCOSUR and NAFTA. The FTAA would account for more than half the present trade of Argentina, Belize, Bolivia, Canada and Mexico, Colombia, and most of the Central American countries. It would also take more than half the trade of the larger Caribbean countries, including Jamaica and Trinidad and Tobago. It is not as important for the smaller. It takes half the imports, but not the exports, of Chile and Peru. It would still account for only just under half of Brazil's trade and about a third of the US. Brazil and the US, therefore, on these aggregate figures, have the smallest trading interests in the FTAA, although they are effectively leading the negotiations.

Even for Brazil, Peru and Chile, however, the FTAA would take more than 50 per cent of manufactured exports (Table 7.5). An analysis of the products exported by Chile to the region, however, found that most did not face significant tariffs; those which were obstructed by high tariffs were often those for which the most important competitors were Canada and Mexico (Agosín, 1994, p. 31). Therefore, 'given the geographic proximity [to the US] of Chile's most important competitors', an FTAA would probably not be a major assistance. In contrast, the barriers to Chile's exports within the Latin American region were greater, and therefore the potential benefits from an FTA were greater (p. 37)

For the MERCOSUR countries as a group, more than 40 per cent of their current exports to a potential FTAA are to MERCOSUR itself (Table 7.6). Adding the Andean countries to this, as is under negotiation, would take this share over 50 per cent. The NAFTA countries are only 36 per cent. For imports, however, those from the NAFTA countries would be more than from the current MERCOSUR members. This suggests that liberalizing their trade with the NAFTA countries would be potentially much more difficult: there would be a large impact on domestic markets and on tariff revenues, made potentially more serious by the greater competitiveness. Argentina follows this pattern, but for Brazil NAFTA is a more important export market than its fellow members of MERCO-SUR, and even MERCOSUR plus the Andean countries would not raise the share to more than about 40 per cent. For Chile, NAFTA is important for imports and exports, but its share of exports is falling, in favour of MERCOSUR and the Andean countries, and these two groups together now slightly exceed it in importance. The attraction for Chile of an agreement with NAFTA over one with MERCOSUR thus clearly fell

Table 7.6 MERCOSUR and Andean countries' trade with FTAA countries by region (%)

	MERCOSUR		Argentina		Brazil		Chile		Andean		Bolivia		Colombia		Ecuador		Peru		Venezuela	
Exports (% of trade with FTAA)	1992	1995	1992	1995	1992	1995	1992	1995	1992	1994	1992	1995	1992	1995	1992	1994	1992	1995	1992	1995
MERCOSUR	32.6	43.2	43.2	57.8	26.5	31.2	30.4	32.0	4.7	5.3	42.1	21.6	3.3	2.8	2.2	3.2	13.4	11.9	3.1	10.4
Andean Group	10.3	10.3	14.3	10.5	9.3	10.7	16.5	19.5	12.0	14.9	23.1	29.6	22.5	31.6	9.0	15.8	17.8	20.6	6.6	12.7
NAFTA	47.4	36.0	30.0	17.3	55.5	49.4	50.9	47.0	72.9	66.8	30.4	43.5	64.7	56.5	74.0	68.6	62.0	57.0	79.7	70.9
Chile	7.2	8.3	10.6	12.6	6.0	6.1	0	0	2.5	2.1	4.4	3.5	2.3	2.2	7.7	6.7	5.1	8.0	1.2	1.2
LAC	58.8	66.0	74.3	83.9	51.6	53.1	51.9	55.4	29.2	35.8	71.3	56.6	36.9	44.9	27.7	34.5	44.1	48.0	22.2	22.2
Total FTAA	100.0	100.0	100.0	100.0	100.0	100.0	100.0	100.0	100.0	100.0	100.0	100.0	100.0	100.0	100.0	100.0	100.0	100.0	100.0	100.0
Imports (% of trade with FTAA)																				
MERCOSUR	35.6	na	44.5	43.1	24.8	31.6	38.0	32.5	12.4	12.7	38.9	34.3	11.0	8.4	14.3	13.5	19.7		8.9	10.4
Andean Group	5.9	na	4.5	3.3	7.6	5.6	10.3	9.2	11.9	17.3	5.8	12.8	15.9	21.5	11.9	24.3	22.8		7.4	12.7
NAFTA	50.6	na	41.4	47.1	61.4	57.0	50.8	57.2	68.9	64.5	42.5	40.2	67.2	66.4	65.0	55.1	48.1		77.9	70.9
Chile	6.4	na	7.6	5.7	5.4	5.0	0.1	0.1	2.5	3.0	11.2	11.9	1.8	2.3	4.4	3.1	6.7		0.8	1.6
LAC	52.5	na	61.0	56.1	42.5	46.7	53.1	50.1	34.5	40.0	59.0	62.0	36.8	39.4	38.4	52.3	55.5		25.3	33.6
Total FTAA	100.0	100.0	100.0	100.0	100.0	100.0	100.0	100.0	100.0	100.0	100.0	100.0	100.0	100.0	100.0	100.0	100.0		100.0	100.0

Source: OAS, Foreign Trade Information System

in the 1990s. For the Andean countries, NAFTA is much more important than any Latin American group: an alliance with MERCOSUR would only cover about 20 per cent of their exports and 30 per cent of their imports. Bolivia is an exception and its trade interest in joining MERCOSUR is clear. For Central America (see Table 7.A12), trade with other regions in Latin America is of minor importance; only trade with the NAFTA countries is important.

APEC

APEC is the largest area, with about 45 per cent of total world trade; only the EU, at just under 40 per cent, is of the same magnitude. The share of intra-regional trade is higher, and sufficiently so to give a slightly higher intensity for imports, although the export figures are similar. (For Taiwan, trade by partner countries was used to get consistent data.) The intensity has, however, been falling, as the increase in intra-regional trade has not kept pace with the region's increase in share of world trade, the opposite pattern from the EU. A longer perspective confirms this fall in intensity, from 1.75 in 1980 to 1.65 in 1985 for exports, and 1.83 to 1.7 for imports (Bora, 1995, p. 25).

APEC is the major trading partner for all its members, not surprisingly as it includes two of the three major trading areas of the world (Table 7.A13). The countries for which the share of APEC has fallen have been Indonesia for exports, and the Philippines, South Korea and Thailand for imports, while there has been little change for China, Hong Kong and Malaysia. Some of the increases in APEC's trade have been in countries in regions with trade arrangements, notably in NAFTA but intra-regional trade has also risen in a range of other countries, such as Taiwan, with no special arrangements.

AEC

Even if all the potential members of an African FTA are included, the share of intra-regional trade would only be about 10 per cent (Table 7.1). This is lower than in the other continents, but the share of Africa in world trade is less than half that of Latin America. The intensity is higher than Latin America, much higher than the FTAA or APEC, and growing. But the low absolute intra-regional share is an important handicap. The AEC is neither a compact sub-region, like the Andean group, CACM, or CARICOM, with a low regional share but very high intensity, nor a major trading area like the FTAA or APEC, with much higher intra-regional trade. Like the Latin America and Caribbean group, it is neither very integrated nor very important to its individual members. An AEC would account for more than 20 per cent of imports in some of the smaller countries, mostly in west and central Africa, including Burkina Faso, the Central African Republic, Chad, both Congos, Malawi, Somalia, Tanzania, Togo, Uganda, Zambia and Zimbabwe. It would be important for exports for Djibouti and for both imports and exports for Mozambique. But these data reflect more trans-shipment than actual trade. Many are landlocked countries. In a few cases, for example in East Africa, the figures do not correspond to current integration schemes and seem to suggest that sub-regions might be more integrated. But Tanzania is in SADC and Uganda is not, and the political reasons for Tanzania's membership were more important than the economic. The major trading countries trade mainly with the rest of the world.

Summary

On the various measures used here, the areas that seem integrated are the EU, MERCOSUR, CACM, NAFTA, ANZCERTA, perhaps CARICOM and parts of the Andean group and the Group of Three (Tables 7.1 and 7.7). SADC shows some integration, but it is asymmetric. Integration is minor for ASEAN and SAARC. A Latin America group or the FTAA would mean significant increases in integration for many of the Latin American countries, but the AEC shows less promise. APEC shows a high degree of integration, but the decline in intensity as its share in world trade has risen, in spite of the fact that it contains a group (NAFTA) for which there is significant evidence of integration, suggests that the integration is not as deep as in the other regions.

It is striking that manufactures, and cars and car parts in particular, are the major vehicle of integration in a wide range of groups, not only in the western hemisphere, where they receive special sectoral treatment in NAFTA, MERCOSUR, and the Andean group, but also in ASEAN. This appears to stem from two different causes. In some cases, notably NAFTA and ASEAN, it comes from the nature of the industry, with a high degree of integration across borders and therefore of inter-industry trade. Combined with its large scale, this makes regions, if they are available, the obvious production and marketing areas once countries are supplied. In MERCOSUR, however, and historically also in the Andean countries, it was seen as a key strategic industry, to be protected and encouraged by a special regime. A more obvious reason for cars, like

Table 7.7 Changes in regional trade, summary

	EU	MERCOSUR	CARICOM	Andean	CACM	NAFTA	G3	ANZC	ASEAN	SAARC	SADC	LAIA	FTAA	APEC	AEC
Exports															
Intra-regional trade	–	+	=	+	+	+	=	+	+	+	+	+	+	+	+
Share of world trade	–	+	=	=	+	=	+	=	+	+	–	+	+	+	–
Intensity	+	+	=	+	=	=	–	+	–	=	+	–	=	–	+
Imports															
Intra-regional trade	–	+	–	+	+	+	+	+	+	+	+	=	+	+	+
Share of world trade	–	=	–	=	+	=	+	=	+	+	–	+	+	+	–
Intensity	+	+	–	+	+	=	–	+	–	+	+	–	=	–	–
Which sectors are more important than average for exports?															
Manufactures	x	x		x	x		x	x			x	x	x		
Cars	x	x		x		x	x	x	x	x	x	x	x		
Agriculture	x										x				
Fuels	x	x													

fuels, to be an important element in many of these regions is simply their high share in all trade, when barriers are removed.

Notes

1 In principle, the ratios for individual countries should subtract that country from the 'world' because a country cannot import from itself, but as the principal focus here is on regions, which can import from themselves, and all the developing countries have very low shares, this is not done.
2 Data on intra-SACU trade are controversial and subject to serious error because there is no effective control on what trade represents transit or re-exports, and most trade in the region goes through South Africa. South Africa and the other members also have notoriously inefficient customs services so that the data are suspect even for absolute flows.
3 The low intra-regional share for imports for the Netherlands may reflect Rotterdam's role as an entrepot.

Table 7.A1   EU 15, Intensities (%)

	Exports		Imports	
	1990	*1996*	*1990*	*1996*
AUSTRIA				
Share of intra-region trade	67.85	59.74	70.85	74.84
Intensity	1.50	1.59	1.64	1.92
BELGIUM–LUXEMBOURG				
Share of intra-region trade	78.56	65.86	88.29	73.56
Intensity	1.73	1.75	2.05	1.89
DENMARK				
Share of intra-region trade	66.37	62.03	66.24	64.00
Intensity	1.46	1.65	1.53	1.64
FINLAND				
Share of intra-region trade	62.52	53.36	60.61	58.49
Intensity	1.38	1.42	1.40	1.50
FRANCE				
Share of intra-region trade	63.27	58.54	62.53	63.17
Intensity	1.39	1.56	1.45	1.62
GERMANY				
Share of intra-region trade	62.46	55.58	59.49	53.80
Intensity	1.38	1.48	1.38	1.38
GREECE				
Share of intra-region trade	69.22	56.39	67.93	69.53
Intensity	1.53	1.50	1.57	1.79

Table 7.A1   Continued

	Exports		Imports	
	1990	*1996*	*1990*	*1996*
ITALY				
Share of intra-region trade	62.92	55.31	61.78	60.88
Intensity	1.39	1.47	1.43	1.56
IRELAND				
Share of intra-region trade	78.08	66.00	70.15	53.62
Intensity	1.72	1.76	1.63	1.38
NETHERLANDS				
Share of intra-region trade	80.10	70.24	65.86	53.45
Intensity	1.77	1.87	1.53	1.37
PORTUGAL				
Share of intra-region trade	80.69	80.37	72.36	76.11
Intensity	1.78	2.14	1.68	1.96
SPAIN				
Share of intra-region trade	71.51	71.05	62.91	66.30
Intensity	1.58	1.89	1.46	1.70
SWEDEN				
Share of intra-region trade	61.36	55.02	62.61	66.37
Intensity	1.35	1.46	1.45	1.71
UNITED KINGDOM				
Share of intra-region trade	57.49	52.33	57.71	49.36
Intensity	1.27	1.39	1.34	1.27

Source: IMF, *Direction of Trade Statistics Yearbook*

Table 7.A2   MERCOSUR 4/6, Intensities(%)

	Exports		Imports	
	1990	*1996*	*1990*	*1996*
ARGENTINA				
Share of intra-region trade (4)	14.84	33.28	21.49	24.45
Intensity (4)	16.95	20.09	16.05	17.44
Share of intra-region trade (6)	19.11	41.93	30.03	27.42
Intensity (6)	17.02	20.70	18.68	16.04
BOLIVIA				
Share of intra-region trade (6)	38.01	19.61	41.63	26.85
Intensity (6)	33.84	9.69	25.90	15.71
BRAZIL				
Share of intra-region trade (4)	4.20	15.30	10.07	15.95
Intensity (4)	4.80	9.23	7.52	11.38

Share of intra-region trade (6)	6.32	18.62	12.51	17.84
Intensity (6)	5.63	9.19	7.78	10.44
CHILE				
Share of intra-region trade (6)	8.66	12.82	14.91	15.99
Intensity (6)	7.71	6.33	9.28	9.35
PARAGUAY				
Share of intra-region trade (4)	39.52	57.49	30.76	45.34
Intensity (4)	45.14	34.70	22.97	32.34
Share of intra-region trade (6)	43.07	61.08	32.94	47.21
Intensity (6)	38.34	30.16	20.49	27.62
URUGUAY				
Share of intra-region trade (4)	35.09	48.10	40.21	44.00
Intensity (4)	40.08	29.04	30.03	31.38
Share of intra-region trade (6)	36.21	49.98	41.70	45.71
Intensity (6)	32.24	24.68	25.94	26.74

Source: IMF, *Direction of Trade Statistics Yearbook*

Table 7.A3 CARICOM, Intensities (%)

	Exports		Imports	
	1990	*1996*	*1990*	*1996*
BAHAMAS				
Share of intra-region trade			0.22	0.05
Intensity			1.55	0.46
BARBADOS				
Share of Intra-region trade	21.05	32.19	14.71	18.87
Intensity	102.13	163.21	105.39	162.42
BELIZE				
Share of intra-region trade	6.87	1.79	6.16	3.91
Intensity	33.33	9.05	44.13	33.62
DOMINICA				
Share of intra-region trade	25.45	31.11	20.34	12.99
Intensity	123.48	157.74	145.67	111.77
GRENADA				
Share of intra-region trade	23.81	17.65	23.85	17.14
Intensity	115.50	89.47	170.84	147.53
GUYANA				
Share of intra-region trade	6.90	4.55	13.26	2.18
Intensity	33.46	23.05	94.98	18.79
JAMAICA				
Share of intra-region trade	6.44	3.14	4.77	1.98
Intensity	31.26	15.93	34.14	17.05

Table 7.A3   Continued

	Exports		Imports	
	1990	*1996*	*1990*	*1996*
ST VINCENT AND THE GRENADINES				
Share of intra-region trade	33.73	29.24	22.06	23.03
Intensity	163.65	148.28	157.99	198.23
TRINIDAD AND TOBAGO				
Share of intra-region trade	9.90	9.72	4.07	2.44
Intensity	47.88	49.26	29.11	20.96

Source: IMF, *Direction of Trade Statistics Yearbook*

Table 7.A4   ANDEAN, Intensities (%)

	Exports		Imports	
	1990	*1996*	*1990*	*1996*
BOLIVIA				
Share of intra-region trade	6.48	22.69	4.22	8.38
Intensity	12.40	32.92	4.70	10.39
COLOMBIA				
Share of intra-region trade	5.51	17.40	8.44	13.51
Intensity	10.55	25.25	9.40	16.76
ECUADOR				
Share of intra-region trade	6.93	7.93	9.72	22.05
Intensity	13.26	11.51	10.82	27.34
PERU				
Share of intra-region trade	6.25	7.12	7.75	14.85
Intensity	11.97	10.33	8.62	18.41
VENEZUELA				
Share of intra-region trade	2.79	9.14	2.95	9.84
Intensity	5.35	13.25	3.29	12.21

Source: IMF, *Direction of Trade Statistics Yearbook*

Table 7.A5   CACM, Intensities (%)

	Exports		Imports	
	1990	*1996*	*1990*	*1996*
COSTA RICA				
Share of intra-region trade	9.19	8.10	7.26	8.43
Intensity	47.38	30.92	57.75	45.30

EL SALVADOR

Share of intra-region trade	30.07	44.24	16.47	18.87
Intensity	155.11	168.84	131.09	101.44

GUATEMALA

Share of intra-region trade	24.76	29.25	8.31	7.57
Intensity	127.74	111.62	66.13	40.67

HONDURAS

Share of intra-region trade	3.37	5.43	7.22	9.92
Intensity	17.38	20.71	57.44	53.32

NICARAGUA

Share of intra-region trade	14.50	12.76	10.82	31.43
Intensity	74.81	48.68	86.09	168.95

Source: IMF, *Direction of Trade Statistics Yearbook*

Table 7.A6   NAFTA, Intensities (%)

	Exports		Imports	
	1990	*1996*	*1990*	*1996*
CANADA				
Share of intra-region trade	75.12	82.14	63.80	69.68
Intensity	3.80	4.01	4.03	4.06
MEXICO				
Share of intra-region trade	70.26	85.26	67.43	73.81
Intensity	3.56	4.16	4.26	4.30
USA				
Share of intra-region trade	28.29	30.32	24.10	28.60
Intensity	1.43	1.48	1.52	1.66

Source: IMF, *Direction of Trade Statistics Yearbook*

Table 7.A7   Group of Three, Intensities (%)

	Exports		Imports	
	1990	*1996*	*1990*	*1996*
COLOMBIA				
Share of intra-region trade	3.62	8.20	7.85	13.46
Intensity	2.89	3.70	5.29	5.67
MEXICO				
Share of intra-region trade	0.90	0.90	0.57	0.35
Intensity	0.72	0.40	0.38	0.15

Table 7.A7   Continued

	Exports		Imports	
	1990	*1996*	*1990*	*1996*
VENEZUELA				
Share of intra-region trade	3.18	6.90	3.42	12.67
Intensity	2.54	3.11	2.31	5.34

Source: IMF, *Direction of Trade Statistics Yearbook*

Table 7.A8   ANZCERTA, Intensities (%)

	Exports		Imports	
	1990	*1996*	*1990*	*1996*
AUSTRALIA				
Share of intra-region trade	4.92	7.17	4.41	4.69
Intensity	3.43	4.97	3.10	3.36
NEW ZEALAND				
Share of intra-region trade	18.20	20.30	20.32	24.22
Intensity	12.69	14.08	14.31	17.34

Source: IMF, *Direction of Trade Statistics Yearbook*

Table 7.A9   ASEAN, Intensities (%)

	Exports		Imports	
	1990	*1996*	*1990*	*1996*
BRUNEI				
Share of intra-region trade	14.49	8.89	16.10	10.47
Intensity (ex Sing)	4.83	1.90	6.14	2.63
Share of intra-region trade	21.88	16.92	42.00	50.61
Intensity	4.55	2.36	10.14	8.02
INDONESIA				
Share of intra-region trade (ex Sing)	2.49	5.66	2.61	5.86
Intensity (ex Sing)	0.83	1.21	1.00	1.47
Share of intra-region trade	9.90	11.13	8.49	10.01
Intensity	2.06	1.55	2.05	1.59
MALAYSIA				
Share of intra-region trade (ex Sing)	6.32	7.68	4.17	5.16
Intensity (ex Sing)	2.11	1.64	1.59	1.30
Share of intra-region trade	29.28	28.15	18.89	18.51
Intensity	6.09	3.93	4.56	2.94

PHILIPPINES

Share of intra-region trade (ex Sing)	4.39	8.42	6.63	6.29
Intensity (ex Sing)	1.46	1.80	2.53	1.58
Share of intra-region trade	7.36	14.42	10.52	11.23
Intensity	1.53	2.01	2.54	1.78

SINGAPORE

Share of intra-region trade	24.37	29.69	20.15	24.11
Intensity	5.07	4.14	4.86	3.82

THAILAND

Share of intra-region trade (ex Sing)	4.10	7.25	5.11	7.35
Intensity (ex Sing)	1.36	1.55	1.95	1.85
Share of intra-region trade	11.45	19.34	12.53	12.80
Intensity	2.38	2.70	3.03	2.03

VIETNAM

Share of intra-region trade (ex Sing)	5.11	6.36	1.13	9.34
Intensity (ex Sing)	1.70	1.36	0.43	2.35
Share of intra-region trade	12.84	12.09	18.62	22.64
Intensity	2.67	1.69	4.49	3.59

Source: IMF, *Direction of Trade Statistics Yearbook*

Table 7.A10   SAARC, Intensities (%)

	Exports		Imports	
	1990	*1996*	*1990*	*1996*
BANGLADESH				
Share of intra-region trade	3.59	1.73	7.03	17.61
Intensity	3.20	1.45	8.87	18.80
INDIA				
Share of intra-region trade	2.71	3.87	0.41	0.41
Intensity	2.41	3.24	0.52	0.43
MALDIVES				
Share of intra-region trade	13.46	29.46	8.70	13.51
Intensity	11.98	24.68	10.97	14.42
NEPAL				
Share of intra-region trade	6.94	10.98	11.50	24.50
Intensity	6.18	9.20	14.51	26.14
PAKISTAN				
Share of intra-region trade	3.99	2.54	1.64	2.64
Intensity	3.55	2.13	2.07	2.82
SRI LANKA				
Share of intra-region trade	3.48	2.64	6.85	11.95
Intensity	3.10	2.21	8.64	12.75

Source: IMF, *Direction of Trade Statistics Yearbook*

Table 7.A11   SADC, Intensities (%)

	Exports		Imports	
	1990	*1996*	*1990*	*1996*
MALAWI				
Share of intra-region trade	14.01	17.21	41.37	58.42
Intensity	18.29	23.84	45.17	78.12
MAURITIUS				
Share of intra-region trade	0.83	1.14	9.07	12.22
Intensity	1.08	1.59	9.91	16.34
MOZAMBIQUE				
Share of intra-region trade	1.82	21.67	7.01	61.73
Intensity	2.38	30.02	7.65	82.56
SOUTH AFRICA				
Share of intra-region trade	1.71	11.81	0.44	1.69
Intensity	2.23	16.36	0.48	2.26
TANZANIA				
Share of intra-region trade	1.93	3.68	1.46	21.95
Intensity	2.51	5.10	1.59	29.36
ZAMBIA				
Share of intra-region trade	4.60	9.80	23.32	44.86
Intensity	5.99	13.58	25.46	59.99
ZIMBABWE				
Share of intra-region trade	28.57	35.30	26.89	56.49
Intensity	37.26	48.90	29.36	75.55

Source: IMF, *Direction of Trade Statistics Yearbook*

Table 7.A12   Latin America and Caribbean, and FTAA, Intensities, 1996 (%)

	Latin America		FTAA	
	Exports	*Imports*	*Exports*	*Imports*
ARGENTINA				
Share of intra-region trade	47.44	31.15	56.17	52.29
Intensity	8.84	6.67	2.33	2.61
BAHAMAS				
Share of intra-region trade	2.41	3.15	31.14	24.97
Intensity	0.45	0.67	1.29	1.24
BARBADOS				
Share of intra-region trade	32.62	23.38	54.51	83.10
Intensity	6.08	5.01	2.27	4.15

BELIZE

Share of intra-region trade	5.95	21.09	50.60	77.73
Intensity	1.11	4.52	2.10	3.88

BOLIVIA

Share of intra-region trade	44.06	37.31	72.74	66.06
Intensity	8.21	7.99	3.02	3.29

BRAZIL

Share of intra-region trade	23.95	22.57	44.50	47.85
Intensity	4.46	4.84	1.85	2.39

CHILE

Share of intra-region trade	19.66	26.49	37.24	51.83
Intensity	3.66	5.67	1.55	2.58

CANADA

Share of intra-region trade			83.70	72.25
Intensity			3.47	3.60

COLOMBIA

Share of intra-region trade	27.08	24.53	68.09	66.26
Intensity	5.05	5.26	2.83	3.30

COSTA RICA

Share of intra-region trade	13.88	25.12	67.09	78.25
Intensity	2.59	5.38	2.79	3.90

DOMINICA

Share of intra-region trade	31.11	19.48	4.11	36.80
Intensity	5.80	4.17	1.71	1.83

DOMINICAN REPUBLIC

Share of intra-region trade	5.52	25.06	60.86	44.18
Intensity	1.03	5.37	2.53	2.20

ECUADOR

Share of intra-region trade	24.54	40.92	65.91	79.22
Intensity	4.57	8.77	2.74	3.95

EL SALVADOR

Share of intra-region trade	50.39	38.56	70.12	79.37
Intensity	9.39	8.26	2.91	3.96

GRENADA

Share of intra-region trade	20.59	21.91	32.35	61.91
Intensity	3.84	4.69	1.34	2.90

GUATEMALA

Share of intra-region trade	38.65	28.67	88.33	78.23
Intensity	7.20	6.14	3.67	1.36

GUYANA

Share of intra-region trade	4.72	4.37	51.57	27.37
Intensity	0.88	0.94	2.14	1.36

Table 7.A12   Continued

	Latin America		FTAA	
	Exports	Imports	Exports	Imports
HAITI				
Share of intra-region trade	0.55	12.49	77.90	74.91
Intensity	0.10	2.68	3.23	3.73
HONDURAS				
Share of intra-region trade	6.44	17.99	77.89	76.86
Intensity	1.20	3.85	3.23	3.83
JAMAICA				
Share of intra-region trade	5.24	11.34	56.75	73.81
Intensity	0.98	2.43	2.36	3.68
MEXICO				
Share of intra-region trade	5.26	2.35	90.52	76.16
Intensity	0.98	0.50	3.76	3.80
NICARAGUA				
Share of intra-region trade	15.28	49.91	68.98	76.88
Intensity	2.85	10.69	2.86	3.83
PANAMA				
Share of intra-region trade	22.26	5.25	35.49	13.37
Intensity	4.15	1.12	1.47	0.67
PARAGUAY				
Share of intra-region trade	63.18	47.41	66.62	64.43
Intensity	11.77	10.16	2.77	3.21
PERU				
Share of intra-region trade	16.25	31.29	38.73	63.23
Intensity	3.03	6.70	1.61	3.15
ST VINCENT AND THE GRENADINES				
Share of intra-region trade	29.25	24.72	34.91	53.93
Intensity	5.45	5.30	1.45	2.69
SURINAME				
Share of intra-region trade	3.27	19.48	23.93	62.78
Intensity	0.61	4.17	0.99	3.13
TRINIDAD AND TOBAGO				
Share of intra-region trade	20.67	19.54	62.22	63.31
Intensity	3.85	4.19	2.58	3.16
UNITED STATES				
Share of intra-region trade			38.44	34.80
Intensity			1.60	1.73
URUGUAY				
Share of intra-region trade	54.03	51.43	61.74	64.40
Intensity	10.07	11.02	2.56	3.21

VENEZUELA
Share of intra-region trade	28.22	26.29	90.63	80.32
Intensity	5.26	5.63	3.76	4.00

Source: IMF, *Direction of Trade Statistics Yearbook*

Table 7.A13   APEC, Intensities, 1996 (%)

	Exports	Imports
	1996	*1996*
AUSTRALIA		
Share of intra-region trade	72.48	65.99
Intensity	1.54	1.51
BRUNEI		
Share of intra-region trade	77.59	66.16
Intensity	1.64	1.52
CANADA		
Share of intra-region trade	90.31	82.20
Intensity	1.91	1.89
CHILE		
Share of intra-region trade	51.48	46.43
Intensity	1.09	1.07
CHINA		
Share of intra-region trade	75.91	71.78
Intensity	1.61	1.65
HONG KONG		
Share of intra-region trade	76.30	83.90
Intensity	1.62	1.92
INDONESIA		
Share of intra-region trade	77.33	71.66
Intensity	1.64	1.64
JAPAN		
Share of intra-region trade	74.86	68.13
Intensity	1.59	1.56
MALAYSIA		
Share of intra-region trade	78.10	77.65
Intensity	1.65	1.78
MEXICO		
Share of intra-region trade	88.56	83.46
Intensity	1.88	1.91
NEW ZEALAND		
Share of intra-region trade	68.41	72.19
Intensity	1.45	1.66

Table 7.A13   Continued

	Exports 1996	Imports 1996
PHILIPPINES		
Share of intra-region trade	79.31	69.49
Intensity	1.68	1.59
SINGAPORE		
Share of intra-region trade	78.18	75.32
Intensity	1.66	1.73
SOUTH KOREA		
Share of intra-region trade	68.93	66.42
Intensity	1.46	1.52
TAIWAN		
Share of intra-region trade	89.49	71.60
Intensity	1.90	1.64
THAILAND		
Share of intra-region trade	70.59	68.34
Intensity	1.50	1.57
USA		
Share of intra-region trade	62.31	66.95
Intensity	1.32	1.54
VIETNAM		
Share of intra-region trade	59.48	72.44
Intensity	1.26	1.66

Source: IMF, *Direction of Trade Statistics Yearbook*

8
Regulation and Liberalization of Investment in Regions

Traditional theory on customs unions and FTAs does not deal with the consequences of freer movement of capital flows among members of a regional group. In the pre-Viner regions, capital movements were either completely free, within and outside the group, or controlled within each country.

Even without special arrangements for capital, the formation of a region will affect investment within the region and outside it. Foreign investment can be to serve a local market or to exploit a resource that is more abundant in the host than the home country, whether a natural resource or an economic one like different types or costs of labour. Investment to supply a market is a substitute for trade; if lowering trade barriers within the region makes it more efficient to supply markets through exports, this type of investment will fall within the region. Investment may increase and perhaps relocate within the region, to exploit opportunities for trade creation or any increased income. If there is trade diversion, investment to exploit this may be diverted from non-member countries. Such increased investment can be either from within the region or from outside. Outside investment will respond in the same ways as regional investment to trade creation or diversion opportunities; in addition, increased growth (relative to the rest of the world) could make the region more likely to attract investment. Particularly for relatively small or poor countries forming a region, the increase in total income or the potential for more rapidly increasing income in the future may give the necessary minimum size for an investment in production capacity or for investment to have cost advantages over exports to supply the market, and cause more than marginal increases in investment. Increases in the integration of the market, including reductions in non-tariff barriers, but also increased similarities, will reinforce this effect.

Investment to exploit a natural resource may increase within a region. If the resource extends across more than one member, increasing returns to scale mean that there is a potential for increased efficiency in its use (whether economies in exploitation, processing, and transport of a natural resource or complementary production of different products using larger supplies of low-cost labour).

A third type of foreign investment may also be attracted by a region. Because lowering internal barriers effectively raises the relative protection against the rest of the world, investment to get behind tariff barriers, the direct substitution of investment for exports, may also rise within a region.

As will be discussed in Chapter 10, there are other types of integration within regions which can also have effects on investment through their trade or growth effects. These include regional preferences for services trade, special rules on government procurement, common standards or regulations for products (or for companies), deeper macroeconomic integration, or the establishment of common legal approaches. Investment is also probably even more sensitive than trade to the 'new partner' or awareness effect. The increased information and discussion of the fellow members of a region may give a stimulus to look for investment opportunities there, rather than in already well-known or still unfamiliar areas.

Two trends of policy on capital flows are tending to reinforce these indirect effects of regions on investment. The first is that all the customs unions considered here have had an objective of freer, and eventually free, capital movement within the region, while secondly an increasing number of other regions have also had special arrangements for investment. Discrimination between the region and the rest of the world has become the norm for investment as well as trade. For all the customs unions, there has been an implicit objective of going beyond a customs union to a single market; all conditions of economic business therefore had to be opened to the group. In other groups, where the region was part of a state-directed programme of development including encouragement and direction of investment, it seemed unavoidable to extend national regulation to the regional level to obtain the full intended effects of the region.

Two influences act against an increased effect of regions on investment flows. In parallel with trade liberalization, countries have tended to reduce their barriers to both inward and outward investment in the last 50 years. This was led by the developed countries, but liberalization of trade and domestic policy in developing countries is also increasingly accompanied by liberalization of capital and exchange-rate controls. Since the 1950s, both on their own initiative and under pressure from major investors, countries have also signed bilateral agreements to restrict their ability to control foreign investment, requiring either minimum standards of liberalization or full national treatment. These were first encouraged by the European countries, and the US only began to sign them from 1982. Both general liberalization and bilateral treaties cut across regions and therefore reduce their relative liberalization. The earlier treaties concentrated on financial questions, of remission of profits and disinvestment, and regulating the conditions for expropriation. In recent years, provisions have restricted national legislation limiting the entry or allocation of foreign investment, or imposing requirements on exports or local content (Parra, 1993). Some require national treatment, or at least MFN. Normally, in the case of disputes, they allow recourse to the World Bank or UN procedures (UNCTAD, *World Investment Report* 1996). The growth of this system, like that of bilateral MFN trading agreements in the late nineteenth century, is starting to give a *de facto* common minimum standard for investment regulation at international level. By including the international dispute procedures, it provides some enforceability. Both the regional agreements and the proposals for multilateral agreements build on this.

At the multilateral level, the increasing awareness of the role of international investment and of large multinational companies led to attempts to regulate both their activities and the potentially conflicting attempts by national governments to control the companies. At the time the GATT was established, most countries had tight controls on capital flows, and there was no attempt to include either liberalization or regulation of the controls in the GATT. There was therefore no equivalent of MFN rules for regulation of investment, leaving countries free to give special access or apply special controls to all investment, or on a discriminatory basis, whether by bilateral agreements or regional arrangements. There were provisions attempting to regulate the use of trade-related restrictions on investment, in particular the imposition of minimum export or local content rules, because these could be held to interfere with commitments on non-discriminatory treatment of trade and national treatment of traded goods, but these were not enforced. In the Uruguay Round, Trade-Related Investment Measures (TRIMS) were one of the major issues in the opening stages, but the final agreement did little more than restate the GATT provisions. The move to include services within the WTO, however, was used to bring in increased regulation of investment in service industries. It was argued that 'establishment', a commercial presence in the importing country, was likely to be an essential part of trade in services, and therefore that the General Agreement on Services (GATS), should include commitments to permit investment for this purpose. The services agreement was not universal, with each country permitted to offer to include under the GATS from 1 to 11 of the sectors into which services were classified, and then to specify in detail exactly which aspects of these would be included or excluded. With no common minimum requirements, no general effects can be expected.

The importance of the agreement was, first, that it made the regulation of at least some types of investment clearly part of the multilateral regime; second, that it required countries to specify all their existing regulations (in the sectors they specified) and to 'bind' them (thus making any increase in regulations contrary to the GATS); and third, that it required countries to specify from the adoption of the GATS any partner countries to which they wished to give special, non-MFN, treatment. In order to give special treatment to fellow members of a region, therefore, the group must either conform to the full integration requirements (discussed in Chapter 5) or have recorded the exceptions.

The World Bank has sponsored a series of agreements on different aspects of foreign investment. There are procedures for settlement of disputes (the Convention on the Settlement of Investment Disputes between States and Nationals of Other States), and for providing insurance against political risks (the Multilateral Investment Guarantee Agency, MIGA), but effectively these apply only when countries agree that they should, or apply for coverage. There are also extensive guidelines on aspects of treatment of foreign investment by host states, but these are advisory. Under the UN system, there are guidelines on the regulation of foreign investment and on the activities of multinational firms, but again these are voluntary. There are also agreements among the OECD countries on particular aspects of the treatment of investment, with proposals for a new agreement on investment, which could be expanded to other countries.

All these multilateral agreements indicate the growing consensus that the regulation and legal treatment of investment, as for trade, are no longer exclusively matters for national governments and that there are limits to countries' discretion in discriminating among investors, by company or by country of origin. The agreements limit the scope and

Table 8.1 Investment regulations

	EU	SACU	MERCOSUR	CARICOM	CACM	ANDEAN	NAFTA	G3	ANZCERTA	ASEAN	SAARC	SADC
Liberal within region	X	X	X			X	X	X	X	X		
Liberal to world	X		X			X	X	X	X			
Major regional advantage?		X	X	X								

167

the potential effect of regional initiatives, but also help to legitimize them. Regions can still differ in whether they liberalise more to the region (Table 8.1).

The EU

Europe has liberalized capital movements within the EU, but also with the rest of the world. The move to a common currency will reduce the practical barriers to intra-regional investment, and therefore give it an effective preference. Increasingly there are common requirements of company law which increase the transparency and further lower barriers to investment. All the members are also members of the OECD and World Bank arrangements, and made relatively large offers under the GATS in all eleven areas.

SACU

Four of the SACU members (excluding Botswana) are in a common monetary area, with no capital controls. All five have common elements in company legislation because of their colonial history. While capital controls with the rest of the world are being liberalized, all still regulate inward and outward investment, and impose exchange controls. The countries made offers in only seven of the GATS areas. Only South Africa has signed more than a few bilateral investment treaties, and even it is well below the average for most major recipients of investment in Latin America or ASEAN. Therefore there is significantly greater freedom of capital movements inside than outside SACU.

MERCOSUR

MERCOSUR requires national treatment of almost all intra-regional investments, following the Colonia Protocol of 1994 (Blömstrom and Kokko, 1997, p. 32; UNCTAD, *World Investment Report*, 1996). This includes treatment of the transfer of profits and repatriation. In addition, the sectoral promotion provisions, especially the special rules for the car sector, effectively encourage investment in the region, although the car sector is the only sector in which performance requirements are still permitted on intra-MERCOSUR investment. There are also legislative provisions for a common company regime, dating from the Argentine–Brazilian agreement of 1985 (Lucángeli, 1996, p. 92). These have full national treatment, but the provisions have not been much used:

there are twelve in Brazil. The final goal of MERCOSUR is a single economic market, including full liberalization of capital (and labour) movements. One of the MERCOSUR working groups is working on harmonizing policies in banking and stock markets (OAS Compendium).

There are still restrictions on foreign investment in both Argentina and Brazil, which apply to the MERCOSUR countries as well as to non-members. Argentina restricts investment near the frontier, in naval construction, nuclear energy and uranium, and also in insurance and finance. Brazil restricts it in mining, hydroelectricity, health services, radio and telecommunications, banking and insurance, construction and shipping (Lipsey and Meller, 1996, p. 110) and its restrictive provisions on government procurement further limit opportunities for all foreign investment. But there has been substantial general liberalization in the region. The countries had already moved to fewer restrictions on national treatment before the establishment of MERCOSUR, and all the members have recently signed a large number of bilateral agreements. MERCOSUR and ASEAN have the highest number of treaties. In MERCOSUR, as elsewhere in Latin America, there has been a major shift from a regime of controlling foreign investment to trying to promote it. This is true also of the associate members, Chile and Bolivia. Now most give what is effectively national treatment and have few controls on profit remittances and disinvestment. They also recognize the World Bank dispute settlement procedures; these can still be used for intra-MERCOSUR disputes, as well as for disputes with third countries. Argentina has joined the World Bank MIGA scheme. Brazil still requires authorization for investment, although Argentina has dropped this (Bouzas in de la Balze, 1995, p. 320). Their services offers were also restricted to only five to seven sectors. As discussed in Chapter 10, there is still no liberalization of services within MERCOSUR.

In MERCOSUR, therefore, there is some discrimination in favour of members, but the major changes in recent years have probably been its general liberalization.

CARICOM

The only regional liberalization of investment applies to banking, although there are provisions in the agreement for a regional regime for investment and for looking at the possibility of national treatment (OAS, Compendium). The CARICOM countries also have joint agreements on the regulation of third-country investment. They issued joint Guidelines on Foreign Investment in 1982, and have specified performance criteria (including on employment, local content, and external financing) and the conditions for expropriation, etc. (ibid).

The Caribbean countries have signed very few bilateral agreements (even the major recipients of investment, Jamaica and Barbados, have fewer than any of the MERCOSUR countries or than South Africa). Jamaica liberalized only seven services in the GATS. The CARICOM regime is still restrictive, for both intra-regional and external foreign investment.

ANDEAN Group

The Andean Pact in its original 1970s form had extensive joint regulation (Decision 24 of the Pact) of foreign investment, including its direction and requirements on performance and remittance of profits. The region was seen as the appropriate area for a development strategy, which necessarily included the regulation of investment and of the balance of payments. This lapsed, and was formally changed in the revisions of the 1980s. The current regime dates from Decision 291 of 1991. This represents a complete reversal of the previous regime, with an emphasis on liberalization and minimal controls, and, although a joint Andean initiative, it gives equal treatment to third-country investors. The purpose was to encourage foreign investment, including offering the regional advantages of a regional market and common rules, rather than to regulate it. Like the MERCOSUR countries, most of the Andean countries have signed a large number of bilateral investment treaties. But, also like the MERCOSUR, their services regimes, within the Andean region and under the GATS, remain restricted.

Andean countries give investors national treatment, permit profit remittances, and do not allow performance requirements. There are still a few reserved sectors, which apply to Andean and other investors. The Decision revived the old concept of the Andean company, a multi-national operating in the region, which was given some preferences (OAS, Compendium; UN ECLAC, *Evolución*, 1997).

Andean liberalization is now explicitly directed at attracting investment from outside, not at promoting intra-regional investment.

CACM

The Central American countries do not have a common investment regime, either within the region or with respect to the rest of the world. They have tended to sign fewer bilateral agreements than the MERCO-

SUR or Andean countries, although more than the Caribbean. Investment does not seem to be an important part of the regime, and there has been little opening on services.

NAFTA

Mexico traditionally exercised extensive regulation on foreign investment, with major sectoral exclusions, but the NAFTA agreement required it to remove most restrictions. The NAFTA agreement goes much further than the average bilateral treaty; it requires national and MFN treatment, and removes pre-investment authorization and other obstacles. It covers the normal subjects – remittances and expropriation. It also forbids performance requirements, both in general and as a condition for special privileges (Parra 1993; OAS, Compendium) Given the nature of previous Mexican regulation, among the most important elements is the removal of sectoral restrictions on financial services and mining.

Following the negotiations, and before NAFTA was implemented, Mexico liberalized its general investment regime to almost the same extent. Previously, it had signed very few bilateral treaties. The US and Canada already had few restrictions on investment flows, except in specified sectors. Mexico included nine of the eleven services sectors in its offer under the GATS (more than Canada, at seven, but fewer than the US at eleven), and more than the other Latin American countries.

Therefore, at the outset of NAFTA there was a general liberalization of investment by Mexico, not restricted to the other NAFTA members. The special advantage of NAFTA was that it introduced dispute procedures for investors at the national level, as well as the facility to use the international means.

Group of Three

The agreement covers national and MFN treatment, although some exceptions are allowed, and expropriation is not covered because Colombia did not want to include it. As the agreement was signed after both NAFTA and the 1991 Decision of the Andean Pact, there was little further to offer in liberalization, either within the region or outside.

ANZCERTA

Australia and New Zealand have liberalized capital flows generally. Australia, however, continues to screen foreign investments (Bora, 1997, p.13). Although there is no specific investment provision in the agreements (ibid.), they have moved to harmonize some business legislation, with the ultimate objective of common procedures. There is thus some effective preference for regional companies because of the removal of practical barriers.

ASEAN

There is an investment agreement for ASEAN. However, it does not apply to all intra-regional investments but only investments made specifically under its provisions. There is no general concession of national treatment, although the specified investments can receive it. It does provide MFN treatment, and recourse to international dispute procedures. The provisions, therefore, do little more than guarantee ASEAN members a minimum standard of treatment, which in practice is given by these countries to all investors. The ASEAN countries have signed large numbers of bilateral agreements which require similar standards of treatment to non-regional countries. They offered on average about six sectors in the GATS negotiations. There is no declared objective of a single market for investment. They have a relatively liberal regime for foreign investment with all countries, but there have been no important recent changes or preferences for the region.

SAARC

There is no regional preference for investment in the SAARC countries, and only Sri Lanka, followed by India and Bangladesh, have signed as many bilateral treaties as most of the Latin American or ASEAN countries. Sri Lanka has encouraged foreign investment, but until recently India was extremely restrictive. They remain restrictive on services, with India and Pakistan opening five sectors under the GATS, and Bangladesh and Sri Lanka only one each.

SADC

There is no proposal for investment preferences within SADC, but the integration on infrastructure and provisions for consultations on agriculture and investment mean that there is some *de facto* encouragement of investment within the region. There is a working group on investment. Only South Africa and Zimbabwe have signed more than four bilateral treaties, and even they are below the average numbers for

ASEAN or Latin America, or even for SAARC. The members other than South Africa (seven sectors) opened very few services sectors, with Zimbabwe again less closed with three sectors open.

Summary

For the EU, the Andean Pact, NAFTA, ANZCERTA and the Group of Three, regional liberalization has been accompanied or followed by full liberalization. There are regional advantages in simplicity, common company rules, sometimes in disputes procedures and in the EU and SACU in exchange-rate coordination. For CACM, ASEAN, SAARC and SADC neither the regional nor the multilateral regime has been liberalized. The only regions where there is significant discrimination in favour of members are SACU, MERCOSUR, and CARICOM (Table 8.1).

9
Investment in Regions

The discussion in Chapter 8 suggested a range of effects of a region on investment, with or without special arrangements. Unfortunately, the direction of these effects is ambiguous, making it more difficult than for trade to find a simple measure of integration or intensity. Conventional trade creation and increasing demand will increase investment within the region, by both regional and external investors. This could suggest an increased share for the region in total world investment, which might include an increased share within the region by regional investors if they have advantages of proximity and familiarity. Their relative importance increases with any decline in artificial barriers. Regional investment is more likely to rise if there is institutional preference for regional investors. Investment outside the region by regional (and foreign) investors would rise less rapidly, and it is possible that this could affect regional investors more strongly, lowering their share in external investment. Investment to exploit the increased effective barriers to the rest of the world could increase the role of foreign investment in the region, while the reduced need for this within the region could reduce intra-regional foreign investment. Any general reduction in barriers to foreign investment could increase both regional and non-regional investment. These factors suggest that the effects of a region could appear as an increase in non-regional foreign investment and perhaps in intra-regional investment within the region. The strongest evidence of diversion would be a decrease in regional investment outside the region. The general reduction in barriers to inward and outward investment, however, could mask any of these effects.

Even in countries with no change in trade policies, there have been important increases in foreign investment in recent years. The total more than doubled between 1991 and 1996 (UNCTAD, *World Investment*

Report, 1997). The increasing number of large firms, in developing countries as well as in the traditional foreign investors among the developed countries, means a growing number of potential investors with the global markets, and therefore demand for production facilities, that encourage foreign investment. Increased liberalization gives more scope for the growth of these firms. These trends mean that increased investment, even at a very high rate, cannot be assumed to derive from reasons peculiar to a region. Even within a region, it is possible that the new potentially multinational firms may choose to invest in the region for reasons of similarity or familiarity, so that we should expect simple measures of intensity for investment for geographical regions to be greater than 1 (as they are for trade) even if there are no forces for integration from policy.

An analysis of regional and inter-regional investment in the years up to 1990, before the period examined here, found a tendency by most major investors to become less regionally orientated (Wyatt-Walter in Fawcett and Hurrell, 1995, pp. 106–9). For the US, Western Europe became a more important destination, replacing Canada and Latin America, while Japanese investment shifted from Asia to North America and Europe. This is attributed partly to the fact that 'companies competing in global markets were increasingly likely to establish a local presence in the three main markets' (p. 108), with the exception that there was no growth in investment in Japan. If new multinational companies in Latin America and Asia follow a similar pattern, of investing first in their own region before diversifying, we could observe an apparent increase in regional investment in the 1990s, but this could only indicate a large number in the first stages of expansion, not a trend to follow formal regions.

There are two other difficulties for analysing investment in a way similar to that for trade. The first is the extreme concentration of all direct investment. This makes the use of any measure of intensity difficult. The evidence for both the world and the EU region is that there are likely to be very uneven flows by and to countries, so that we would not expect to find similar ratios among members of a region, or to find that comparisons among regions can be made directly. The US accounts for a quarter of foreign investment, the UK for 15 per cent; if Germany, France, Japan, and Hong Kong are added, these six countries make up 70 per cent of the total. This is very different from the pattern of trade. Among recipients, the US is again a quarter of the total, with the other important recipients being the UK, France and China. Among developing countries, ten countries, six in Latin America, four in Asia, account for three-quarters of receipts. If a region contains one of these major investors or recipients, the numbers will be distorted.

The second obstacle is the poor quality of the data, and the lack, for many countries, of data by source and destination. Data on investment flows on a comparable basis by direction and source are only available in one international series, by UNCTAD, with detailed figures for some regions only to 1990, and for none beyond 1994 (UNCTAD, *Directories*). Where available, these have been supplemented by data from individual countries, but these are poor for direction and rarely permit the analysis by sector which can be done for trade data. There are no regions for which there are sufficient comparable data to make intensity calculations.[1] The Canadian Government attempted some calculations for the APEC countries in 1992, and these are quoted in Table 9.14, but they need to be used with caution. The data are becoming less reliable because of the liberalization of capital flows. Countries that no longer require prior authorization for new investment or for repatriation can only obtain data from indirect methods or sample surveys. This is now a particular problem for Latin America, where most of the major recipients and the significant regions are located.[2] This chapter will not therefore attempt to calculate intensities for investment, but only indicate whether the trends seem to be related to what we observe for regulation of investment and for trade.[3]

SACU

The SACU countries (with the exception of Botswana) offer a common monetary area for foreign investors, but with continuing restrictions. Recent liberalization has covered relations with outside countries, so any effect would be expected to be on inflows from outside. However, these are complicated by the change in regime in South Africa in 1994 which meant an end to sanctions on investment, and also improved expectations for its growth. Investment in South Africa did change from disinvestment in the second half of the 1980s to an inflow in 1994, but this was extremely low. Inflows increased in 1995 and 1996 (Table 9.A1)[4] but South African investment abroad rose much more rapidly, suggesting a loss of confidence in the region. The data for the other countries suggest that any outflow was not to them, as they also saw outflows and low inflows. These data do not suggest any regional effect on investment within SACU in recent years. Estimates for the stock of South African investment (Table 9.13), suggest that in 1994 2.5 per cent of the total was in the other SACU countries (although this was a quarter of its investment in Africa). For inward investment, the figure for all Africa was under 1 per cent; there was disinvestment in Namibia, and therefore in the SACU countries as a whole. About two-thirds of investment in Namibia has been from South Africa.[5]

The region has, however, been important in particular cases. During the period of sanctions on South Africa, foreign investors went into the other countries, notably into Swaziland, to produce both for South Africa and for other African (and developed) markets. The customs union should have encouraged investment more generally in the other countries to meet the South African market, with its higher labour costs, but this may have been discouraged by their small size and poor transport links. There are isolated examples, a refrigerator factory in Swaziland and a car assembly plant in Botswana, but these may be too small to affect the recorded aggregate figures.

MERCOSUR

The general liberalization by Argentina and Brazil explains some of the increase in foreign investment, intra-regional and from other countries; this has been reinforced by substantial inflows in both countries because of their privatization programmes. Only a marginal advantage would be expected from the limited regulation in favour of regional investment. The massive increase in intra-regional trade, however, could suggest an increase in trade-induced investment. There has been a sharp increase in investment in the MERCOSUR countries, especially Brazil, followed by Argentina; outflows have risen slightly, but the net inflow is significant (Table 9.A2). These are two of the six major Latin American recipients of foreign investment, with Chile a third. Data on intra-regional investment are only available in non-comparable forms, and for selected years.

For Argentina, investment by other members accounted for 1 per cent of foreign investment in the 1980s and only 1.3 per cent in 1990, but it was 5.7 per cent of stocks by 1992, when investment was starting to rise (Table 9.1). By then investment inflows from Chile had risen to 6 per cent of the total (IDB and IRELA, 1996). Measured by stocks, Brazil was an important investor in Argentina before 1992. Using data on individual projects, Chudnovsky (Chudnovsky, López, Porta, in Chudnovsky 1996, pp. 124–5) found that Brazilian investors accounted for about 5 per cent of foreign investment in 1990–4, and Chile for 14 per cent. These figures support those from the aggregate data. A survey by an Argentine investment institute (Fundación Invertir Argentina,

Table 9.1   MERCOSUR: Intra-regional capital stocks (% of total)

	Inward		
Origin		*Destination*	
	Argentina	**Brazil**	**Chile**
1992			
Argentina		0.12	0.55
Brazil	5.42		1.05
Paraguay		0.12	0.01
Uruguay	0.33	0.18	0.42
MERCOSUR 4	5.74	0.42	2.03
Chile	6.00	0.02	
MERCOSUR 6	5.74	0.45	2.03
Latin America and Caribbean	12.22	6.04	26.51

	Outward		
Destination		*Source*	
	Brazil (1992)	**Chile (1992)**	**Brazil (1995) (% MERCOSUR)**	**Chile (1990–6)**
Argentina	2.10	43.65	75	46.6
Brazil		1.11		6.10
Paraguay	1.41	0.03	14	
Uruguay	0.88	12.38	11	
MERCOSUR 4	4.39	57.17	100	53.10
Chile	1.21			
MERCOSUR 6	5.60	57.17		52.70
Latin America and Caribbean	60.18	90.83		78.00

Source: UN ECLAC, *Directorio sobre Inversión Extranjera en América Latina y el Caribe, 1993*; UNCTAD, 1994, UN, *World Investment Directory*; Inter American Development Bank Data bank; IDB, INTAL, 1997

1996) of investments planned in 1994–5, found only 2 per cent (by value) from Brazil, mainly in breweries, and 6 per cent from Chile. There was one investment, worth 0.2 per cent from Uruguay, but the major investor was the US, accounting for 40 per cent of the total. A third of the Chilean investment was purchase of a privatized electricity plant, with other investments in improving other electricity plants. Argentine surveys of investors show increasing interest in MERCOSUR, rising from 5 per cent in 1991 to 45 per cent by 1995 (Lucángeli, 1996, p. 93). but there is little evidence of this in data on Argentine outward investment.

Table 9.2 MERCOSUR: Intra-regional investment (% of total)

	Inflows		
Origin		*Destination*	
	Brazil	**Paraguay**	**Chile**
1990			
Argentina	0.01	0.28	0.00
Brazil		13.94	0.00
Paraguay			
Uruguay	0.14	0.28	0.00
MERCOSUR 4	0.15	14.51	0.01
Chile	0.02	13.94	
MERCOSUR 6	0.18	28.45	0.01
Latin America and Caribbean	6.55	15.49	9.86
1992			
Argentina		2.73	1.26
Brazil		39.97	1.61
Paraguay			0.00
Uruguay			0.85
MERCOSUR 4		42.70	3.72
Chile		0.00	
MERCOSUR 6		42.71	7.44
Latin America and Caribbean		42.95	7.47

	Outflows to Brazil	
	1990	**1992**
Argentina	0.25	10.91
Brazil		
Paraguay	0.18	
Uruguay	0.04	
MERCOSUR 4	0.47	10.91
Chile	−0.09	−0.61
MERCOSUR 6	0.38	10.30
Latin America and Caribbean	37.81	3.64

Source: UN, ECLAC, *Directorio sobre Inversión Extranjera en América Latina y el Caribe*, 1993; UN, *World Investment Directory*

There was no comparable rise in the early 1990s in MERCOSUR investment in Brazil. In 1991, under 1 per cent of investment in Brazil came from the other MERCOSUR countries or went to them (Table 9.2), although the share was higher in 1992 when total Brazilian foreign investment fell sharply (Table 9.A2). A survey of Brazilian data suggested that only 70 companies from the other three countries had invested in Brazil (Neto and Bannister, 1997, p. 13). There had been some investment by Argentina in Brazil in the 1980s (Lucángeli, 1995, p. 89), but this ended by 1990, with the recession in Brazil and expansion in Argentina. But in 1991, there was a large increase in investment in Argentina; the data for stocks suggest a higher share in the past (Table 9.1). Most Brazilian investment is in developed countries, especially the US, but it is argued that MERCOSUR is an 'incubator for Brazilian emerging multinational companies. Depending on the source, 1/3 to 1/2 of all Brazilian emerging multinational companies started their overseas operations in the MERCOSUR region' (Neto and Bannister 1997, pp. 7–8). This suggests that some of the investment is not because of MERCOSUR as an institution, but merely as a step to world investment.

Most Brazilian foreign investment is in services (about 60 per cent) and manufacturing (about 30 per cent) (Neto and Bannister, 1997, p. 6), but in Argentina it is mainly in manufacturing.[6] One hundred and thirty nine Brazilian companies are operating there, principally in transport equipment, financial services, and metal products. The importance of transport is consistent with the importance of this sector in trade. Financial services have been liberalized in Argentina, making this a logical direction for investment, especially as the large Brazilian banks are among the largest in Latin America, and are taking advantage of a more advanced use of automation. It is, however, still impossible for Argentine banking and insurance companies to operate in Brazil on the same basis as Brazilian in Argentina. The investment in breweries, visible in both Argentine and Brazilian data, is because the Brazilian firm already held almost half the Brazilian market, and was looking for expansion (ibid., p. 11). In Paraguay, almost all Brazilian investment is in services. In Uruguay, two-thirds is in services, but there is also investment in chemicals, wood, and textiles (IDB, INTAL, 1996, p. 16), similar (except for the absence of transport equipment) to the investment in Argentina.

The greater investment by Brazil in Argentina than by Argentina in Brazil is partly because of lack of liberalization in Brazilian services, but it may also indicate the advantage, at least initially, of a country with larger companies, already accustomed to operating on a wide geographical scale. Surveys of Brazilian industry in 1994 and 1995 (Confederação Nacional de Industria 1994, 1995) suggested that, while almost all sectors saw this having an important effect on exports (the only exceptions were mining, leather, food, and drink), those expecting to invest abroad as a response were in transport, consistently in both years, then in a spread of other manufactures, with less consistency between the two years, except in chemicals, perfumes, and drink.

The MERCOSUR countries are important investors for Paraguay. In 1992, about a third of inward investment there came from Brazil, and Chile had been important in 1991. But both these observations date from before regional integration. MERCOSUR countries account for 7 per cent of investment in Bolivia.

MERCOSUR investors already accounted for 3.7 per cent of flows into Chile in 1992 (Table 9.2), but for only negligible amounts in 1990–1; they accounted for 2 per cent of the stock (Table 9.1). Chile's important role is as an investor, particularly in Argentina. There have been parallel investments by two Chilean power companies, perhaps, like the Brazilian breweries, finding the Chilean market too small for expansion. For Chile, in contrast to Brazil, Argentina represents a much larger market than the domestic one. Chile, however, has also been investing in other Latin American countries. A total of 78 per cent of Chilean investment went to Latin American countries in 1990–6. While Argentina received most of this, other important recipients were Brazil, Peru, Bolivia, Colombia, Mexico and Panama (IDB, INTAL, 1997, p. 6), so again the explanation for investing in Argentina may not be the regional access. The investments recorded here preceded Chile's associate membership, and most preceded even the beginning of negotiations. For Argentina, Brazil and Chile account for almost all its receipts of investment from Latin America; Brazil and Chile have more sources (and destinations). On investment, therefore, Argentina seems more 'regional' than the others.

The increase in total foreign investment in both Argentina and Brazil coincides with the increase in their privatization programmes, with Brazil coming slightly later, and continuing beyond 1997. UNCTAD (1997, p. 73) estimates that a quarter of investment inflows to Latin America were accounted for by privatization in the first half of the 1990s, but the shares for Brazil and Argentina are estimated to be much higher, perhaps as much as a half. The Chilean purchases of electricity companies indicate that regional investors are also participating in the privatization process, but this is more likely to reflect common interests and experience (the Chilean and Argentine electricity industries) than regional preference. MERCOSUR effects can be seen in investment patterns, but are not the major explanation for the regional flows.

CARICOM

There has been no reduction in restrictions on regional or other investment and recent changes in trade do not provide a strong reason for
new investment. There are no data on intra-regional investment for
CARICOM, and the data on investment in the region are too distorted
by the presence of financial centres to be useful. There has been some
increase in investment in the region, but it is unlikely that this is associated with regional incentives.

ANDEAN Group

The 1991 change in the investment regime for the Andean countries was intended to increase investment from the rest of the
world, not specifically regional investment. The level and the
increase of intra-regional trade, however, could have encouraged
regional investment. Total investment in the region has increased
spectacularly since the second half of the 1980s or 1990 (Table
9.A3). It now includes two of the principal developing country
recipients of investment, Colombia and Peru, a transformation
from the 1980s.

The most recent intra-regional data date from 1992. Only about 1
per cent of investment in Colombia and Ecuador came from the
region, but there was significant investment by Venezuela in Peru
(Table 9.3). The pattern had not changed greatly from 1990. The high
percentages for Peruvian investment in Bolivia and Colombian investment in Venezuela show mainly how little these countries invest, but
do suggest a strong preference for regional investment by small investors. Unfortunately, the large increases in total investment in Colombia and Peru come after these data, so it is not possible to identify the
sources. The small investment by countries in the region, however,
suggests that they are not the principal source. Other Latin American
countries, already important in 1990, notably Chile, are important.
The figures for stocks (Table 9.4) support the view that some of the increase was coming from other Latin American countries, and show
clearly that investment by Colombia is largely confined to Latin America. Figures for US investment do not show an increase in its investment in these countries sufficient to explain the increase shown in
their totals (Table 9.5).

CACM

Investment in this region will not have been stimulated by the regulatory regime, but the high and increasing level of intra-regional trade could encourage regional investment. There are no data on this. Costa

Table 9.3 Andean Group: Intra-regional investment (% of total)

	Inflows				
Origin		*Destination*			
	Bolivia	**Colombia**	**Ecuador**	**Peru**	**Venezuela**
1990					
Bolivia				0.00	
Colombia			0.88	0.64	0.00
Ecuador		0.26		0.00	
Peru	0.59	0.26			0.00
Venezuela		0.52	0.22	2.99	−0.01
Total of above	0.59	1.04	1.11	3.63	−0.01
Latin America and Caribbean	31.62	21.75	30.09	34.83	21.42
1992					
Bolivia				0.06	
Colombia				0.00	
Ecuador		0.09		0.00	
Peru		0.42			
Venezuela		1.21		1.11	
Total of above		1.72		1.17	
Latin America and Caribbean		27.25		28.95	

	Outflows		
Destination		*Origin*	
	Colombia (1990)	**Colombia (1992)**	**Peru (1991)**
Bolivia			80.00
Colombia			
Ecuador	−0.96	0.81	0.00
Peru	−0.96	0.14	
Venezuela	−5.77	7.58	10.00
Total of above	−7.69	8.53	90.00
Latin America and Caribbean	−56.73	20.97	100.00

Source: UN ECLAC, *Directorio sobre Inversión Extranjera en América Latina y el Caribe*, 1993; UN, *World Investment Directory*

Table 9.4 Andean Group: Intra-regional
capital stocks (% of total)

Inward		
Origin	*Destination*	
	Colombia	**Peru**
1992		
Bolivia	0.01	0.28
Colombia		0.60
Ecuador	0.70	0.07
Peru	0.20	
Venezuela	2.22	0.74
Total of above	3.13	1.69
Latin America and Caribbean	10.80	23.10

Outward	
Destination	*Source*
	Colombia
Bolivia	
Colombia	
Ecuador	1.33
Peru	3.00
Venezuela	7.78
Total of above	12.11
Latin America and Caribbean	63.71

Source: UN ECLAC, *Directorio sobre Inversión
Extranjera en América Latina y el Caribe*, 1993; UN,
World Investment Directory

Rica has seen an increase in inflows in this period, but not the other
countries.

NAFTA

Mexico liberalized its investment regulation at the time of the establishment of NAFTA, but to the rest of the world as well as NAFTA. This
could give an increase in total investment in Mexico. The increase in
trade, particularly the evidence of diversion and increased integration
of sectors like cars and clothing, could be expected to lead to an increase
in intra-regional investment. In recent years, Mexico has returned to its
position as one of the major recipients of foreign investment among
developing countries (Table 9.A4). The share of NAFTA in US foreign

investment was high in 1990, but then declined in 1992 (Table 9.5). It recovered in 1994, with large increases to both Mexico and Canada, but the share fell back to around 10 per cent since then in 1995 and 1996.

Table 9.5 FDI in the US (%)

	Inflows				Outflows			
	1990	*1994*	*1995*	*1996*	*1990*	*1994*	*1995*	*1996*
NAFTA	4.22	13.21	9.52	6.63	18.81	15.28	13.38	11.25
Canada	3.76	10.55	10.20	7.19	12.59	9.90	9.91	8.04
Mexico	0.46	2.66	−0.68	−0.57	6.22	5.38	3.47	3.21
MERCOSUR (4)	0.01	0.05	0.30	−0.13	4.03	6.57	8.51	4.07
Argentina	0.10	0.08	0.19	0.00	1.22	1.36	2.69	0.49
Brazil	−0.09	−0.02	0.14	−0.13	2.83	5.15	5.76	3.58
Paraguay		0.00	0.00	0.00	0.01	0.00	0.00	0.00
Uruguay	0.00	−0.01	−0.03	0.00	−0.03	0.05	0.05	0.00
Chile	−0.07	−0.02	−0.03	0.00	1.68	2.28	1.65	1.16
Bolivia	0.00	0.00	0.00	0.00	0.06	0.11	0.14	0.00
MERCOSUR (6)	−0.07	0.03	0.28	−0.13	5.76	8.95	10.30	5.23
ANDEAN	−0.15	0.25	−0.01	0.29	0.51	2.20	1.55	2.58
Bolivia	0.00	0.00	0.00	0.00	0.06	0.11	0.14	0.00
Colombia	...	−0.03	−0.03	0.00	0.25	0.54	0.23	1.16
Ecuador	0.00	−0.01	...	0.00	−0.10	0.27	0.16	0.03
Peru	...	...	0.01	0.00	−0.27	0.34	0.37	0.94
Venezuela	−0.15	0.29	0.00	0.29	0.57	0.94	0.65	0.46
ASEAN	0.88	2.38	0.23	0.00	6.41	8.01	4.26	5.74
Brunei	...	0.00	0.00	0.00	0.02	−0.01	0.02	0.00
Indonesia	−0.03	0.09	0.01	0.00	2.23	2.94	0.82	1.01
Malaysia	0.04	0.32	−0.06	0.11	0.56	0.82	1.02	1.20
Philippines	−0.01	0.06	−0.01	0.02	0.57	0.55	0.30	0.76
Singapore	0.76	2.01	0.27	−0.13	2.00	2.62	1.22	1.67
Thailand	0.11	−0.09	0.02	0.00	1.02	1.09	0.87	1.11
SAARC	0.00	0.01	0.03	0.00	−0.02	0.38	0.20	0.39
Bangladesh	0.00	0.00	0.00	0.00	0.00	...	...	0.00
Bhutan	...	0.00	0.00	0.00				0.00
India	0.01	...	0.02	0.00	...	0.24	0.22	0.39
Maldives				0.00				0.00
Nepal				0.00				0.00
Pakistan	...	0.01	0.01	0.00	−0.02	0.13	−0.01	0.00
Sri Lanka	0.00	...	0.00	0.00	0.00	0.00	0.00	0.00
SACU	−0.03	−0.02	0.00	−0.05	0.25	0.23	0.40	0.30
S. Africa	−0.03	−0.02	...	−0.05	0.25	0.23	0.39	0.30
Bostwana	0.00	0.00	0.00	0.00	...	0.00	0.00	0.00

Table 9.5　Continued

	Inflows				Outflows			
	1990	*1994*	*1995*	*1996*	*1990*	*1994*	*1995*	*1996*
Lesotho				0.00	...	...	...	0.00
Namibia (part of S. Africa until 1990)		0.00	0.00	0.00	0.00	...	0.00	0.00
Swaziland	...	...	...	0.00	0.00	...	...	0.00
SADC	**−0.03**	**−0.03**	**0.00**	**−0.05**	**0.24**	**0.38**	**0.47**	**0.30**
SACU	−0.03	−0.02	0.00	−0.05	0.25	0.23	0.40	0.30
Angola	0.00	0.00	0.00	0.00	−0.01	0.15	0.11	0.00
Malawi	...	0.00	0.00	0.00	0.02	−0.01	0.02	0.00
Mauritius				0.00	0.00	0.00	...	...	0.00
Mozambique				0.00	−0.01			0.00
Rwanda				0.00	0.00	...	...	0.00
Somalia				0.00	−0.03	...	...	0.00
Tanzania	...	0.00	0.00	0.00	−0.01	...	−0.02	0.00
Uganda	...	...	...	0.00	0.00	...	...	0.00
Zambia				0.00	0.01	0.01	0.01	0.00
Zimbabwe	...	0.00	0.00	0.00	0.04	0.03	0.02	0.00
CACM	**0.00**	**−0.05**	**−0.02**	**0.00**	**0.27**	**0.52**	**0.32**	**0.44**
Costa Rica	−0.01	−0.03	0.01	0.00	0.14	0.39	0.31	0.39
El Salvador	...	−0.01	0.00	0.00	0.07	0.05	−0.03	0.00
Guatemala	0.01	−0.01	−0.02	0.00	0.03	0.03	0.03	0.08
Honduras	0.00	−0.01	...	0.00	0.01	0.06	0.02	−0.04
Nicaragua	...	...	...	0.00	0.03	...	...	0.00
CARICOM	**3.46**	**−0.73**	**−4.51**	**0.04**	**1.16**	**0.74**	**0.07**	**−0.04**
Antigua and Barbuda	0.00	0.00	0.00	0.00	0.00	0.00	0.00	0.00
Bahamas	3.25	−0.17	−4.33	0.04	−0.10	0.17	−0.53	−0.37
Barbados	0.21	−0.57	−0.18	0.00	0.36	0.10	0.29	0.14
Belize	...	...	...	0.00	0.00	...	...	0.00
Dominica	0.00	0.00	0.00	0.00	...	...	...	0.00
Grenada	...	...	...	0.00	0.00	...	...	0.00
Guyana	...	0.00	0.00	0.00	0.02	...	...	0.00
Jamaica	...	...	...	0.00	0.91	0.37	0.17	0.00
Montserrat				0.00				0.00
St Kitts	0.00	0.00	0.00	0.00	0.00	...	...	0.00
St Lucia				0.00	...	...	...	0.00
St Vincent				0.00	...	0.00	...	0.00
Trinidad and Tobago	0.00	0.01	...	0.00	−0.03	0.10	0.14	0.18
All countries	100.00	100.00	100.00	100.00	100.00	100.00	100.00	100.00

Source:　US *Survey of Current Business*

In investment in the US, the NAFTA share also rose in 1994, and remained high in 1995 and 1996, but this was because of increases in Canadian investment in the US, not Mexican (the Canadian–US FTA had been in force for several years); Mexican investment in the US remains low. Not only do these small and fluctuating changes not suggest a strong regional effect, but the small overall share of NAFTA in US inward and outward investment is strikingly lower than its share in trade. The share of MERCOSUR in US outflows also rose in the early 1990s, although with a decline in 1996; the only other developing region with a significant share is ASEAN. Both of these are much closer in share to NAFTA on investment than they are in trade. There are, however, no other developing countries with as high a share in inward investment in the US as Mexico.

Table 9.6   US Foreign investment stocks (%)

	by destination		by origin	
	1990 % of total	1996 % of total	1990 % of total	1996 % of total
NAFTA	**18.54**	**13.85**	**7.63**	**8.72**
Canada	16.15	11.50	7.48	8.55
Mexico	2.40	2.35	0.15	0.17
MERCOSUR (4)	**3.96**	**4.36**	**0.20**	**0.18**
Argentina	0.59	1.01	0.11	0.09
Brazil	3.34	3.29	0.10	0.09
Paraguay	0.01	0.01		0.00
Uruguay	0.02	0.05	0.00	0.00
Chile	0.44	0.85	0.00	0.00
Bolivia	0.05	0.04	0.00	0.00
MERCOSUR (6)	**4.45**	**5.25**	**0.20**	**0.19**
ANDEAN	**0.89**	**1.29**	**0.14**	**0.01**
Bolivia	0.05	0.04	0.00	0.00
Colombia	0.39	0.44	0.01	0.00
Ecuador	0.07	0.11	0.00	0.00
Peru	0.14	0.26	. . .	0.00
Venezuela	0.25	0.45	0.13	0.00
ASEAN	**2.75**	**4.47**	**0.40**	**0.36**
Brunei	0.01	0.00	. . .	0.00
Indonesia	0.74	0.95	0.01	0.02
Malaysia	0.34	0.66	0.01	0.07
Philippines	0.31	0.42	0.02	0.01
Singapore	0.92	1.78	0.33	0.23
Thailand	0.42	0.66	0.04	0.03

Table 9.6   Continued

	by destination		by origin	
	1990 % of total	1996 % of total	1990 % of total	1996 % of total
CACM	**0.17**	**0.22**	**0.00**	**0.00**
Costa Rica	0.06	0.15	0.00	0.00
El Salvador	0.02	0.02	0.00	0.00
Guatemala	0.03	0.03	0.00	0.00
Honduras	0.06	0.02	0.00	0.00
Nicaragua	. . .	0.00	0.00	0.00
CARICOM	**1.25**	**0.71**	**0.44**	**−0.26**
Antigua and				
Barbuda	0.00	0.00	0.00	0.00
Bahamas	0.93	0.25	0.39	−0.30
Barbados	0.06	0.11	0.05	0.03
Belize	. . .		. . .	0.00
Dominica	. . .		0	0.00
Grenada	0.00	0.00	. . .	
Guyana	0.00		0.00	0.00
Jamaica	0.15	0.21	. . .	
Montserrat	. . .	0.00	. . .	0.00
St Kitts	0.00	0.00	0.00	0.00
St Lucia	. . .			0.00
St Vincent	0.00	0.00		0.00
Trinidad and	0.11	0.13	. . .	
Tobago				
All countries	**100.00**	**100.00**	**100.00**	**100.00**

Survey: US, *Survey of Current Business*

In 1994 and 1995, most US investment in Mexico was in manufacturing equipment, and within that in transport (Table 9.7). But in 1996, there was a sharp fall in the latter, while investment in food products became much more important. Mexican investment in the US has also been mainly in manufacturing. US investment in Canada has also been largely in manufacturing, with a high share of transportation equipment, and showed the same fall in 1996. Canadian investment in the US has been more varied, with a high share in services.

The US is the principal foreign investor in Mexico, with 61 per cent of past investment by 1992, and a share of about 60 per cent in most years (Table 9.8). Canada, however, has been only a minor investor. Although the first post-NAFTA figures for 1994 show a decline for the US and a rise for non-NAFTA countries in the share, incomplete figures

Table 9.7 NAFTA–US investment by sector (%)

Investment by NAFTA in US

Year	All industries	Petroleum	Manufacturing						Wholesale trade	Retail trade	Finance				Services	Other industries
			Total	Food and related products	Chemicals and related products	Primary and fabricated metals	Machinery	Other			Depository institution	ex. depository institution	Insurance	Real estate		
Canada																
1992	100	-11.54	93.96	20.48	4.70	2.75	41.16	24.78	-2.80	-8.79	3.80	16.33	-9.54	9.49	3.70	5.34
1996	100	6.01	43.30	6.21	14.02	7.55	3.84	11.66	-0.42	3.07	13.23	-25.08	28.20	5.26	8.10	18.32
Mexico																
1992	100	0.15	44.98	3.55	-0.93	0.15	-2.94	45.29	3.55	0.62	-9.43		0.00	-0.15	14.53	0.00
1996	100	1.34	9.62	-5.15	23.04	-1.12	4.70	-11.86	-53.24	0.00	14.32	38.70	0.00	0.22	0.00	6.49
NAFTA																
1992	100	-8.68	81.99	16.35	3.32	2.11	30.39	29.78	-1.25	-6.49	0.57	0.00	-7.21	7.13	6.34	4.04
1996	100	6.41	46.18	7.18	13.25	8.29	3.77	13.67	4.10	3.33	13.13	-30.54	30.61	5.69	8.79	19.34
TOTAL																
1992	100	-6.90	39.80	9.97	17.30	0.72	4.92	6.90	18.62	3.33	14.08	7.03	8.94	4.47	5.70	4.91
1996	100	10.29	36.93	3.09	8.73	6.70	-0.04	18.46	12.43	2.71	0.71	9.86	9.82	0.49	10.93	5.81

Table 9.7 *Continued*

Investment in US by NAFTA

Year	All industries	Petroleum	*Manufacturing*						Wholesale trade	Retail trade	*Finance*			Real estate	Services	Other industries
			Total	Food and related products	Chemicals and related products	Primary and fabricated metals	Machinery	Other			Depository institution	ex. depository institution	Insurance			
Canada																
1994	100	3.25	66.01	5.09	8.98	2.04	1.24	2.17	34.82	11.64	5.50	0.98	7.44	4.32	12.51	
1996	100	0.29	23.30	4.25	10.47	-1.40	6.71	2.36	-11.27	12.10	10.95	1.56	18.68	9.66	35.68	
Mexico																
1994	100	0.00	63.85	17.28	8.46	0.00	0.00	2.29	27.16	6.37	8.00	0.00	5.88	1.17	15.08	
1996	100	0.73	66.76	39.28	22.82	2.37	4.59	0.15	-17.22	14.82	1.46	3.79	22.50	4.51	0.29	
NAFTA																
1994	100	2.11	65.25	9.38	8.80	1.32	0.81	2.21	32.13	9.79	6.38	0.63	6.89	3.21	13.42	
1996	100	0.42	35.64	14.25	14.00	-0.32	6.10	1.73	-12.97	12.88	8.24	2.19	19.77	8.19	25.58	
TOTAL																
1994	100	2.86	49.97	3.37	2.17	2.27	6.21	5.87	5.45	5.09	10.00	0.84	14.12	9.05	13.06	
1996	100	7.18	33.35	3.83	9.16	5.58	2.36	5.27	0.83	6.03	8.24	1.55	33.88	4.26	11.55	

Source: US, *Survey of Current Business*

for 1996 show the US returning to a position of about two-thirds, and a fall in most European and Japanese investment. Data by investor country and type of investment are not available, but for all foreign investment, manufacturing accounts for a third to a half of the total in the 1990s, suggesting that the US share in manufacturing may be relatively high. The calculated intensity figures were already high between Mexico and the US in 1992 (Table 9.14).

The figures support some effect from the region on both Canada and Mexico, but suggest that the region is much less integrated in investment than it is in trade. The figures show clearly the extent of integration in the car industry, but suggest some regrouping in 1996 perhaps in response to NAFTA.

Group of Three

The extensive liberalization by the Andean countries, and by Mexico on entry into NAFTA, means that these countries have liberalized to the rest of the world in the 1990s, but with no discrimination in favour of the region. Nor does the evidence of low trade integration suggest a strong impulse to regional investment. As indicated in the data for the Andean Pact and for NAFTA, there has been a substantial increase in investment in the region, but this is unlikely to be related to the Group.

ANZCERTA

The only regional preference on investment is through harmonization of procedures; any other effects would from the two countries' trade integration. After a period of restrictions on foreign investment, Australia and New Zealand liberalized their regimes in the 1980s; there has been no change in recent years. Both are net recipients of foreign investment,

Table 9.8 Investment in Mexico (%)

	US	Canada	UK	Germany	Japan
Stocks					
1994	61	2	7	5	5
Investment					
1993	72	2	4	2	2
1994	50	2	14	5	9
1996, first half	67				3

Source: *Mercado de Valores*, April 1994, April 1995, May 1996, September 1996

Table 9.9   ANZCERTA: Share of inward and outward FDI stock, 1992 (%)

	US	N Am-erica	Japan	China	NIEs	ASEAN	Asia	ANZ	Non-Asia	APEC
Inward	27.21	30.09	15.53		3.50	0.41	19.44	7.85	37.94	57.38
Outward	20.17	23.45	0.96	0.02	1.10	3.55	5.63	26.92	50.37	56.01

Source: Data compiled by Industry Canada; Pangestu and Bora 1996

In 1992, 8 per cent of the stock of inward investment came from within the region, but also more than a quarter of outward investment (Table 9.9). This gives a much higher intensity figure than for trade (Table 9.14). By 1995, New Zealand accounted for 4 per cent of the stock of investment in Australia, but 16 per cent of Australia's investment abroad (UNCTAD, 1997). The latter figure is much higher than the share of its trade within the region; as in the smaller Latin American countries, a relatively small investor is more concentrated in its own region. Most investment in Australia is from the US and the UK (together accounting for about a half), and these are also the most important destinations. Only about half of investment (in both directions) comes from the APEC region, whether for Australia in 1995 or ANZCERTA in 1992. Although trade with the Asian countries has increased in recent years, investment has moved away from them (UNCTAD, 1997, p. 51).

ASEAN

The ASEAN agreement offers little specific encouragement for regional investment, and the relatively low intensity of trade in the region might also be considered to restrict the region's effect on trade. What is important in ASEAN is that it has been a rapidly growing region, and this growth has attracted substantial investment, regional and non-regional. It is a major net recipient of investment (Table 9.A5), with three of the four major Asian recipients of foreign investment: Singapore, Malaysia, and Indonesia; Thailand is also important. For this reason, it is not surprising that although 20 per cent of ASEAN outward investment is intra-regional, only 1 per cent of inward investment is from the region (Table 9.10). This share of outward investment is higher than the share for trade, and gives high intensity figures (Table 9.14). For inward investment, the ASEAN share is much less than for trade. This is the same contrast as is found for ANZCERTA, and again supports the view that the local bias for new investors is high, and not dependent on

Table 9.10   ASEAN: Share of inward and outward FDI stock, 1992 (%)

	US	N Am-erica	Japan	China	NICs	ASEAN	Asia	ANZ	Non-Asia	APEC
Inward	8.63	8.86	22.55	0.13	25.65	1.23	49.57	2.32	11.18	60.75
Outward	8.09	9.82	0.21	1.97	42.46	19.51	63.17	5.67	15.49	78.66

Source: Data compiled by Industry Canada; Pangestu and Bora 1996

Table 9.11   ASEAN: Composition of stock of foreign direct investment in 1992, by origin (%)

		1992			Up to 1989	1988–95
Origin	Total	Indonesia	Malaysia	Thailand	Singapore	Vietnam
Hong Kong		7.4	3.0	6.6	6.7	13.6
Republic of Korea		5.7	2.9	1.5		8.6
Singapore		4.1	6.7	6.3		8.9
Taiwan Province of China		7.7	22.8	9.2	0.4	19.3
Total NIEs	25.8	24.9	35.4	23.6	7.1	50.4
Japan	26.1	15.7	22.7	38.1	20.5	9.9
United States	9.5	6.5	7.0	11.9	20.3	4.3
Other countries	38.6	52.9	35.0	26.4	52.1	35.4

Source: Ministry of International Trade and Industry, *White Paper on International Trade 1994*, Tokyo, 1994; UNCTAD, *World Investment Report 1996*; Chia, 1992; Asian Development Bank data

regional integration. Outward investment to the NICs (which here include Singapore) is greater than to other ASEAN countries, suggesting that the geographical or common interest effect is more important than the regional. The NICs account for about a quarter of investment in the ASEAN countries, and Japan another quarter. These shares are not new (Table 9.11); Singapore is an exception: it does not receive a high share from the other NICs. An analysis in the early 1990s of the reason for this pattern stressed natural resources, low wages, preferential access under the GSP, proximity, ethnic and cultural affinity, and good infrastructure; there was no mention of ASEAN or other regional arrangements (Chia, 1992, p. 16). The suggestion of tiered investment, with Japan and the developed countries investing in the NICs and the NICs in ASEAN is supported by the pattern for Vietnam, where the NICs at a total of 42 per cent are much more important than Japan, and Malaysia also appears as an investor.

The linkages among the Asian countries show an important regional influence, but the links are from the NICs to the ASEAN countries, individually, not among the ASEAN countries. They do not, therefore, correspond to the institutional ties, or show a particular need for institutional ties based on the ASEAN set of countries.

SAARC

The only major recipient of foreign investment among the SAARC countries is India. It is probable that the trade links found among the SAARC countries are based on sub-contracting or other firm-to-firm arrangements, not foreign investment. None of the countries is a significant outward investor, so that there is no basis for intra-regional investment to develop.

SADC

As the proposals for trade liberalization in SADC are not sufficiently specific or advanced towards implementation to provide firm indications for investors, it is unlikely that any investment has yet relocated within or to the region because of SADC trade policies. There is, however, a possibility that the discussion of South Africa's role in the region could have led to an 'introductory' effect.

South Africa has seen itself and been seen by others[7] as a centre of growth for the region, with regional investment an important part of this, both to provide capital to the poorer countries in the region and as technology transfer (UNCTAD, 1997, p. 66) Labour costs are substantially lower in most of the other SADC members than in South Africa, so that if trade were liberalized this could encourage an increase in investment to take advantage of trade creation, and perhaps also diversion. There could be a parallel development to that from the NICS to the ASEAN countries. There are, however, important differences. South Africa does not have the same technological advantages that the NICs had. It is not as advanced. It has not itself developed on the basis of developing manufactured exports, and therefore does not have the same experience to transfer. The other SADC countries are not as developed in terms of infrastructure as the ASEAN countries, and the data suggest that they are not as attractive to foreign investors in general; therefore they are less likely to attract even a local investor. Finally, unlike the Latin American and NIC countries which have invested primarily in their respective regions, South Africa has had more investments outside

Table 9.12 South African investment in
SADC, stocks (%)

	1991	1994
Share in SADC:		
SACU	68.20	92.17
Botswana	*23.45*	*21.91*
Lesotho	*3.39*	*4.06*
Namibia	*13.89*	*9.07*
Swaziland	*27.47*	*57.13*
Malawi	3.09	0.76
Mozambique	1.24	0.28
Zambia	1.24	0.66
Zimbabwe	26.23	6.14
Share of SADC in total	1.45	3.16
Share of Africa in total	8.00	11.24
Total, value	8053	9425

Source: UNCTAD, *World Investment Report 1997*

Africa than within it. In 1994, only 6 per cent of South African outward
investment went to Africa (UNCTAD, *Africa*, 1996); in 1993 it was 3 per
cent. On stocks, 11 per cent were in Africa in 1994 (Table 9.12).

The total SADC figures (Table 9.A6) show that only Angola and South
Africa are important recipients of foreign investment; they are two of
the three major recipients in sub-Saharan Africa (the third, Nigeria, is
also a mainly primary exporter, suggesting that investment in Africa
still has a very different pattern from that in Latin America and Asia). As
South Africa is a major investor abroad, the only important net recipients in SADC are Angola and Tanzania. Namibia, as indicated in the
section on SACU, gets two-thirds of its investment from South Africa;
geographical distribution is not available for most of the other SADC
members. Zimbabwe also receives most of its SADC investment from
South Africa, but this is only a small share of its total inflows.

Almost all of South Africa's investment in SADC is accounted for by
the investment in SACU; the only other significant recipient is Zimbabwe. But total SADC investment is less than a third of the total in Africa,
indicating a very weak regional effect. Data on South African acquisitions
of firms in SADC countries for 1991–6 suggest that there has been a substantial increase in 1995 and 1996 over 1991–4 (from 1–2 a year to 5
and 9; this could reflect the changed climate for South African-owned
firms with the new government. Of the firms for which information is

available, only Botswana, Namibia, and Zimbabwe have more than one example (UNCTAD, 1997, p. 273). Most are in manufacturing.

APEC

There is no reason of trade or investment policy to expect increased investment among the APEC countries, although the same general rea-

Table 9.13   APEC: Share of inward and outward FDI stock, 1992 (%)

	US	N America	Japan	China	NIEs	ASEAN	Asia	ANZ	Non-Asia	APEC
Inward	17.58	22.62	19.26	0.10	7.58	0.57	27.51	2.06	24.68	52.19
Outward	20.97	29.90	2.77	2.69	5.67	5.14	16.27	5.23	35.13	51.40

Source: Data compiled by Industry Canada; Pangestu and Bora 1996

Table 9.14   FDI intensities for APEC members, 1992

	Can	US	Mex	Jap	China	Kor	HK	Taiw	Sing	Indo	Mal	Thai
Can	0.00	1.39	20.33	0.05	...	...	0.17	3.00	0.19	219.00	0.70	...
US	4.38	0.00	90.67	0.38	...	6.50	1.13	11.50	3.44	60.00	2.90	...
Mex	0.11	1.86	...	...	...	...	...	...	...	...	...	...
Japan	0.55	0.54	74.67	0.00	...	78.00	3.61	50.50	16.00	1212.00	17.80	...
China	0.13	1.08	...	0.26	0.00	...	29.52	...	0.63	...	4.00	...
Korea	0.02	0.37	...	0.17	...	0.00	1.05	...	5.13	1790.00	0.50	...
HK	0.23	0.08	...	0.24	1055.50	16.25	0.00	416.50	99.13	2595.00	121.50	...
Taiw	...	0.97	...	0.13	...	9.75	4.64	0.00	43.81	888.00	30.60	...
Sing	...	0.04	...	...	...	...	13.06	38.50	0.00	230.00	60.80	...
Indo	0.18	−0.05	...	...	11.50	...	...	777.00	478.63	0.00	49.50	...
Mal	0.03	0.07	...	...	...	...	0.27	710.50	417.13	521.00	0.00	...
Thai	...	1.02	...	...	...	...	54.88	...	37.69	...	...	...
Phil	...	0.57	...	...	49.00	...	3.89	3123.00	11.88	1491.00	1.80	...
Aus	0.02	0.32	...	...	27.50	1.00	0.28	5.00	34.31	1127.00	76.40	...
NZ	...	0.46	...	...	...	...	...	...	...	...	...	...
NA	0.52	0.13	84.00	0.35	...	6.00	1.05	10.50	3.13	74.00	2.70	...
NIEs	4.05	0.10	...	0.20	835.00	13.00	2.11	335.50	79.44	2172.00	187.80	...
ANZ	...	0.34	...	...	25.00	1.00	0.25	4.50	30.81	1013.00	68.70	...
ASE	4.01	0.25	...	...	17.50	...	2.35	1357.50	275.69	792.00	3.20	...
Asia APEC	0.49	0.49	64.00	0.02	101.50	68.25	3.47	110.50	28.75	1318.00	38.10	...
Other APEC	0.58	0.13	83.00	0.35	...	5.75	1.04	10.50	3.44	84.00	3.40	...
APEC	3.49	0.18	80.33	0.30	15.00	15.00	1.40	25.50	7.25	267.00	8.50	...
EU	0.83	0.64	14.33	0.10	3.00	0.50	1.28	1.00	16.38	11.00	7.10	...
RoW	1.00	1.00	1.00	1.00	1.00	1.00	1.00	1.00	1.00	1.00	1.00	...

... Data are zero, negligible or unavailable
Source: Industry Canada, taken from Bora, 1995

sons of high growth that could explain high trade shares could be important. Only half of APEC inward and outward investment is within the region, a much lower share than for trade (Table 9.13). This gives a very low intensity (Table 9.14). The share is particularly low for investment in the US (about a third for both inward and outward); the ASEAN countries have a high share. For ANZCERTA, again, it is clear that they invest largely in local countries.

Latin America and FTAA

For most Latin American countries, other Latin American countries are not important investors, with only Bolivia and Colombia (as discussed under the Andean Group), Paraguay (MERCOSUR), and El Salvador as exceptions (Table 9.15) . A Latin American grouping would not, therefore, include a high share of investment and would add little to existing groups. If the US were included, however, this would raise the share of

Phil	Aus	NZ	No Am	NIEs	ANZ	ASEAN	Asia APEC	Other APEC	APEC	EU	RoW
4.00	5.35	5.20	1.27	0.22	5.34	14.94	0.37	1.32	1.14	0.49	1.86
9.50	7.25	5.20	0.47	1.89	7.06	9.53	0.74	0.54	0.57	1.09	3.81
...	3.06	...	1.69	...	2.77	0.00	...	1.71	1.45	0.44	...
28.17	12.35	17.00	0.59	9.23	11.85	98.06	3.05	0.71	1.05	0.05	3.49
...	...	...	0.99	23.43	...	2.35	3.11	0.98	1.30	0.06	2.81
17.83	2.88	16.40	0.34	1.61	4.15	137.41	2.69	0.38	0.72	0.88	3.56
22.50	9.31	...	0.09	23.66	8.43	250.59	10.43	0.18	1.70	0.02	...
162.83	1.85	...	0.88	10.71	1.68	155.65	4.47	0.89	1.59	0.00	2.14
19.17	7.71	...	0.04	11.06	6.98	318.59	8.75	0.11	1.39	0.09	1.97
...	5.63	...	−0.05	87.73	5.09	35.76	11.36	0.01	1.69	0.03	...
1.33	15.56	...	0.07	77.31	14.09	46.59	10.29	0.22	1.71	...	...
...	...	...	0.93	48.17	...	0.00	7.00	0.92	1.64	0.08	0.12
0.00	...	...	0.52	54.84	...	97.18	8.56	0.51	1.70	0.01	...
22.33	0.00	575.20	0.35	5.59	54.25	120.76	3.11	0.92	1.24	0.81	...
...	134.67	0.00	0.42	...	102.91	...	...	1.50	1.28	0.38	1.53
9.00	7.06	4.52	0.55	1.72	6.89	10.00	0.71	0.61	0.63	1.03	3.63
24.67	8.69	0.60	0.11	20.66	7.92	263.00	9.77	0.19	1.61	0.06	0.48
20.00	11.48	517.00	0.35	5.02	59.17	108.53	2.80	0.98	1.25	0.77	0.15
0.83	9.46	...	0.23	69.72	8.57	60.59	9.68	0.32	1.70	0.01	0.00
27.00	13.92	6.00	0.52	11.84	11.28	117.12	4.00	0.64	1.13	0.28	3.06
9.17	13.35	12.60	0.54	1.76	7.45	11.06	0.73	0.62	0.63	1.03	3.59
11.83	7.81	10.00	0.54	3.25	8.02	26.76	1.21	0.62	0.71	0.92	3.51
0.67	9.63	7.60	0.67	3.53	9.43	5.41	0.63	0.76	0.74	0.95	3.14
1.00	1.00	1.00	1.00	1.00	1.00	1.00	1.00	1.00	1.00	1.00	1.00

Table 9.15   Latin America: origin of capital stocks, 1995 (%)

	US	Latin America & Caribbean	Europe	SE Asia	Other
Bolivia	59.5	22.1	9.0	0.4	5.0
Brazil	36.7	6.2	44.0	7.7	5.4
Chile	40.0	7.4	24.7	3.9	24.1
Colombia	55.7	21.7	18.4	1.9	2.3
Ecuador	66.9	9.2	21.6	0.3	2.0
Mexico	59.5	0.0	23.4	5.1	12.0
Paraguay[a]	9.8	46.3	38.9	0.9	4.1
Peru	14.5	11.2	69.0	0.7	4.6
Venezuela[b]	53.2	10.3	29.1	3.8	3.6
Costa Rica[c]	75.1	11.8	9.3	3.6	0.2
El Salvador	36.0	19.8	24.6	1.9	18.3
Guatemala[d]	55.2	8.8	5.8	5.2	25.1
Panama[e]	74.5	6.0	3.5	3.8	12.2[f]
Dominican Republic	29.2	3.2	10.0	0.3	57.3

[a] 1992–4
[b] 1993
[c] 1990–4
[d] 1990–4; other includes some European countries; Canada is 11.5%
[e] 1994
[f] Canada
Source: UN ECLAC, 1993

investors to above a half for all countries except Brazil, Chile, the Dominican Republic, and Peru. For all countries except Paraguay, the US is more important than all the other Latin American countries. The importance of the US in investment is thus greater than for trade. Brazil remains a major exception, as it was for trade, with 44 per cent of its investment from Europe (and 8 per cent from Asia).

None of the Latin American countries is a major foreign investor. Brazil comes the nearest. It is not therefore surprising that there is a limited investment linkage within the continent.

Summary

In MERCOSUR and NAFTA, there is some evidence of a regional effect on investment (Table 9.16). (There are also special cases in SACU.) In the Andean Pact, ANZCERTA, and ASEAN, there is what seems to be more a neighbouring country effect: newly investing countries have

Table 9.16 Changes in regional investment, summary

	SACU	MERCOSUR	CARICOM	Andean	CACM	NAFTA	G3	ANZC	ASEAN	SAARC	SADC
Investment high?	no	yes	no	yes	no	yes	yes	no	yes	yes	no
Regional effect											
on outward	possibly	yes	no	yes	no	yes	yes	possibly	yes	no	yes
on inward	possibly	possibly	no	no	no	yes	no	no	no	no	no
Rules on integration?	complete	some	limited	yes	no	yes	yes	yes	limited	no	no
Different from the rest of the world?	yes	little	little	no	no	limited	no	limited	no	no	no

gone first to nearby countries, but this is not associated with formal regional pacts, and other investors are more important.

Notes

1   Country-to-country differences in data for investment between them are far greater than those for trade, so that even using the UNCTAD data on ASEAN countries produced figures for regional investment which exceeded total investment in or by the region.

2   'Al no registrar más la entrada de inversiones extranjeras, se pierde casi toda posibilidad de analizar éstas en cuanto a su lugar de procedencia y a su destino sectorial. Cada vez son más los países que tienen tan sólo una noción global de los montos de recursos financieros que acuden desde afuera, a partir de los cálculos que efectúen para elaborar sus balances de pagos'. UN ECLAC, *Evolución*, 1997, p. 16.

3   Using correlation among interest rates as a proxy would be an alternative way of measuring the integration of capital markets, but there are now few regions where capital flows have been more liberated within the region than with the rest of the world, and in these internal controls suggest that interest rates are unlikely to move freely. There would also be the usual difficulties of finding comparable rates and ensuring that they were not correlated because of other influences, perhaps from outside the region.

4   Data on total inflows are given (in the tables at the end of this chapter) only where the region is important enough to affect totals.

5   The share is exactly 65% for every year from 1991 to 1995 (UNCTAD, Africa, 1996 p. 297), suggesting that it has been estimated. Botswana, Lesotho and Swaziland only record investment by developed countries.

6   Brazilian data for investment in Argentina are lower than Argentine data for investment from Brazil; Neto and Bannister (1997) attribute this to lack of controls and poor data.

7   'To become a regional growth pole, South Africa would need to contribute to the development of the neighbouring economies, mainly through trade and FDI' (UNCTAD, 1997 p. 65).

Table 9.A1   SACU FDI inflows and outflows (US$ m.)

	1984–9 (Annual average)	1990	1994	1996
Botswana				
Inward	64	96	−14	23
Outward				
Balance	64	96	−14	23
Lesotho				
Inward	8	17	19	28
Outward				
Balance	8	17	19	28

Namibia				
Inward	2	29	52	52
Outward		1	4	7
Balance	2	28	48	45
South Africa				
Inward	−3	−5	339	330
Outward	63		327	718
Balance	−66	−5	12	−388
Swaziland				
Inward	38	39	81	67
Outward	7	8	58	103
Balance	31	31	23	−36
SACU				
Inward	109	176	477	500
Outward	70	9	389	828
Balance	39	167	88	−328

Source: UNCTAD, *World Investment Report* 1996, 1997

Table 9.A2 MERCOSUR FDI inflows and outflows (US$ m.)

	1984–9 (Annual average)	1990	1994	1996
Argentina				
Inward	653	1836	603	4285
Outward	31	50	126	264
Balance	622	1786	477	4021
Brazil				
Inward	1416	989	3072	9500
Outward	184	665	1037	971
Balance	1232	324	2035	8529
Paraguay				
Inward	6	76	180	225
Outward				
Balance	6	76	180	225
Uruguay				
Inward	29	42	155	169
Outward	3	−1		
Balance	26	43	155	169
MERCOSUR (4)				
Inward	2104	2943	4010	14179
Outward	218	714	1163	1235
Balance	1886	2229	2847	12944

Table 9.A2   Continued

	1984–9 (Annual average)	1990	1994	1996
Bolivia				
Inward	−2	11	145	527
Outward	1	1	2	2
Balance	−3	10	143	525
Chile				
Inward	614	590	1773	3140
Outward	8	8	925	956
Balance	606	582	848	2184
MERCOSUR (6)				
Inward	**2716**	**3544**	**5928**	**17846**
Outward	**227**	**723**	**2090**	**2193**
Balance	**2489**	**2821**	**3838**	**15653**

Source: UNCTAD, *World Investment Report*, 1996, 1997

Table 9.A3   Andean FDI inflows and outflows (US\$ m.)

	1984–9 (Annual average)	1990	1996
Bolivia			
Inward	−2	11	527
Outward	1	1	2
Balance	−3	10	525
Colombia			
Inward	563	600	3000
Outward	27	16	225
Balance	536	584	2775
Ecuador			
Inward	105	126	447
Outward			
Balance	105	126	447
Peru			
Inward	9	41	3556
Outward			
Balance	9	41	3556
Venezuela			
Inward	71	451	1300
Outward	129	375	622
Balance	−58	76	678

ANDEAN			
Inward	746	1229	8830
Outward	157	392	849
Balance	589	837	7981

Source: UNCTAD, *World Investment Report* 1996, 1997

Table 9.A4   NAFTA FDI inflows and outflows (US$ m.)

	1984–9 (Annual average)	1990	1994	1995	1996
Canada					
Inward	4718	7855	7299	10786	6681
Outward	4664	4725	7447	5761	7543
Balance	54	3130	−148	5025	−862
Mexico					
Inward	2436	2549	10972	6963	7535
Outward	128	224	1045	597	553
Balance	2308	2325	9927	6366	6982
USA					
Inward	43938	47918	49903	60848	84629
Outward	16847	27175	51007	92929	84902
Balance	27091	20743	−1104	−32081	−273
NAFTA					
Inward	51092	58322	68174	78597	98845
Outward	21639	32124	59499	99287	92998
Balance	29453	26198	8675	−20690	5847

Source: UNCTAD, *World Investment Report* 1996, 1997

Table 9.A5   ASEAN FDI inflows and outflows (US$ m.)

	1984–9 (Annual average)	1990	1996
Brunei			
Inward		3	9
Outward			
Balance	0	3	9
Indonesia			
Inward	406	1093	7960
Outward	16	−11	43
Balance	390	1104	7917

Table 9.A5   Continued

	1984–9 (Annual average)	1990	1996
Malaysia			
Inward	798	2333	5300
Outward	233	532	1906
Balance	565	1801	3394
Philippines			
Inward	326	530	1408
Outward	4	−5	182
Balance	322	535	1226
Singapore			
Inward	2239	5575	9440
Outward	286	2034	4800
Balance	1953	3541	4640
Thailand			
Inward	676	2444	2426
Outward	41	140	1740
Balance	635	2304	686
Vietnam			
Inward	2	16	2156
Outward			
Balance	2	16	2156
ASEAN			
Inward	**4447**	**11994**	**28699**
Outward	**580**	**2690**	**8671**
Balance	**3867**	**9304**	**20028**

Source: UNCTAD, *World Investment Report*, 1996, 1997

Table 9.A6   SADC FDI inflows and outflows (US$ m.)

	1984–9 (Annual average)	1990	1994	1995	1996
Angola					
Inward	172	−335	340	300	290
Outward		1	−2		
Balance	172	−336	342	300	290
Botswana					
Inward	64	96	−14	70	23
Outward					
Balance	64	96	−14	70	23

Lesotho					
Inward	8	17	19	23	28
Outward					
Balance	8	17	19	23	28
Malawi					
Inward	14	23	9	13	17
Outward					
Balance	14	23	9	13	17
Mauritius					
Inward	16	41	20	19	21
Outward		1	1	4	13
Balance	16	40	19	15	8
Mozambique					
Inward	2	9	28	33	29
Outward					
Balance	2	9	28	33	29
Namibia					
Inward	2	29	52	47	52
Outward		1	4	6	7
Balance	2	28	48	41	45
South Africa					
Inward	−3	−5	339	327	330
Outward	63		327	562	718
Balance	−66	−5	12	−235	−388
Swaziland					
Inward	38	39	81	58	67
Outward	7	8	58	17	103
Balance	31	31	23	41	−36
Tanzania					
Inward					
Outward					
Balance	0	0	0	0	0
Zambia					
Inward	71	203	56	67	58
Outward					
Balance	71	203	56	67	58
Zimbabwe					
Inward	−8	−12	35	43	47
Outward	−4				
Balance	−4	−12	35	43	47

Table 9.A6   Continued

	1984–9 (Annual average)	1990	1994	1995	1996
SADC					
Inward	376	105	965	1000	962
Outward	66	11	388	589	841
Balance	310	94	577	411	121

Source: UNCTAD, *World Investment Report* 1996, 1997

Part III
Other Regional Linkages

10
Regionalism beyond Trade and Investment

Formal regional coordination and cooperation have extended to related areas, namely, other international economic linkages and national policies which affect trade. The perceived need to deepen regional (or multilateral) arrangements stems partly from the fact that, as a result of the close association of activities, non-tariff restraints, for example on services such as transportation or communications, or different rules on intellectual property or different national technical standards can interfere with the movement of goods. Beyond this, however, the increased contacts and integration that come from increased trade flows lead to common interests and common approaches to other problems. The regional initiatives are parelleled by what has happened at the multilateral level with the extension of the responsibilities of the GATT and the WTO to services, labour mobility, intellectual property, technical and health standards, and rules for public procurement, and the proposed extension to questions of competition policy, the environment, and labour policy. At the regional level, the groups have non-economic common interests even before any increased trade or investment integration.

Needs for new linkages can be dealt with (and usually are initially) on a case-by-case basis, by negotiation or using provisions like the GATT/WTO rule that allows actions to counter 'nullification or impairment' of benefits granted under a trade agreement. But these provide only uncertain and unpredictable remedies. The new areas therefore become subject to international or regional rules. The process is, of course, cumulative, with the increasing contacts from the new regime in turn leading to increased demand for further new rules. This chapter will

209

examine each of a range of practical, economic, and more political and institutional linkages, but in understanding regions it is the network of all the linkages discussed in Chapters 6 to 11 that is important.

Multilateral negotiations provide a context and limits for regional links. The inauguration of the GATT in the 1940s was a move to a universal system, with the same obligations on trade for all members. It was in part a reaction to the discrimination and complications of the system of differing and changeable bilateral agreements and national legislation of the 1920s and 1930s. The exceptions, like agriculture, were important, but clearly set off as exceptions to the universalist principle. The GATT then moved, first, to discriminate in favour of developing countries and later, in the initial moves into non-trade areas in the 1980s, on some non-trade barriers and public procurement, to allowing members to apply only some parts of the system ('plurilateral' agreements). The GSP applied only to developing countries, and developed countries could choose what products, and eventually which countries, to include. The new GATT measures were drafted as separate protocols or conventions, which countries could choose to accept or not; only the trade elements among developed countries were universal. The Uruguay Round of negotiations included a reaction to universal rules, against several parts of this modified system: to bring in the excluded sectors; and to simplify, if not abolish, the discrimination by countries. Partly to avoid the complications that this caused, but also because of a stronger revived belief in a universal reciprocal system, it was agreed that the WTO would be presented as a 'single undertaking'. Countries which wanted to join the revised organisation had to accept all the elements of the agreement, including the new areas. This followed the example of the EU, and served as an example to the new regions forming at the same time.

The more extensive links in the multilateral system and in the older regions have three effects on new regions. The first is example. They create expectations in the private and public sectors of what is 'normal' for a regional group; these now go far beyond simple trade areas or the textbook model of even customs unions. The second is a response reaction. Groups which do not yet have the linkages face pressure to establish them in order to offer their members the same opportunities for efficiency, coordination or economies of scale as their competitors receive from their regions. Finally, as the new multilateral requirements supersede regional arrangements, this encourages regions to find new links to distinguish themselves from the rest of the world. The last effect holds if regions have a self-identity; if the region itself, not just the advantages of liberalization, is the purpose.

The combination of the growing coverage of trade negotiations and the shift to emphasis on the role of the private sector has meant that private sector actors have participated more actively, and in some cases more directly, in negotiations of regions. Business links have been more important than those among social or labour groups in most regions, and have been the only linkages encouraged in APEC. Institutionally, this has meant the development of formal and informal linkages at non-governmental level. In coverage, it may have influenced the agenda of regionalization towards measures to reduce practical barriers to business, and away from the more traditional agenda of legal integration.

Non-trade areas are important for regions with a strong commitment to trade opening, but also as an alternative way of showing regional commitment for countries which do not want to integrate on trade or investment, or which want to emphasize multilateral commitments on these. It is for this reason that regions which come well down the ranking in terms of trade linkages can seem more linked on the non-trade aspects included in this chapter. APEC is explicitly seen as a way of promoting informal cooperation among its members, rather than legal liberalization, but in practice moves to coordinate legal systems on standards or trade procedures have been more acceptable than tariff negotiations. The MERCOSUR, and particularly the Brazilian, position on the FTAA is that progress must be made on trading procedures and non-tariff barriers before tariff liberalization, partly because these are considered in practice more important barriers than the remaining low tariffs in the US.

The customs unions, on the whole, maintain a leading position because some of these linkages are close to essential for the full implementation of economic union; both MERCOSUR and SACU are intended to be closer to common markets. For MERCOSUR, this is still work in progress. It has working groups on communications, mining, technical standards, financial services, transport and infrastructure, the environment, industry, agriculture, energy, labour affairs and social policy. At present it is less integrated than some of the FTAs. But there is official commitment in both the original agreements and in current political discourse to move in the direction of a single market. SACU has acquired linkages and consistency more by the dominant position of South Africa than by active coordination. Table 10.1 (p. 247) summarizes the links discussed in this chapter. It includes the WTO as a (minimum) standard of comparison.

Services

Services seem the most obvious immediate sequel to liberalization of trade in goods, but in fact they have not always progressed ahead of more technical linkages like standards or intellectual property rules. Services tend to be more regulated by governments than goods. Some are in areas where health or safety requirements may be particularly important: these include some of the most directly trade-related, for example in transportation. Some are in areas which have close links to national security: communications can come into this class. But almost all services are by their nature harder to treat as purely market transactions. The service usually does not exist, in a visible and testable form, before payment is made, requiring the service provider, rather than the service itself, to be regulated; normally for goods it is the product rather than the provider which is controlled. This can be particularly important in financial services where banking and insurance, for example, require contracts over time. This requirement for regulation means that there is normally either a legal requirement that they be supplied nationally (100 per cent protection) or *de facto* barriers from regulatory provisions. Therefore, as in other highly protected industries, liberalization is a particularly strong shock to providers because there may be significant differences in ways of providing the services as well as in competitivity. This makes it likely that there will be strong opposition to liberalizing them. Some services, of course, also have long established providers that can resist liberalization. Others, notably those involving infrastructure in transport or energy, are identified as important conditions, or even pre-conditions, for development, and therefore make a case for national provision. The multilateral rules for regions have not required them to be included, thus removing one incentive which has led to regional liberalization of goods which may have been highly protected for similar reasons. The services requirements under the GATS, as described in Chapters 5 and 8, remain less binding than those for goods, and have not yet been tested against any regional agreement. They still effectively allow services to be completely excluded.

In addition to these explanations for barriers, services sometimes require the physical presence of either the provider or the recipient in the other's country. This means that barriers to the movement of capital or labour can act as barriers to trade in services even without formal barriers to the services themselves.

Balance of payments data for services rarely distinguish by destination or origin so that it is difficult to measure intensity.

The *EU* has liberalized the provision of most services, but some, even in basic trade-related areas like transport, remain subject to national limits. Many of the regulations continue to have the effect of making it difficult for non-national firms to comply with requirements. This has slowed progress in the integration of financial services, while different national systems are *de facto* barriers in many professional services. More commercial services are liberalized, but integration has remained slow. Much of the regional integration has been accompanied by provision for national treatment, limiting the possibility of trade diversion.

In *SACU*, the history of joint administration of the members as colonies of the UK, and then of Namibia by South Africa, combined with the dominance of South African providers of commercial and financial services, has meant *de facto* integration. Recent reforms have come in opening to the rest of the world; South Africa has strengthened its commitments under the WTO financial services agreement.

CARICOM, like SACU, has the legacy of common administration as colonies. It has preserved not just access, but the joint provision of services like education, health and transportation, as well as being well integrated in commercial services and tourism and sport. In this, therefore, it has gone further than most other groups.

ANZCERTA has liberalized all trade in services, subject to a negative list.

Services have been an important part of *NAFTA*; they had been covered, but less comprehensively, in the Canadian–US FTA. The members, particularly the US, wanted their inclusion because of the Mexican history of highly protected and regulated services, but all three members made relatively extensive offers under the GATS (extended under the 1997 financial services agreement by the US and Mexico), reducing the initial obstacles to a regional agreement. The general liberalization required national and MFN treatment (Primo Braga and de Brun, 1997, p. 17), except in those cases specifically excluded. An important additional negotiating objective and achievement for the US, and not a traditional aspect of services agreements, was that NAFTA removed some requirements by Mexico for local establishment (USITC, 1997, pp. 2–8), a major past barrier to service provision in Mexico. Transportation services between the US and Canada had already been liberalized. The agreement provided for Mexico and the US to liberalize transportation first along the border (by 1995), and then more broadly (by 2000), and then to negotiate for further liberalization (OAS, Compendium). The first stage has, however, not been implemented in full. The arguments used against concern safety, but the transport industry is highly protected in both the US and Mexico. Air transport is excluded. For tele-communications services, NAFTA liberalized private, but not basic services. On financial services, integration has been limited allowing establishment and requiring national treatment, not changing the regulatory structure of the industries (Zahler and Budnevich, 1997, p. 11). The liberalization of services has thus gone beyond what could be expected of a full implementation of the GATS in a few industries, but is not as complete as in the EU and SACU. Some of the provisions have been extended to other countries through national treatment rules, but some discriminate in favour of the region.

Following the example of NAFTA, the Group of Three also provided for MFN and national treatment, and added the provision of removing requirements for national presence. The liberalization was to apply to all services, except those in a negative list or those provided by the government. As in NAFTA, most financial services were excluded from full liberalisation, but commercial telecommunications were included. Transportation was included in principle, but is still subject to negotiation (OAS, Compendium).

The *Andean Group* and *CACM* have liberalized transport services, but the members remain generally restrictive on services. As in investment policy, they have concentrated on multilateral, not regional, liberalization, most recently in the 1997 financial services negotiations.

Integrating services is an objective of *MERCOSUR*, but the very different regulatory regimes for financial services, energy, and telecommunications have meant slow progress in the working groups. The first meeting of the working group on services was only in September 1995, more than a year after the formal completion of the customs union on goods (Lucángeli, 1996, p. 3). In December 1997, MERCOSUR adopted a target of free trade in services in ten years. There remain significant differences in the Argentine and Brazilian regulation of financial services which have made coming to a regional arrangement difficult. Argentina is effectively open to all suppliers (Abreu, 1997), but Brazil still has strong preferences for local suppliers. Argentina has little to offer in a regional negotiation; for Brazil it is a highly protected industry. These differences are reflected in Brazil's high investment in Argentina in this sector, without corresponding Argentine investment (see Chapter 9). Both still have restrictions on foreign insurance companies, and there has been no progress in regional preferences. Both countries made very limited offers on financial services under the GATS. In the 1997 negotiations on a financial services agreement: Brazil made some further offers, but these are subject to delay and to administrative controls;

Bolivia made its first offer on financial services; and Uruguay slightly extended its offer. These may help to open the prospect of a regional agreement. Pressure for an agreement on services, particularly financial services, was already coming from the pressure for their inclusion in the FTAA (see below). If MERCOSUR is to remain more integrated than the rest of the FTAA, it has to make faster or deeper progress on financial services, which has suggested that there might be progress at the MER-COSUR level. This is a clear example of integration in one group acting as a stimulus for integration in another. The proposals for rules of origin in services would confine any regional preference to firms with 80 per cent MERCOSUR ownership (Primo Braga and de Brun, 1997, p. 20). This would be a major regional preference compared with the provisions of the EU or NAFTA, and would therefore make trade diversion more likely.

The associate members of MERCOSUR, Chile and Bolivia, are not formally part of the services negotiations and are not committed to joining any common market in these. Chile has a more liberalized regime for services, and therefore (as in the Argentine negotiations with Brazil) a mercantilist approach to liberalization would make finding an acceptable bargain difficult. Chile, however, wants to be part of an integrated services region (Insulza, 1997, p. 7), and could sign a framework agreement, if not the detailed provisions. For the original four MERCO-SUR countries, however, the integration of services is seen as one of the elements in their deeper integration, and perhaps therefore not appropriate for the free trade arrangements with the associate members. The example of other FTAs moving toward free trade in services without the deeper integration of a customs union or common market may encourage MERCOSUR to bring the others in.

ASEAN has had a framework agreement on services which did not impose any obligations beyond those of the GATS where, as mentioned in Chapter 8, the members' offers had been relatively restrictive for their level of development. In 1997, they added to this target liberalization in telecommunications, tourism, transport, construction, shipping, business, and financial services, with partial liberalization starting in 1998 and full liberalization by 2020, but the programmes and extent of liberalization had not yet been negotiated. At the multilateral level, however, they made much stronger offers in the financial services negotiations. The regional measures were explicitly targeted at improving conditions for trade and investment. While the coverage is probably sufficiently broad to meet the requirements of GATS Article V, the 22–year transition period is well beyond WTO limits. As in trade, the regional liberalization has been limited and involves long periods of transition; multilateral liberalization is more important.

SADC and *SAARC* have made no progress on liberalization of services, although it has been proposed in SADC. SADC has a history of co-operation on infrastructure, transport, and energy services, and, as in SACU, there is extensive dependence on South African services, so that the *de facto* integration is greater than might appear. The SAARC countries remain restrictive at both regional and multilateral level.

APEC and the *FTAA* both have working groups on services, but only the FTAA has the objective of liberalization, with the NAFTA members pressing for similar provision to be extended to the whole continent.

Integration on services has thus been mixed. MERCOSUR may be following the pattern of the EU towards full integration, but the members' approaches to policy perhaps vary more, thus creating obstacles to a harmonized regime. In NAFTA and the Group of Three, there has been considerable progress on services liberalization, without any intention of full integration, and with services treated simply as an extension of goods liberalization. In CARICOM and SACU, the integration comes for historical rather than policy reasons. In ASEAN, the area with the most rapid growth in total, although not regional, trade, both MFN and regional liberalization of services have been limited, while the Andean countries have moved to liberalize both. For both of these, it is clearly the multilateral policy which is driving reform. This suggests that services are not a necessary part of integration, and that their integration depends on national situations: on protection and the role of services in the economy. Services should be considered as simply a group of sectors which may or may not be included. There is an above-normal probability of exclusion because of the greater role of national governments and regulations, and because of the more limited international regulation on integration. These forces seem strong enough to counterbalance the apparent logic of services being liberalized to help trade.

Labour mobility

Free movement of labour is still rare in regional groups. Under the GATS, countries could include provisions for allowing the entry of particular types of service provider, but few countries did this, and those that did made very limited offers, normally restricted to a few sectors and often only to senior labour. Only the EU explicitly includes full freedom of movement. There is extensive movement within SACU and ANZCERTA. In CARICOM, graduates have been allowed to work in other members since 1996 (Nogueira, 1997, p. 5), and there are provisions for easier movement for tourists. CARICOM, MERCOSUR, and SADC, as well as the EU, have different immigration treatment at their borders for regional members, providing a visible sign of the region as well as easier entry. MERCOSUR has introduced a joint travel document, and has full mobility as a goal, but has not yet made progress even on easier entry for service providers. It has, however, arranged that workers from one country will have minimum labour rights in another (UN ECLAC, Panorama, 1996, p. 131). NAFTA has provision for temporary entry for business visitors. 'Professional' labour is allowed to enter Mexico and Canada, and Canadians can enter the US, but there remains a quota on Mexicans entering the US (OAS, Compendium). This makes the US restrictions on Mexico tighter than some countries have given on an MFN basis under the GATS. The Group of Three and CACM allow temporary entry. None of these allows unlimited mobility, and the NAFTA agreement specifically excludes it from the agreement (ibid). There are no provisions for labour in the other agreements.

The regions thus offer a sharp contrast between capital and labour mobility in creating a regional market. This implies that, in most of them, integration is seen as a way of improving the returns to capital more than to labour. Either or both may benefit from the trade liberalization, but capital gains also increased flexibility in its use. Any consumer surplus or non-financial welfare benefits from increased choice and mobility for labour are also excluded. This implies a sharp contrast between the basic purposes, and therefore the measures of success, of most regions and those of countries. For regions it is a combination of national income and the interests of particular sectors of the economy; for countries it is individuals. This is consistent with the greater presence of business interest groups in most regions' negotiations, but may imply only limited political support for such regions.

Harmonization of business conditions

The next set of possible regional policies are those which can affect the conditions of production in the different member countries, and therefore the competitiveness of companies within the region. They also affect competitiveness with respect to the rest of the world, so countries may have an interest in the policies of trading partners even outside a region, but they are more likely to be regulated within a region. The countries are major trading partners; other barriers are lower, so the relative weight of other influences on differences in competitiveness is greater; increased integration and the continuing negotiations make the countries more aware of their fellow members' different policies. They are all questions which are also becoming subject to multilateral discussion and regulation.

Labour standards

Rules for minimum standards for labour conditions vary widely among countries, and this has become an issue in multilateral negotiations. It had been discussed in connection with special preferences, notably as a condition for inclusion or level of preference in the GSP; proposals to include minimum regulations at multilateral level were also made at the end of the Uruguay Round. Within regions, the EU has gone furthest on this, with rules on minimum health and safety standards, but also regulations about how labour representation is organized within companies. SACU, in contrast, has not included it. For MERCOSUR, it is assumed that the goal of a single market will ultimately require some common rules on labour, but the working group has not yet made its proposals. It has established a programme to coordinate regulation of work relationships (individual and collective), migration, training, health and safety, and social security (OAS Compendium). The co-ordinating group (like the Forum, discussed below under institutional structures) includes representatives of labour and employees, as well as governments. These arrangements do not include Bolivia and Chile.

NAFTA has the most extensive coverage, after the EU. 'Improving working conditions and living standards' is one of the declared purposes in the NAFTA agreement. In principle, NAFTA's labour provisions are based on setting minimum requirements for national legislation, with national enforcement. The North American Agreement on Labour Cooperation (NAALC) has a Secretariat and National Administrative Offices in each country. These prepare reports and provide information on labour conditions and legislation in the member countries and consider complaints from individuals and unions as well as governments. In 1997, for the first time, labour in all three countries filed a joint complaint against a US firm operating in Mexico. This suggests that the system is moving to encourage joint union action across borders, as well as the original aim of US unions taking complaints against actions in Mexico. The NAALC has conciliation and dispute procedures, although still based on national legislation, not regional rules, and can levy fines on countries (OAS, Compendium, 1996; US Government 1997, pp. 94–9). The procedure has been used since 1994. This is effectively reinforced by US government reviews (US Government 1997) which examine not only the outcome of NAALC discussions, but the degree of enforcement within Mexico.

The Andean Pact in 1973 had the objective of harmonizing labour laws and social security (UN ECLAC, Panorama, 1996, p. 136), and securing equal treatment for workers from other countries of the region, but this was not implemented. CACM adopted the goal of harmonizing social policies in 1995.

Other regions have no provisions on labour standards, with strong opposition in the Asian regions. The Chile–Canadian bilateral free trade agreement does have provisions similar to those of NAFTA, based on national legislation and a Commission for Labour Cooperation (*El Mercurio*, 11 July 1997). The proposals by the US for an FTAA included labour standards, similar to the NAFTA provisions, but this was opposed by the Latin American countries.

All three regions with labour standards – EU, MERCOSUR, NAFTA – have them explicitly as part of a common approach and common market, not simply to ensure fair competition among the members. In NAFTA, there is a contrast between the relatively advanced integration on labour standards enforcement and the relatively limited provision for migration. From a welfare point of view the two can be substitutes: rather than permitting labour to improve welfare by mobility, NAFTA attempts to guarantee better conditions throughout the region. This gives no weight to freedom of choice, however. From an economic point of view, both can be considered ways of making trade less subject to artificial differences among countries. It could be argued that common labour standards, if they reduce competitive differences among countries, reduce trade creation, and therefore reduce the benefits of a region (or the costs, to protectionists), but the circumstances in which the provisions were introduced in the EU and MERCOSUR, at least, make it clear that the objective was not to remove what were considered 'unfair' or inappropriate competitive advantages.

Competition policy

Within countries, competition legislation can regulate what types of behaviour are permitted, in order to make markets function efficiently. It can regulate sizes of firms and pricing policy. Between countries, regulation takes the form of anti-dumping actions, which, by WTO rules, can look only at the relationship between a company's prices and its costs, and then at its potential market-disrupting effect. There are proposals for a multilateral competition regime.

If a region adopts a common competition policy, it should be able to dispense with anti-dumping actions within the region. A customs union might be expected to have a common external anti-dumping policy, if external firms price in the same way throughout the region (with the market completely open) and if the internal industrial conditions are the same. Free trade areas might have a more diverse internal market and therefore face different behaviour by the same trading partner. In practice, customs unions are more diverse than this would assume. Only the EU and ANZCERTA have formally abolished intra-regional anti-dumping actions (Winters Conference, 1997, p. 20), although only South Africa among the SACU countries has an anti-dumping procedure, and it has never been used within SACU. Anti-dumping actions against third countries are taken by the EU, not by the member states.

MERCOSUR has the intention of setting up a common competition policy (it is in the 1991 Asunción Treaty), and then coordinating its anti-dumping policy and possibly unifying it. Until this is achieved, the member countries can still take anti-dumping action against each other and independent actions against outsiders. In 1996, a framework was established for a competition policy (Tavares and Tineo, 1997, pp. 9–13). It provides explicitly for controlling anti-competitive practices which affect competition at the MERCOSUR level, by harmonizing domestic legislation. There will be enforcement by a MERCOSUR Trade Commission with representatives from the individual countries (ibid., p. 10). It is not clear if its scope will extend only to effects on the MERCOSUR market as a whole, (Rowat, 1997, p. vi); the division of responsibilities between national and regional agencies has not been determined. As Paraguay and Uruguay do not have internal competition laws, implementation may be slow. The Canada–Chile bilateral agreement has provisions for phasing out anti-dumping between them.

The other regions have not moved to harmonize competition law. This suggests that there is not a strong motivation to improve competition, which in turn suggests that other initiatives to create similar market conditions may come from other motives. These may be reducing the costs of doing business in the case of harmonizing standards, or may be non-economic for labour standards.

Environment

There has been more progress on common standards for the environment at the multilateral level than for labour, but these also remain unusual within regional groups. The EU has made progress on coordinating and harmonizing legislation on environmental standards, and the environment has been included in the NAFTA agreement, but not in other agreements. The limited interest may reflect the extent to which this is a developed country issue.

In NAFTA, the Agreement on Environment Co-operation (NAAEC), established a Commission, with a Cabinet-level council, a secretariat, and a joint Public Advisory Committee as well as National Advisory Committees. This is a more extensive, but similar structure to that for labour. The Commission can both study environmental questions and consider complaints about non-enforcement of environmental legislation; like the NAFTA provisions for labour, the environmental regime is based on national legislation. The Commission has the power to settle disputes and levy fines on member countries (OAS, Compendium). It only covers traded goods, not all types of production (Nadal, 1995, pp. 16–18).

The ASEAN countries have been criticized because of environmental concerns about the production of wood. ASEAN established defensive institutions, first the Senior Officials group on the environment, then a Plan of Action (1994), to coordinate a common position (Weibe, 1997). They have taken no action and have no dispute resolution power or public role. After the smoke and smog crisis of 1997, they adopted a regional action plan, based on new national legislation, but regional monitoring.

Intellectual property

Patent and copyright law has been subject to international agreements for more than a century, but the Uruguay Round brought these into the trade regime, with an agreement on Trade Related Intellectual Property standards (TRIPS) included in the WTO. The EU has introduced its own standards, which go further than the multilateral rules or than some of its members' rules. It also has some common procedures for registration and enforcement.

The Andean Pact had its own rules for intellectual property from its foundation. In its early years, these included rules limiting the use of patents and the royalties paid to foreign owners for their use. It has reformed these provisions, but still has a regional regime. (OAS, Compendium). CACM envisaged harmonization of intellectual property regulations from its foundation, but it was only in 1994 that the first agreement was made.

NAFTA preceded the TRIPS agreement, and anticipated many of its provisions. Like it, it was based on requiring minimum standards of legislation and enforcement within countries, unlike the earlier Latin American agreements with their common provisions. It required adoption of the international conventions on copyright and patents, but also offered additional protection of computer programs, longer-term protection for copyright, and anti-pirating provisions. It also included minimum standards for the enforcement mechanisms. The Group of Three followed the NAFTA/TRIPS model (OAS, Compendium).

MERCOSUR has a technical group considering harmonization of intellectual property legislation, and some common standards for marking have been agreed (OAS, Compendium). ASEAN has had a framework agreement on intellectual property since 1995. In both CARICOM and SACU there is *de facto* coordination because of a common legislative background, and a similar background exists in ANZCERTA.

Intellectual property has been an important issue in Latin American relations with foreign investors since the 1960s, and the inclusion of joint provisions in the regions may reflect this history and the desire to act together. The more recent NAFTA and Group of Three rules stem more from attempts by the US to strengthen intellectual property protection at the multilateral level. The two traditions have different roots: the attempt by Latin American countries to avoid paying 'too much' for patents created elsewhere and the insistence of the US on receiving full payment for its inventions. In the Asian countries, the problem has been more one of informal resistance to paying for foreign property, and therefore has not given rise to national or regional legislation. There are also two different approaches: regional rules in the more integrated regions, and regional supervision of national rules in the others.

Standards

Different national standards can obstruct trade, and this becomes increasingly important as products became more complicated and more regulated. They can also be used as intentional barriers, and this became important in the 1980s as other barriers to imports became more controlled by the GATT. Even if a country sets a standard with the objective of greater efficiency or minimum acceptable health or safety provisions, it is likely that producers in other countries will find it more difficult to meet the standard than domestic producers. As outsiders, they have not themselves been involved in setting it, and their existing procedures will not have been taken into account. Traders may have to meet different standards in their home markets and in other markets, so increasing their costs. For a region, therefore, setting common standards may have the same effect internally as removing non-tariff barriers. The regional standards will benefit outsiders less (for the same reasons as for country standards), even if they gain by a reduction in the number of standards they need to meet in their export markets. This gain itself will be less than the gain to the members if members have a high share of intra-regional trade.

There are two possible approaches to coordination of standards: harmonization or mutual recognition. The Uruguay Round settlement made a start on regulating standard setting by defining international agreements for some standards, and requiring that countries normally accept these; countries are required to justify any alternative standards. This represents a choice of harmonization. It creates more efficiency advantages for traders, and may be needed where countries (or consumers or business within the countries) believe that a single policy is essential, for example for safety or health, rather than simply desirable for practical convenience. Recognition is the policy countries adopt *de facto* when they accept an import without harmonization: the need to adopt it as a legal provision arises only where there is no agreed standard and countries are using differences in standards as a reason for constraining trade.

For the EU, common standards have been one of the most visible signs of integration. These have normally started with traded goods, but integration means that they now effectively cover all goods. In most cases, the EU has set its own standards (in some cases these were industry standards).

Some regions follow the WTO pattern of formally specifying international standards as the regional standard. This includes the Andean Pact and MERCOSUR. NAFTA also does so, but with the possibility of using alternative standards if these would provide a 'higher level of protection than would be achieved by . . . international standards' (OAS, Compendium). The Group of Three followed this form, but with a more tightly limited exception for 'fundamental factors of climatic nature' or technological reasons. NAFTA's commitment is to review and improve international standards, not necessarily to use them, and again the Group of Three follows the same model. NAFTA has provision for member countries to establish their own sanitary and phytosanitary standards.

MERCOSUR has a working group on technical standards, which is proceeding by harmonizing national rules, the European model. The MERCOSUR Committee on Standards had approved about 87 standards by mid-1996, and hoped to complete 500 standards by the end of 1997. This is very low compared with the approximately 8000 standards which Brazil and Argentina have (Machado, 1996, p. 46). MERCOSUR's agricultural working group is also looking at plant and sanitary standards, but the problems here lie more in the lack of appropriate testing and enforcement mechanisms than lack of harmonization (ibid., p. 48).

CACM has no provisions for common standards. CARICOM countries normally use British standards, and thus have harmonized standards based on history. ANZCERTA has some common standards, and the common historical tie to British standards.

ASEAN countries found lack of common standards as important barrier (Sree Kumar in Imada and Naya, 1992, p. 83), but there has been no progress beyond WTO standards. APEC has a committee on standards, but is encouraging the use of international standards, not the development of separate standards. Its proposals are for adoption in 2000 or 2005. The SADC Trade Protocol has also suggested the use of international standards.

Use of international standards is satisfactory as an initial form of integration, but it does not allow a region to go further than the international system in efficiency or other gains. If regional integration is to go further or faster than multilateral, there will be cases where regional reconciliation of national standards will be needed because there is not yet an international standard, or where the region wants to use the WTO authorization to set a higher or more precise standard. This may be less common in smaller regions than in larger, because their relatively small share of total regional trade makes it more likely that the need for new standards will appear first in trade with a non-member, and will therefore provide an incentive to encourage a new international standard, rather than a regional one.

Trade facilitation

This term is used by APEC and MERCOSUR (in its negotiations in the FTAA) to mean slightly different concepts, but in both cases it concerns measures that promote trade by removing barriers which are not tariffs, but which are not conventionally classified as non-tariff barriers. In the Asian context, it normally means removing differences in trading or customs rules or documentation. For MERCOSUR, it has a broader meaning of technical standards for goods.

Identifying such differences as a problem is not new. Viner (1950, p. 59) argued that 'the costs involved, for exporter and importer, in meeting the customs regulations, and the costs involved, for the tariff-levying government, in administering the customs machinery ... are often, in fact, more important than the duties themselves as hindrances to trade'. He identified the US as 'an outstanding offender in this respect. In the case of most other tariffs, their removal would not involve comparable administrative economies.'

In APEC, removing differences in the way the member countries trade, and more generally in the way their companies and even their industrial policies function, is considered to be more important to increasing trade than removing tariffs (Bora, 1995, p. 21). There are working groups and proposals on simplifying administrative documents. Technical assistance has the implicit aim of encouraging the developing members to adopt the procedures of the developed. These are problems that affect the difficulty of doing business in the region, and thus perhaps reflect the extent to which APEC is business- rather than government-led.

In the FTAA negotiations, this has become a major issue. MERCOSUR is arguing that the negotiations should begin with 'trade facilitation', meaning simplification of customs procedures, a common nomenclature and removal of anti-dumping duties (IRELA, 1997 FTAA, p. 5) and probably also more explicit barriers in the forms of standards. Only once these have been negotiated will removal of tariffs begin.

The APEC and MERCOSUR arguments do not follow the precedent of the EU or indeed of MERCOSUR (Machado and Veiga, 1997, p. 37). Simplified documentation came in Europe in the 1970s, after the completion of the customs union; other administrative harmonization came in the 1980s and with the completion of the single market in 1992. MERCOSUR negotiated first on tariffs, and all other forms of integration are following. But the new emphasis on procedural barriers may still be partially derived from the EU experience. The EU's emphasis on the gains from completion of the single market, at a time when tariffs and conventional NTBs had long been eliminated, brought the cost of the remaining obstacles to trade to international attention. They also have an important advantage over tariffs in negotiations. If administrative barriers are not designed as intentional barriers, they have a cost to traders, without bringing income to governments: they are therefore more of a welfare cost than tariffs, and politically less difficult to remove. In many cases, however, they are designed (or at least preserved) as barriers, so that it might be naive to assume that they will be easier to eliminate.

The emphasis in the FTAA has force to the extent that Viner's singling out of the US as the least open is still true. Such barriers are probably more important for exporters from Latin America to the US than from the US to Latin America (at least now, following the liberalization in Latin America); they are therefore the most important barriers, and those where reciprocity will have least impact, for the Latin Americans;

the US preference for beginning with tariffs or negotiating on all simultaneously is similarly consistent with its negotiating interests. No progress has been made in the FTAA, but the momentum of the working groups is likely to produce recommendations.

Economic Policy

Public procurement

External access to public contracts was introduced as a side agreement to the GATT in the 1980s, i.e. it was not required of all members. It was extended after the Uruguay Round, but remains a 'plurilateral' agreement, not part of the 'single undertaking', the required core of WTO obligations. Regional access to public contracts (subject to minimum sizes) was already accepted in the EU, and in the EU's preferential agreement for the Lomé countries. It is also found in ANZCERTA, NAFTA, and the Group of Three but not in other regional agreements.

NAFTA goes beyond the GATT requirements. It is asymmetric, with a higher threshold for the US and Canada with Mexico, than for US–Canada relations. The Group of Three agreement followed the NAFTA precedent, and is also asymmetric. Here, Mexico accepted stronger obligations than Colombia and Venezuela (OAS, Compendium). As Mexico had already opened to the US, there was little reason for it not to permit the Group of Three the same access. But illustrates a difficulty of successive regional negotiations: a country's bargaining position with the next region will be weakened by what it may have agreed already.

MERCOSUR has a committee studying current rules, but no proposals for opening procurement to the region. Argentina already allows firms in its territory to have national treatment for this.

The step beyond improving the mechanisms of the market is to regulating or coordinating differences in national economic policy. Public procurement could be considered an element in this, if the criteria are political rather than purely economic, and this may help to explain why few regions are willing to advance in this.

Sectoral policy

Providing special coordination for a particular industrial sector is in the tradition of using regions for national development and in particular for obtaining advantages of economies of scale or selective development. It is also closely related to cooperation on infrastructure, which may be a specific advantage of regions over multilateral agreements. Sectoral policies, however, also reflect highly protected products that are excluded from the full liberalization of some regions. They were the basis of the first version of the European Community, the Coal and Steel Community, and sectoral policy remains important in European energy and agriculture. There is also European support for infrastructure linkages in transport and communications.

NAFTA had to incorporate Mexico's traditional regulation of the energy industry, and Canada also retains the right to restrict exports for security reasons. The first agreement between the US and Canada was for cars, the Autopact of 1965. The NAFTA rules of origin are particularly strict for cars, at over 60 per cent NAFTA content (see Chapter 6), and the member countries also have their own technical standards for cars and car parts. An Automotive Standards Council is trying to set common standards. The Mexican industry is effectively incorporated into the US industry, with outside producers excluded.

The Group of Three also had to accept both Venezuela's and Mexico's desire to be able to impose controls on trade in oil. It has a Committee on the automobile sector, and cars will be among the last to be liberalized, in 2007. Textiles are also specially protected.

Brazil has an active industrial policy, promoting several sectors including cars and informatics. For Argentina, there is protection for some old industries (also including cars), but not a current industrial strategy. There are therefore *ad hoc* arrangements for the most sensitive sectors. This can work as a temporary strategy, but it is not clear that the different approaches will remain reconcilable as priorities change. There is explicit provision in the MERCOSUR agreement for the adoption of new sectoral accords, but it has never been used. Protocols for wheat and iron and steel had preceded the Argentina–Brazil trading agreements. The car sector remains outside the MERCOSUR regime, with a high tariff and exceptionally high origin requirements (70 per cent for Brazil, 60 per cent for Argentina). Argentine and Brazilian parts can be included in this, but only if balanced by trade in the opposite direction (IDB, Intal, 1996, p. 23). The member countries do not export cars outside the region, and the rules 'are aimed primarily at facilitating the integrated production strategies of a small group of global automobile TNCs' (Mortimore, 1997, p. 1). The proposal was to agree a common MERCOSUR automotive regime by 1998 to come into effect by 2000, and to replace the national regimes; there would therefore still be a separate sectoral policy (OAS, Compendium 1996), but even this agreement has not been reached. Because textiles are highly protected in Argentina, there is a special regime for imports. Iron and steel are excluded from MERCOSUR. Sugar is also excluded from MERCOSUR until 2001, to protect Argentine producers (Maletta, in CEFIR, 1995, p. 153) and as in cars, no agreement has yet been reached (IDB, INTAL, 1997).

For the smaller countries in MERCOSUR, Bolivia and Paraguay, joint energy projects with the major members have been important, and Argentina also has electricity agreements with Brazil and Chile. Chile and Argentina have agreed joint mining development along their border. All these are bilateral agreements outside MERCOSUR.

The Andean Pact in its early history had strong industrial policies, but the reforms of the 1980s, as indicated in Chapters 6 and 8, greatly reduced this. The tariff cutting there and in the Group of Three has excepted old industries in need of protection, but has not emphasized sectoral policies.

SADC's administration has a sectoral structure (see below), but its policies have been limited to coordination of infrastructure and of research (Ndlela, 1997, pp. i, 28). The Asian groups have not had regional sectoral policies.

The importance of cars as an integrating sector reflects not only their importance in trade, but the importance of large companies with a strategy of cross-country production. This offers support for the view of the regions as more orientated towards business.

Border coordination

The strongest impact of a region can be where transport costs are least, at the country borders within the region. This is sometimes directly promoted through duty-free zones, but there is almost always *de facto* greater freedom of movement of people and goods at the borders than within the rest of the country. These are the areas where the rigid distinction between countries may already be weak. The trend has been emphasized as one of 'growth triangles' in Asian areas like Malaysia–Singapore–Indonesia and Hong Kong–Guandong, but older examples can be found on the France–Germany and Germany–Netherlands–Belgium, or US–Mexico, US–Canada, and Paraguay–Brazil–Argentina borders. More broadly, both the EU and MERCOSUR have at their centre traditional regions which cross borders, centring on the Rhine and the Plate. Such areas can provide a signal for where formal regional integration may have an economic advantage. Where they have been promoted by policy (for example, the assembly plants on the Mexican border with the US), they may provide an experiment in more formal regionalism. There is no necessary relationship, however: there are artificially created duty-free-zone-based industries from the US and Europe in Malaysia and Thailand, and from Asian countries in Mexico, with no implications for further regional integration. If they are on a border, however, they may become more strongly linked. In NAFTA, the border zone was established in 1966. Any effect on the formation of NAFTA was therefore long-term, but the well-established advantages of using cheap labour near a rich market were an element in support for NAFTA, and the need for these operations to expand beyond the border, to find new plots and new supplies of labour in duty-free zones within Mexico, made extending the duty-free entry to all parts of Mexico a logical step. The legal integration has encouraged further border growth, in trading services.

In MERCOSUR, there is no similar promoted industrial zone. The duty-free zones are at almost the most distant points of Brazil (Manaus) and Argentina (Tierra del Fuego). The concentration of cities, some industry, and agriculture around the northern part of Argentina and southern Brazil produced a situation more like the central corridor of the original six-member European Community.

In ASEAN, since 1990 Singapore has promoted the Singapore–Malaysia–Indonesia border zone, planning it to provide three levels of sophistication of production (high, middle and low), and thus potential for complete production. This did not depend formally on the (already existing) ASEAN, although related to it in motive: namely, tying Indonesia more closely to Singapore (Higgott et al., 1993, pp. 236, 239). It may face the same difficulties that other regions have faced when industrial plans suggested unequal divisions, with suspicion of reserving the leading position for Singapore (ibid., p. 243)

The other regions do not have important border areas of these types.

An active cross-border relationship must strengthen a region's economic coherence, but it will also be reflected in the countries' intra-regional trade data.[1] It may weaken exclusive political identification with a single nation state, and therefore make a regional identity easier to accept; intra-regional borders, however, often have a history of conflict (e.g. both MERCOSUR and Europe) and thus strong national commitment. The actual importance of these influences will depend on the relative size of the border region and the country: highly important for Benelux; slightly less so for the original EC; decreasingly so as more distant members were admitted, but still a major part, economically and geographically, of the EU. MERCOSUR is similarly extending away from its original centre, but this remains a high share of the total. In contrast, the US–Mexican border is small relative to the US, not near the major internal Mexican centres of industry and population, and very distant from Canada. It is therefore less likely to be a very strengthening factor in NAFTA. For ASEAN, the zone is important for Singapore, but less so for Malaysia and Indonesia.

Exchange rates

A common exchange rate has often extended beyond a single country, unlike fiscal policy or macroeconomic coordination, and therefore may be a possible step for a region at an early stage, not necessarily an indication of a late stage of economic policy coordination. Some currency areas have not included free trade (and are therefore excluded from this study), for example the franc zone in Africa, while only a few of the regions considered here have had a common currency or plans for one. The arguments for a common currency deriving from high dependence on a particular country's trade may hold in a region, but do so in only a few of the regions considered here (NAFTA and SACU, and possibly MERCOSUR for the smaller members); for most regions, other partners are more important. Some of the countries have experienced high or variable inflation, making a tie to a trading partner difficult to sustain. The question of whether exchange-rate instability is in itself damaging to trade remains unresolved, because of the other problems which the instability reflects, and the undesirability of what may be the alternative, a seriously misaligned rate.

The EU is now moving towards a common currency, but in fact three members (Germany, Belgium and the Netherlands) have been effectively tied together since the 1970s, and Austria was tied to the German rate before it entered the EU. The move follows some coordination on fiscal policy: common VAT rates as well as a CET, and is accompanied by provisions for tighter fiscal and macroeconomic policy coordination, so that it is not seen as a separable element of regionalization, when extended to all countries.

The *de facto* use of a currency in trade can be used as a signal of a potential currency zone, but need not imply this: for a common currency of invoicing like the dollar (or increasingly the DM), it may merely indicate an accepted store of value and unit of account, considered better than the home currency for trading contracts. In this case, it is better precisely because it is not subject to the local pressures, and therefore cannot be replaced by a local currency. The frequent use of the dollar in this role might even obscure potential currency links. It has been most used in Latin America where currency volatility has, at least until recently, made any permanent links or common currencies not credible.

SACU has a common currency, except for Botswana; the three smaller countries are effectively in the position of Austria relative to Germany, dependent on a dominant trading partner with little exchange-rate freedom. For all the members (including Botswana), the pre-existing condition at the time of independence was a common currency, so the decision was whether to leave the area, not whether to form one.

Argentina and Brazil have both tried to tie their currencies to the dollar in recent years, but through different mechanisms and with different purposes, so that this did not constitute a tie to each other. When Brazil had a growing trade deficit and higher inflation in 1997, there was fear of devaluation in the other MERCOSUR countries, but the high share of trade between Argentina and Brazil which is either in energy products (priced in dollars) or intra-firm trade (in cars, the major manufacturing industry), and therefore not as subject to price-induced fluctuations, suggests that the risk be smaller than it is perceived to be. Only if trade increased significantly in competing goods would devaluation be a major threat, and therefore suggest advantages in a common exchange rate.

CARICOM has discussed a common currency for several years, but made no moves towards one.

There is no plan for exchange-rate linking in NAFTA, although swap arrangements exist to support the exchange rates against sudden fluctuations, and more extensive support was given by the US to Mexico in its serious currency crises (before and after NAFTA). The CACM also has arrangements for joint support. The 1997 currency crisis in the ASEAN countries has led to support for central bank cooperation there. The APEC countries agreed to a scheme of regional surveillance of financial policy, but this seems to be informal (*IMF Survey*, 1 December 1997). Indonesia, Malaysia, and Thailand had already established cooperation with Hong Kong and Australia in 1995. For this type of support, there is no reason to expect an established region to be the most appropriate group. Any outside pressure may be more likely to affect a whole region, and therefore support from outside the region may be particularly necessary.

Fiscal coordination

This is more likely to be required in a region than exchange-rate or monetary cooperation. Any free trade area will have a fiscal effect through loss of tariff revenue, and a customs union must involve coordination of the common external tariff. The greater the integration, the more difficult it will be for the countries to maintain very different tax regimes, if there is mobility of companies, consumers, or workers within the region.

For the EU, the common external tariff and a share of a coordinated, but not completely harmonized, VAT provide the revenue for the central funds of the Community. But harmonization has gone beyond this to set limits on excise and other internal duties.

In SACU, coordination is included in the SACU agreement which requires the smaller countries to have the same laws on customs, excise, and sales duty as South Africa. The revenue from customs is divided among the members according to their total trade, but with a formula favouring the four smaller countries.

In MERCOSUR, there is no agreement on taxes or subsidies. There have been major conflicts on subsidies, because Brazil has continued to offer and increase these, while Argentina has been constrained by its budget. Only export subsidies within the MERCOSUR area are explicitly forbidden (IDB INTAL, 1996, p. 24). For Argentina, the establishment of the CET was particularly constraining because it had already adopted a currency board, providing complete binding of its exchange-rate and monetary policy, so non-trade taxes were the only ones left to manage (Lucángeli, 1997, p. 15). Any attempt to harmonize indirect taxes would be opposed by Paraguay which relies on its low rates to attract purchases from the other countries. MERCOSUR seems still to be adjusting to the implications of a CET and constraints on fiscal policy. The awkward arrangement of requiring goods to pay duty at the country of final destination and the differences over the use of subsidies will need to be resolved as trade, particularly in new goods, develops.

The Andean Group and CARICOM do not attempt to coordinate indirect tax rates. For Canada and the US, the loss of tariff revenue from NAFTA was minor; Mexico still has to adjust to the full loss.

There is no provision for coordination of tax rates in any of the FTAs, but as all retain border controls, this situation is in principle no more difficult to sustain than before the FTA. It is, however, a problem for policy acceptance: increased integration and contact in an FTA mean increased awareness of price and therefore tax differences. This is happening at the multilateral level, but will be stronger within regions.

Macroeconomic coordination

It has been argued that a minimum level of stability (or expected stability) in the partners is necessary for a country to be willing to accept external constraints on its policy, or, alternatively, stability in a country is required for its neighbours to be willing to open to it. The need for the first will depend on each country's approach to economic policy: if it has no intention of using trade or other external policies, agreeing not to do so does not have a cost. The second proposition needs to be examined more closely. The question of whether opening an economy through liberalization leads to more stability, because of balancing effects, or less, because of exposure to shocks not 'managed' by the government, is traditional in discussions of the role of government intervention. What is at issue here is whether liberalizing just to a region requires a higher concern about potentially destabilizing effects. As the opening is incomplete, the benefits from a range of markets and other economies will be less; the number of shocks may be lower, but the impact, if they vary together, may be greater. But there is not a straightforward way of measuring what is meant by stability in this context. Stability is necessarily a relative term: more stable than in the past, or trading partners more stable than others. One way to try to ensure stability in partners is macroeconomic coordination.

Arguments for free trade at the international level do not require macroeconomic stability to produce an increase in welfare. A reason for making higher demands on a region for stability is the existence of the rest of the world. If that is a significantly larger market than the region, then the region may need to offer some economic advantage. If the outside world is also more stable, the members of the region will have a greater interest in tying themselves to the outside, unless other forces are holding the region together. While it is not essential, macroeconomic stability is an advantage in a region which is a major trading partner, and instability could weaken the region. It can create direct conflicts, for example, if periods of low exchange rates in one partner lead to the growth of protectionist reactions within the region. Macroeconomic coordination is beginning in the EU; the Andean Pact had coordination in its early phase, but no longer does. CARICOM has regular consultations.

There are significant differences in the degree of informal coordination. This has been implemented through ministerial and official meetings in Europe since the 1950s. At the least integrated extreme are regions where members still act without thinking of the implications to the rest of the region. This would be true of the least integrated FTAs, especially where intra-regional trade is small, but is perhaps also characteristic of new regions: in the initial years of MERCOSUR both Brazil and Argentina took fiscal measures without taking into account even the technical needs of the CET and regional obligations. Then there are the regions where a country is dominant, and may be aware of its effects on the smaller countries, but is unwilling to adapt its policy to suit them – assymetric coordination. SACU may fit this model. Regions like NAFTA and ASEAN have a tradition of consultation that may lead to some coordination, without formal mechanisms..

If macroeconomic convergence is not a prerequisite for regions, is it a result of the greater integration? The effect of greater integration depends on the size of the region relative to the rest of the world (and its members' trading partners). For the EU, the evidence is that there has been some convergence, but this experience cannot be assumed to be relevant to most of the developing regions. The EU convergence has been partly deliberate, particularly during the preparations for a single currency. The countries' intra-regional trade is higher than in most of the other regions. Finally, the period of European integration has coincided with greater multinational convergence because of international integration. In regions where smaller members are linked to a dominant partner, convergence might occur without any institutional regionalization.

Mexico was judged to have stabilized its economy before entering NAFTA in 1994, but suffered a crisis in December, and there have been periods in the past (for example, the 1960s) when it also had a strong appearance of stability. The coming together of Argentina and Brazil in the origins of MERCOSUR was at a time when there had been major regime changes, in the government and the economies, which could support an expectation of stability. The history of the other Latin marican groups does not offer support. The ASEAN and SAARC countries do not seem to have moved into periods of stability in performance or perceptions at the time of the formation of their FTAs, and the African economies clearly do not meet such a criterion.

Intra-regional transfers

Many of the regions include countries at widely different levels of development (Chapter 4), and the effects of integration may be more favourable to some members than others. Either of these could justify financial or other transfers within the region. Such differences have been used to justify longer transition periods for the poorer countries, in the EU, NAFTA, MERCOSUR, Andean group, CARICOM, SADC, and APEC, but explicit transfers are less common. The EU and SACU are the only examples. In the EU, there are differences in countries' budgetary contributions; transfers and special programmes in the poorer areas; and transfers to particular industries, including agriculture. In SACU, the system for distributing the customs and excise revenue favours the smaller countries; this is formally a compensation for their loss of free-dom to set their own tariffs and their acceptance of high import tariffs, and therefore higher costs, to help South African industry, but implicit-ly it is accepted because they are poorer. There are now proposals to change the system, to tie the receipts more closely to estimates of the individual countries' shares of imports, and to reduce the subsidy from South Africa to the others. This comes at a time of reduced South African political need for support from its neighbours, following its change of regime – another implicit explanation.

MERCOSUR does not yet have such a transfer system, although the differences in incomes and levels of development are large. In the early years, it was unacceptable to Brazil and Argentina. The 1997 summit brought the first discussion of the possibility, at least partly because Bra-zil had to persuade the smaller countries to accept the increase in the CET which it had implemented when there was pressure on its markets in November 1997. Introducing such a system would be a major shift from a MERCOSUR of individual countries to one with a sense of regional obligations and identity. There is a proposal for a MERCOSUR develop-ment bank, perhaps particularly to help the poorer regions and Bolivia, but this would rely on private funding, with government encouragement.

In some regions, there are development funds, but without a formally redistributive function. NAFTA has a fund for border development, but the contributions from the US and Mexico are equal. When the US assisted Mexico in 1994, this was not as part of NAFTA, and followed the precedent of its assistance in 1982. The Andean Pact had a develop-ment fund established in 1968, and expanded in 1988, but this is for balancing payments, not for long-term development (OAS, Compen-dium, 1996).

APEC has a commitment to use its technical assistance to help its developing members preferentially. For some of the poorer countries, this is an essential part of APEC: a Chinese official has seen economic and technical cooperation as being as important as lowering barriers to trade and investment (Yushang Wang, speech at APEC meeting, May 1996). If the developed members of APEC are diverting their assistance preferentially towards APEC from other developing countries, this could be an additional form of distortion arising from regions, but both the US and Japan have in fact been diversifying their aid programmes. The assistance to APEC may be 'diverted' in a different way, to a greater emphasis on assistance to adopt policies consistent with integration and with the pattern of the donor's industrial planning, thus reinfor-cing the bias already present in EU assistance.

The institutional structure of regions

Administration and initiatives

The approach of all regions (and countries) is to accept every increase in institutionalization and administration reluctantly, but increasing economic activity or, in a region, increasing coverage of activities, normally leads to increases in the scope of regulation. Regulations may bring an essential element of policy predictability, reinforcing one of the advantages of any liberalization. A region needs mechanisms for identifying and considering possible new areas of reponsibility. Once there are rules, means are required to implement and enforce them, and to settle disputes about them.

The regions vary in how they are organized, in the strength of their central institutions, and the role of non-governmental actors, including industry, labour and interest groups. One source of difference is whether the region is regarded as complete, a single agreement, or alternatively as a new institution which will need to adapt to new circumstances and perhaps to take initiatives. The first requires mainly technical or enforcement institutions; the second requires a structure capable of identifying problems and evolving. Normally the central authority involves a combination of political representatives of the members' governments and civil servants, who can be either delegated by the countries or international civil servants with institutional loyalty to the region. Councils of ministers are part of almost every region; they are needed because sovereignty continues to be derived from the member countries. But committees of delegates for whom the regional administration is not their principal responsibility, whether politicians or civil servants, are too cumbersome for routine administration. A more permanent secretariat becomes necessary the greater the responsibilities, and perhaps also the larger the number of countries in the region.

The EU has the most comprehensive institutional structure, and by its basic treaties this is permanent, and not subject to withdrawal. It has the basic elements of a region – summits of heads of government, councils of ministers, and a secretariat or Commission – but the latter has the equivalent of senior ministers as Commissioners, giving it a status between those of a secretariat and of a government. The Council is formally the heads of government, but meets also as the functional ministers; civil servants also meet. The voting is by weighted votes. The combination of voting (other regions still require the consensus of all members) and the executive and initiating role of the Commissioners (Winters, 1997, *World Economy*, p. 893) gives the region a strong central structure and identity. This is reinforced by the independently elected European Parliament, again unique to the EU. The region is still, however, very different from even a federal government. The Commissioners are chosen by the individual countries, not at regional level, and the Commission is responsible to the countries as well as to the Parliament. The civil servants in the Commission, however, are international, not delegated, and there are European programmes funded through taxes belonging to the region. Formally, there is representation of business, labour, and other interests in the appointed Economic and Social Committee. Informal representation is used more often, as in the individual countries.

SACU has meetings of civil servants, but the administration of the customs revenue is within the South African Finance Department, and all decisions on the CET or on taxes are taken by South Africa. There is no secretariat, although there are now proposals for one.

The MERCOSUR basic treaties are incorporated into the basic laws of the members, and are of indefinite duration. There is not, however, an institutional structure giving it legal autonomy with respect to the member states, as in the EU, and there is no structure delegating initiatives to the secretariat (Haines Ferrari, 1993, pp. 424, 427). MERCOSUR has a small secretariat, located in Uruguay, but is still governed entirely by representatives of the national governments, in the Common Market Council, with meetings of the foreign and economic ministers and of the Presidents, and in the Common Market Group, with civil servants from the members' foreign and economic ministries. There are also the working groups on further integration discussed above. Some of the countries have also set up integration ministries, to offer liaison and information from MERCOSUR within the members (Zormelo, 1995, p. 20–1). Restricting regional contacts formally to these ministries is another difference from the EU (or SACU), where ministers or civil servants from any relevant ministry meet. This may restrict the development of a network of contacts and coordination. The civil servants actively involved are only a small number, perhaps 50–100 in the major countries. This already imposes a strain, with the structure of working groups and regular meeting, as well as non-MERCOSUR external relations. Chile, as an associate member, has had the right to be invited to some meetings, but not all. At the 1997 summit, it gained fuller participation, although still without a vote. This meeting, however, put more emphasis on integrating the associate members into the group.

As well as these executive links there is a joint parliamentary Committee, similar to the precursor of the European Parliament, and also the Economic and Social Forum, which has been copied from the EU Economic and Social Committee, but with only business and labour representation. Like its model, it has been purely consultative, with effective representation coming more from joint action by business and labour lobbies based in the countries. It has created a formal context for countries' economic sectors to take a position on regional matters, and thus is perhaps a useful contribution at the early stages. The secretariat has also established information posts in the individual countries to increase awareness.

There is thus no continuing MERCOSUR body with the power to take initiatives, but the governments are beginning to accept that a stronger centre will be necessary as the responsibilities become greater and responses are needed on a routine basis. The associate members parti-cipate in the summits, but are not full members of the institutions. There is no clear structure for including them, and this will become increasingly awkward if other countries are accepted as associates. Some interest groups are developing regular links, including associations of industrialists, and also academic links. There is encouragement of increased linkages of this type. There is, however, no formal participa-tion by the private sector in the working groups, although there are observers in technical groups like that on financial services.

The CACM has summit meetings, a council of ministers, a civil ser-vants' committee, a secretariat, and a joint parliamentary committee. There is also a Central American Court. The formal mechanism of integ-ration, however, is a treaty with an initial duration of 20 years, subject to renewal.

The Andean Pact had a large secretariat from the beginning, with a research function, but with no power to take intitiatives. (It was sup-ported financially by the European Commission.) It has a Commission, of representatives of the governments; a Board, with representatives at official level; a Court of Justice; and the Andean Parliament, of repres-entatives from countries. In 1996, it established separate business and labour consultative councils (UN ECLAC, *Panorama*, 1996, p. 136), with the members selected by organizations in the member countries. Mem-bership is, however, in principle revocable: there was an initial period of 20 years, then 5 years notice is required (Echavarria in Lipsey and Meller, 1996, p. 145).

CARICOM also combines ministerial meetings with a secretariat, but the existence of regional organizations such as air services and the uni-versity gives the region a visible centre, greater than for the other com-mon markets. The Common Market Council is composed of ministers.

It was agreed in 1997 to establish a supreme court (to replace the British Privy Council as the final court of appeal). It has indefinite duration.

The purely free trade areas are much less structured. Members have the right to leave at short notice. NAFTA is intended as a completed creation, legally as a treaty, although with indefinite duration. It has a ministerial committee, the Free Trade Commission, and committees and working groups, as well as the labour and environmental commissions mentioned above. It required congressional ratification in the US, but not in Mexico: individual laws were changed as needed to make them consistent with the agreement (WTO, Mexico, 1997). There is a small secretariat, but without functions of initiation or identification of problems.

The Group of Three follows the NAFTA model, with an Administrative Commission made up of ministers, but with the facility to withdraw at 6 months notice. Secretariat functions are carried out within country governments. The group is administered by working groups on particular topics. Interestingly, it is seen as less permanent than the other groups – with an initial period of only three years, then indefinitely renewable.

ASEAN and SAARC have annual meetings of ministers and of civil servants, and ASEAN has a very small secretariat.

SADC follows the unusual approach of delegating different aspects of policy to different governments. For example, trade is delegated to the Tanzanian Government and finance to South Africa. This can only work while responsibilities are small, and disputes therefore unlikely. SADC has a small secretariat and regular summit and ministerial meetings. Its trade protocol provides for councils of ministers and civil servants, which would presumably replace the trade responsibility of Tanzania, although these are in addition to the existing institutions.

APEC has a deliberately anti-institutional and anti-formal agreement approach. APEC experts (e.g. Garnaut and Drysdale, 1994) take the European Commission as an example to be avoided. The regular structure includes annual summit meetings, for which a group of 'eminent persons' produces recommendations, and a business forum. Enforcement and sanctions are to come from peer pressure. The annual meetings provide an occasion on which member countries are expected to make offers of trade or other liberalization, and they are then expected to implement. The substitute for formal agreements and votes is consensus. Like the delegated responsibility of SADC, this system would be unlikely to work for complex negotiations or serious disagreements. It works because there is no serious expectation or impulse from any member for APEC to achieve detailed objectives.

One aim that does seem to be important (Higgott in Higgott et al., 1993, p. 303) is the gathering of information about the policies and practices of the various members. This is an essential first step, and has a parallel in the early stages of the GATT, when the emphasis was on notifying and binding tariffs, not altering them, or the GATS, which again encouraged countries to provide full information about existing restrictions on services. It is consistent with the current stage in the MERCOSUR–EU negotiations (see Chapter 11), which is compiling a common data base. In these cases, however, it was and is implicit from the beginning that the objective was to use the information to hold trade liberalization discussions. In APEC, there is no such target, as the entire liberalization process is to take place by agreement and consensus. This may make the information-gathering less effective because there is neither a deadline nor a clear intended use. The argument of APEC is that Asia is different: 'Government systems here operate differently. Moreover, the reality of economic cooperation is that the business sectors and not governments can supply much of the knowledge needed for analysing economic issues' (Stuart Harriss, quoted in Higgott et al., 1993, p. 307).

There are, as discussed in Chapter 6, two interpretations of how APEC will liberalize. They have different implications for future institutional development. If it is to be concerted MFN liberalization, then only coordinating organizations are needed, at least in principle. There would be no formal agreement among the APEC members, and their liberalization would be legally implemented and enforced through the WTO. If, however, the US interpretation of reciprocal liberalization is followed, excluding non-APEC countries which are unwilling to join in, then a regional agreement, with regional implementation and enforcement, would be necessary both to enforce the regional commitments (as WTO mechanisms would not be available) and to meet WTO rules on regions. This would require institutions.

The LAIA has a secretariat, but country representatives meet only irregularly.

The FTAA still has only working groups, but they have a clear programme and objectives, and are developing a sense of community as negotiations proceed. The procedure of a prolonged period of parallel negotiations, supplemented by annual summit meetings, is more like the permanent state of APEC than the prior negotiations of other regions. Although MERCOSUR did have technical sub-groups on similar subjects during the period of transition, 1990–4, these were after the treaty establishing the region had been adopted. Up to now the FTAA negotiations have had the advantage over APEC of a goal of establishing formal, and therefore well-defined, links. If the FTAA is not achieved, the results of the technical discussions may be at least as integrating as those held under APEC.

It is important to remember that while informal linkages are expected to give strength to the regions, by increasing integration and interest in continuing it, they do not guarantee it. They have been present in failed regions as well. They were well developed in the early years of the Andean Pact, but this faded in the 1970s and 1980s; they were always important between imperial countries and their colonies. They do not ensure permanence.

Dispute settlement

Once a group has formal agreements among its members, there must be a means of settling disputes between countries and also between firms or other economic actors and member countries which are accused of not meeting their obligations on tariff or other policies. The role of dispute settlement in the regions must be seen against the background of the innovations in the WTO. Strengthening dispute procedures was one of the major changes in the Uruguay Round. Under the old GATT system, there were no time limits on procedures, so that countries could delay in replying to complaints and in any conciliation process, and any report had to be adopted by consensus, meaning that any country could effectively avoid condemnation. Under the WTO, there are strictly time-bound stages; a decision can be appealed against, but can be overturned only by a majority vote. As a result, there has been a massive increase in the number of disputes brought to the WTO. These have included some between members of the same regional group, because the WTO procedure is for obligations under the WTO, while regional procedures are needed for regional obligations.

The EU has a Court of independent judges. It is unusual in having a procedure which gives direct access to non-governmental complainants. The European Court of Justice has been used extensively, although supplemented in practice by negotiations.

The NAFTA labour and environmental procedures have elements of this, and there is provision in the investment chapter for disputes between investors and governments, but the formal dispute procedure for trade obligations is available only to governments. It is similar to that of the WTO, with independent experts, not representatives of countries. Also like the WTO, it can go beyond violations of the treaty to include 'nullification or impairment' of rights granted under the treaty (Endsley, 1995, p. 552). It was used 26 times in the first three years (Schott, 1997, p. 17).

SACU has no formal dispute settlement procedure: the smaller countries have little trade with each other, and South Africa would not accept a decision against itself. As matters like tariffs and other taxes are effectively to be decided by South Africa and accepted by the others, there is relatively little scope for formal dispute rather than lobbying or government representation. Where there have been disputes, as in a recent case of Botswana allowing what South Africa considered an assembly industry without sufficient local content to establish itself for export to the rest of SACU, the issue was resolved by South African pressure.

MERCOSUR set up a procedure, but it has not yet been used. It would use *ad hoc* tribunals, but, unlike those of the WTO or NAFTA, these are to be made up of country representatives. There have been requests for consultation to the Trade Commission, but these have been resolved at that stage, or postponed to further negotiations. Only two disputes have led to panels being established; in both cases the disputes were solved by negotiations (López, 1997 pp. 23–4). Most disputes are settled in direct negotiations between governments, including the presidents. Brazil is unwilling to submit to decisions by the smaller countries, and with only four full members, negotiations are a feasible solution, and accord better with the very interventionist approach of the governments to MERCOSUR (in contrast to the legalistic approach of NAFTA) (ibid.) This may be more effective (and faster), and may allow an evolving approach to problems, but the more legal NAFTA approach may strengthen the institutions, and be more predictable for private companies and individuals.

The Andean Court can settle disputes, and is modelled on the European Count of Justice so that it can accept cases from persons or companies. But it has been used only rarely (UN ECLAC 1996, p. 17). The Group of Three has procedures similar to those of the WTO, with panels of legal experts formed on an *ad hoc* basis for individual disputes. CACM, like MERCOSUR, uses a tribunal of country representatives. CARICOM uses a panel, with each disputant selecting a member, and the third chosen by the two combined.

Military and other security linkages

It was argued in Chapter 2 that peace at least was a prerequisite for a trading region, but in Europe and Latin America, this goes further: regionalism is seen as part of peace-building. Both the original membership of the European Community, which brought together recent enemies, and the current extension to the east are deliberate attempts to use economic ties to prevent war.

For MERCOSUR, including the associate members, military linkages have been stressed as a major confirmation of regional solidarity. Unlike the EU[2], there were not other existing military alliances within which the countries could operate, and there was a very recent history of border tension which would have made joint manoeuvres unthinkable. Therefore, it has been specifically within the MERCOSUR framework that joint manoeuvres have developed, first between the armies and navies of Argentina and Brazil; and in 1997 between Argentina and Chile. Staff colleges are holding joint courses, building up direct linkages. Brazil has proposed moving to a joint foreign policy, including security policy. MERCOSUR has informally moved towards this by exerting joint pressure on Paraguay when a military coup was threatened in 1996.

Similar pressure has occurred in SADC and ASEAN. In SADC, in 1995–6, leading governments put pressure on Lesotho to preserve political legitimacy, and there was discussion of intervention in Mozambique. Although both South Africa, one of the leaders in this initiative, and Lesotho are in SACU, this was done through SADC meetings. In 1997, the decision to invite the Democratic Republic of Congo to join was in part to encourage peaceful development there. Zimbabwe has proposed a security framework, but South Africa has been unwilling to have a permanent forum for intervention in other countries. The 1998 interventions by South Africa in Lesotho and by South Africa and Zimbabwe in the Congo continued this intervention, but illustrated its risks. In this early stage of SADC, and without the formal inclusion of democracy as a criterion for membership as in the EU and MERCOSUR, the grounds and objectives for intervention are not clear.

ASEAN tried to mediate in the change of government in Cambodia in 1997. It sent a mission to try to persuade the new premier to restore the joint administration, and then adopted a policy of 'preventive diplomacy', a step towards accepting intervention. This was a major change in ASEAN policy, which has been rigorously opposed to intervention in national policies, either within the region or from outside. Then, in contrast to its insistence on admitting Burma, in spite of pressure from the EU and the US, it postponed consideration of admitting Cambodia, and (according to comments by the UN Secretary General, AFP 17 December 1997) it has also encouraged Burma to enter discussions with the UN on its elections. In 1998, following the change in government in Indonesia and demonstrations in Malaysia, some members tried to add formal acceptance of an ASEAN interest in internal politics.

In all three regions, there were two possible types of reason for intervention. The first was the interest of the countries in avoiding potentially unstable regimes in their neighbours. This could have brought *ad hoc* joint action even in the absence of a region. Nevertheless the existence of the region was important in making intervention more likely, and potentially more persistent. The regional consultation mechanisms provide a continuing forum for discussion. The habit of acting together was established, and there was a group available to intervene. This suggests a link from economic cooperation to military and security cooperation. The second reason, which was certainly important in MERCOSUR and SADC, and probably in ASEAN in spite of its non-interventionist traditions, was the existence of a common approach to government and in particular to democratic (in MERCOSUR) or at least constitutional (SADC and ASEAN) means of change. The mixed success in SADC and ASEAN suggests that they may not (yet?) be as united on policy as the EU and MERCOSUR.

CACM, which has also emerged out of countries recently at war, set up a coordinating body for its military forces in 1997. The FTAA negotiations include an explicit commitment to democracy, but no commitment to take direct action to support it. The other regions have no military or security aspect, although, as discussed earlier, there are some clear implications for security, for example including China and the US in APEC.

Other political and social linkages

These include some which have been deliberately started as part of the regional integration process, but also others which have appeared as responses by members to the new opportunities or demands of the region. For example, as well as the formal provision for consultation among business groups, business organisations and other groups with an interest in lobbying on policy changes have joined together, whether formally or on an *ad hoc* basis. This section can only indicate some of the examples considered most important by the regions themselves.

In the EU, there are extensive European organizations, which come from a long tradition of joint action as well as from EU encouragement. A description of the MERCOSUR innovations suggests the difference between a tradition of contacts and one of almost completely separate development.

In MERCOSUR, there is emphasis on increased meetings and contacts, at business and academic level in particular. Some of the examples reveal how unintegrated the neighbouring countries were before formal regionalization. New semi-official networks include mayors, provincial governors, and students. There is an annual 'Economic Summit'. Newspapers have greatly increased their coverage of the other members, and have introduced special MERCOSUR sections or supplements. Spanish is now obligatory in Brazilian schools, and the demand for Portuguese teaching has increased in Argentina.Tourism among the countries has greatly increased. The mutual recognition of academic qualifications has helped to encourage joint research programmes.

In SACU, most of this type of linkage is traditional, but probably derived more from the common history and similar business and educational systems than from the region itself. Such links are almost equally important among the SADC countries. In particular, the level of knowledge and awareness of policy found in other members of the region has traditionally been higher than among the MERCOSUR countries.

The CARICOM and CACM countries also have a long history of close linkages, but the Andean countries are more like those of MERCOSUR, with limited contacts, except in the context of the formal region.

In NAFTA, the continuing debate about the costs and benefits to the members means that there is not yet the sense of permanence needed to encourage the development of new linkages. The examination in 1997 of the effects of NAFTA (discussed in Chapter 7) took the form of separate representations from interest groups throughout the US, looking at sectoral interests. The fact that there are no proposals for changing or developing NAFTA means that there is no incentive for lobbying groups to form across borders to influence future development.

APEC has had formal business linkages for longer than the APEC structure itself has existed, but these are separate from the normal structure of business groups. They work together only in the APEC context, and do not develop other linkages (as in the EU). There are extensive business and other linkages among the ASEAN countries, in particular between Singapore and Malaysia. The type of links mentioned for MERCOSUR are well-established, but pre-date and are independent of ASEAN.

In most of the regions, linkages existed before and independently of the regions (or did not exist, and still do not). The most striking exception is MERCOSUR; in contrast to analysis which emphasizes the need for linkages as a condition, it was formed before conventional linkages had developed.

Summary of links

For many of the FTAs, the extent and number of types of linkages are even weaker than the coverage of multilateral organizations, indicating no move further than the average (by analogy with trade, an intensity of 1). The range of practical links varies widely, according to the needs and circumstances of the groups.

Most long-standing groups like CARICOM, CACM, and the Andean Pact have developed strong institutions. The outstanding exception is SACU, with extensive practical links, but almost no institutional structure. SADC is developing practical and institutional links, but from an unusual framework of divided, country, responsibilities. APEC is interesting for its relatively strong consultative structure, with low practical links and no formal institutions. What is evident is that groups that are either strongly integrated or long-lasting normally develop formal institutions. After the EU MERCOSUR has gone furthest in both practical and institutional development.

Notes

1 It may not be fully reflected if there is substantial unrecorded trade and smuggling, but these can exist without an active official border industry, as, for example in SAARC between India and Bangladesh, so this will not necessarily bias the comparison among regions.
2 The membership of some, but not all, EU countries in NATO only started to be a potential difficulty with the adoption of a common approach to security.

Table 10.1 Other linkages within regions

	WTO	EU	SACU	MERC-OSUR	CARI-COM	Andean	CACM	NAFTA	G3	ASEAN	SAARC	SADC	LAIA	FTAA	APEC	AEC
Services	some	most	yes	planned	many	few	few	many	some	frame-work	no	pro-posed		wrk gp		
Exceptions to liberalization	yes	transp.						transp.	transp.							
Labour mobility	no	finan. yes	de facto	v. limited	some types	no	limited	finan. no	finan. limited	no	no	de facto				
Business conditions																
Labour standards	pro-posed	yes	no	planned	no	pro-posed	goal	yes	no	no	no	no	no	no	no	no
Competition policy	pro-posed	yes	no	planned												
Anti-dumping abolished?		yes	de facto	planned	no											
Environment	yes	yes	no	pro-posed	no	no	no	yes	no	frame-work	no	no	no	no	no	no
Intellectual property	yes	yes	de facto	planned	de facto	yes	yes	yes	yes	frame-work	no	no	no	pro-posed	no	no
Standards[a]	some	yes	de facto	planned	de facto	world		world		no	no	pro-posed	no	no	pro-posed	no
Company law	no	yes	de facto	yes	de facto	yes	no	no	no	no	no	no	no	no	no	no
Trade facilitation	no	yes	de facto	pro-posed	yes	yes	yes		yes	no	no	no	no	pro-posed	yes	no

Table 10.1 Continued

	WTO	EU	SACU	MERC-OSUR	CARI-COM	Andean	CACM	NAFTA	G3	ASEAN	SAARC	SADC	LAIA	FTAA	APEC	AEC
Policy																
Public procurement	yes	yes		partial	no	no	no	yes	yes	no	no	no	no	no	no	no
Sectoral	no	yes		allowed		not now		de facto	de facto	yes		limited				
Border linkages		yes	yes					yes								
Exchange rates		yes	yes		pro-posed					yes						
Fiscal coordination		yes	yes													
Macroeconomic coordination		yes			consult-ants											
Transfers		yes	yes	pro-posed											lim-ited	
Institutional																
To initiate policy	no	yes	no	yes	yes	yes	yes	no	no	yes	no	yes			no	
To administer	yes	yes	yes	yes	yes	yes	yes	yes	yes	no	no	no			no	
To enforce	yes	yes	yes	no	yes	yes	yes	yes	yes	no	no	no			no	
Ministerial links	yes	yes	no	yes	yes	yes	yes	yes	yes	yes	yes	yes		yes	yes	
Civil Servant links	no	yes	yes	yes	yes	yes	yes	yes	yes	yes	yes	yes		yes	yes	

Parliamentary links	no	yes	no	yes	no	yes	no	no	no	no	no		no
Ec-Soc Committee	no	yes	no	yes	no	yes	no	no	no	no	no		yes
Secretariat	yes	yes	no	yes	yes	yes	yes	yes	yes	yes	yes	yes	no
Independent?	yes	yes	–	no	yes	yes	no	no	no	no	no	no	no
Court or dispute settlement	yes	yes	no	proposed	yes	yes	yes	yes	yes	no	no	no	no
Public access?	no	yes	–	no	no	limited	no	limited	–	–	–	–	–
Military, security links	no	de facto no	yes	no	no	no	yes			limited	limited		
Constitutional commitment	no	yes	yes	no	no	no	yes	limited	limited	yes	yes		yes
Other linkages													
before region formed	yes	yes	no	yes		yes	some						yes
since region formed	yes	no	yes			yes							yes

a World means specific commitment to world standards

11

The External Relations of Regions

Open regionalism and other models

An analysis of how regions relate to different parts of the rest of the world and to the multilateral system as a whole can give evidence on two types of question. First, how they operate towards outsiders in practice: do they set common international objectives, is authority to negotiate delegated to the region, and if so how is this organized? How far is the region negotiating as a single unit, rather than as a group of countries with common interests but no necessary common policy? This is an area where the differences between customs unions and free trade areas are important, but in practice various outcomes are possible. The second question is in relations with potential new members. How far do they see themselves as a permanent or an evolving unit? It is often difficult to identify a point where the relations of a region with 'outsiders' evolve into relations with potential members.

One model proposed is the 'hub and spokes', with direct, perhaps different, linkages from different partners to a central country (or group). This is intended to allow for different levels of common action. The European experience, the extreme example of hub and spokes, demonstrates the problems it creates, of complicated arrangements and obligations between the 'hub' and 'spokes' when new relationships are formed, and the indirect relationships among the 'spokes'. The EU relations with a variety of different areas are discussed later, and the proposal to reform the EU's preference scheme for the Lomé Convention countries into a series of regional FTAs, with different coverage and timing according to the needs of each region, would follow this precedent.

In discussion on Asia, the tendency is to think in terms of nesting groups, with subsets, but not overlap among groups. Among Latin

American groups, the variety of bilateral FTAs raises the possibility of spokes joining more than one hub, combined with nesting in a Western Hemisphere group. At this point, the mechanical analogue would crash. It seems likely that the economic form would be equally unworkable. Except in the case of unrelated linkages (trade and regional infrastructure development, for example), it is difficult to see how the differing obligations could be guaranteed not to raise conflicts over time, especially as the regions followed the normal progress of moving towards greater linkages. And this process is likely to reduce the potential number of unrelated links.

The way in which regions approach other regions or countries has become an issue in some analysts' judgements about what is 'good regionalization' (for example, Serra, 1997). If 'good' is taken to be from the point of view of the international system, the criteria are: forms which are less rigid, with respect to setting new international standards, or less protectionist, with respect to multilateral liberalization. If avoiding trade diversion is also an objective, an additional criterion can be accessibility to new members. Regions should have fixed rules for new entrants, and be effectively required to admit new members that meet those criteria. It is argued that this will reduce the potential damage from discrimination, as non-members would always have the option of joining. In fact, few agreements are legally open to all, and none is in practice. Such a requirement appears to be inconsistent with the political and historical dimensions of regionalism (unless the criteria are defined so explicitly in political, historical, and often security, terms as effectively to exclude all but the current members). And it ignores the fact that regions evolve. What they include changes, their rules and procedures change, and therefore the requirements for members change. Even the WTO, which comes closest to a purely rule-orientated, purely economic organization, has lengthy negotiations with each new member to fit it into the detailed structure of the different obligations and privileges that have evolved over 50 years. Nevertheless, the identification of 'open' regions with good, or at least harmless, regionalism has become a major strand in analysis.

What is sometimes called Asian open regionalism is a variant. The principle behind this appears to be that a group of countries should negotiate concessions among themselves, but agree to extend these to any country which offers to reciprocate. This is not a traditional, Article XXIV region, because there is no commitment to a target of full free trade and the element of automatic extension means that the group is not fixed. As any country could obtain the reductions, it is not clear that it would be challengeable under Article XXIV, although the position would be anomalous. It would clearly violate MFN if the new member was not considered part of a region. It is also not clear what obligations would rest on one member to consult another before extending reductions to a new partner.

There would clearly be a potential conflict if any of the members of sub-APEC regions implemented this. If a member of an FTA opened to a non-member, it could 'impair' the rights already given to the existing members, by effectively reducing their relative preference. While this would clearly be beneficial from a world welfare point of view, by 'undiverting' trade, it would violate any implicit (or explicit) agreement among the members to treat each other better than the average, perhaps incurred for non-economic reasons.

The broader definition of Asian open regionalism is that any concessions would be extended to all. If regions are purely economic bargaining units, this is similar to the old GATT bargaining technique of reaching agreement for any commodity among the principal suppliers and buyers, and then automatically extending MFN treatment to all, on the grounds that the others did not add significantly to the costs or benefits of those negotiating and that the result could not significantly harm any country outside the principal traders. Where there is substantial regional trade, a similar argument could hold. There would, however, be some difficulty in finding any region except the EU or NAFTA where intra-regional trade was as large a proportion of the total as the GATT commodity-based groups usually involved, and therefore where countries would accept the principle of automatic extension. Extension to all might again conflict with obligations to any sub-APEC FTA. In APEC, there is no procedure for bargaining for tariff changes; the annual meetings provide only a forum for announcing them, and there is no procedure for 'binding' offers (except in the WTO). Where tariffs are low, the bargaining becomes easier, but less worthwhile. As new areas of cooperation become important, the problem of whether reciprocal privileges could be extended in part or only for all subjects would arise.

This form of 'open regionalism' remains at the proposal stage, and it is not clear that any of the present groups, in or outside APEC, would follow it. It seems to be advocated most frequently in the Australia–New Zealand area. Within APEC, the scope has already been challenged, with finance initially excluded but now proposed. For other issues like regulation and standards which are likely to arise in regional groups, it is difficult to see how mutual recognition or harmonization could be defined or achieved without a rather more formal structure than is assumed.

The alternative (ECLAC) form of open regionalism is a slightly more formal concept and closer to the open membership rule: that any group should allow any country which is prepared to accept the agreements already reached to join. It also suggests that the regions should be on the basis of a negative list of exclusions, rather than a positive one of inclusions, on the grounds that this is likely to lead to more integration (UN ECLAC, 1994, p. 13). A negative list is also more likely to meet Article XXIV's criterion of 'substantially all' trade. MERCOSUR has followed the negative list criterion, as far as goods are concerned, but the questions of other forms of cooperation and the new issues, and even services, have not yet been dealt with; by implication all are excluded, except where explicitly included. The openness to new members is a more difficult concept. UN ECLAC (1994, p. 12) suggests that, 'What differentiates open regionalism from trade liberalization and non-discriminatory export promotion is that it includes a preferential element, which is reflected in integration agreements and reinforced by the geographical closeness and cultural affinity of the countries of the region.' The openness is thus limited by an assumption that all Latin American and only Latin American countries meet the political and social conditions. It is difficult to reconcile Mexico's membership of NAFTA or the potential FTAA with this view of 'affinity', and it raises questions about the Caribbean's links to Central America, Colombia and Venezuela. The freedom to join with 'flexible membership criteria' raises a variety of questions and makes several assumptions. It is to be eased by adopting international rather than regional standards. This effectively eliminates regional standards as a component of the agreements, which suggests the question of why there should be a region rather than global integration. Regional investment is to receive national treatment. There is no mention of migration, the environment, or other non-WTO issues. If this is to go beyond simply applying WTO rules, it probably requires more preconditions than trade cooperation. ECLAC also suggests macroeconomic coordination – a major step, which makes the mutual obligations of the members relatively extensive, at the level of some of the most integrated regions. Flexible membership, on the other hand, suggests that some members could have a restricted level of obligations. It is not clear that these are compatible concepts.

Flexible membership also raises the question, particularly important in the context of the range of agreements to be found in Latin America, of whether cross-membership of more than one organization should be permitted, and of whether countries should be able to join more than one regional group without the approval or joint negotiation of all the groups involved. In practice, the greater the degree of integration reached by any group, the less likely it is to be flexible (except in a transition period) with new members. If the existing members have found it necessary to extend and deepen their relationship, they will see a need to do this with a new member. The more an organization becomes established and evolves these new linkages, and the more congruent in their characteristics this in turn makes the economies and countries, the more difficult it will be for a new member, without this history, to meet the conditions for membership. In the terminology of the EU, the '*acquis*' must be adopted, and each increase in this raises the *de facto* barriers to new members.

The problem with both these definitions is that they assume that regions are essentially static in their coverage and degree of integration. It becomes progressively more difficult, and more meaningless, to be 'open', as the number of decisions taken by the existing members, and, therefore, the standard obligations to be accepted increase; accepting existing agreements becomes a moving target.

Outward-oriented regionalism is a more practical term, in that it accepts that regions, like countries, have *de facto* if not *de jure* external policies, which can be judged on the same criteria. Policies which emphasize improving the development and competitiveness of the member countries, while taking full advantage of the opportunities in the rest of the world can be contrasted to concentrating on internal policy and the regulation of agreements with others. This analysis can in principle be applied to non-trade policies as well as trade. The old Andean Pact and the other regional organizations with strong discrimination between national and external flows make the obvious parallel with import-substituting policies, while the new Latin American and most of the Asian organizations appear to be following more externally orientated policies.

From the point of view of the international system and especially the multilateral organizations, regional cohesion is a delay or an obstacle. But from the point of view of members of a region (perhaps particularly of the smaller members), who may have formed the group to increase their bargaining power, the obstruction may be desirable. To be most efficient from both points of view, the scope of the negotiating capacity of the regional representative needs to be carefully specified, as do the negotiating procedures. But this requires the institutional maturity which some discussions of limited or open regionalism consider undesirable. The more amorphous a trading region, the more open it may be to trade, but the more difficult it is to negotiate with.

This chapter will first look at the area where external relations overlap with accession negotiations, and where the most active regional negotiations and revisions of membership can be found. It will then examine the definitely external relations of regions with multilateral institutions, and other regions and countries.

Negotiations in Latin America

FTAA

The FTAA would include all the regions in Latin America.[1] Although when proposed it was considered to be analogous to a widening of NAFTA, and the initial negotiations were in parallel with negotiations for Chile in particular to enter NAFTA, this model was politically unacceptable to MERCOSUR. *De facto*, an FTAA would probably replace all the FTAs because the proposed coverage would go beyond anything they include, unless they make new arrangements and rapid progress during the FTAA negotiations. This is not impossible, but none of the present FTAs seems to be intending to move in this direction. The NAFTA members clearly intend to extend as far as possible all the NAFTA provisions to the FTAA, including non-trade elements like the agreements on labour and the environment, because they do not want to have less favourable agreements with the US than the other FTAA members. The Group of Three modelled all its provisions closely on those of NAFTA, and was intended in part as a deliberate first step to negotiating Colombia and Venezuela into NAFTA.

There has been no example of an FTA forming with 34 members (or even 13 if MERCOSUR, CARICOM, and CACM are each counted as one member), so the negotiations are likely to be prolonged. After starting in 1994, by 1998 they reached the point of deciding to initiate trade negotiations. The US ability to negotiate is in doubt without fast-track authority,[2] and MERCOSUR, in particular Brazil, has been hesitant from the start. The negotiating questions for the customs unions are more complicated, because they do have elements in common that will not be superseded in the FTAA, and they will therefore eventually need to decide whether to remain as units within the FTAA. More immediately they face the question of whether they should negotiate as regions or as individual countries.

After the start of negotiations, eleven working groups were formed; membership was on a country basis. Many cover subjects which are not included in some of the regions, including the customs unions. On some, however (for example services), there are simultaneous negotiations in the FTAA and a region (MERCOSUR). On tariffs, it should have been obvious that for the customs unions, at least, namely MERCOSUR, CAR-ICOM, and perhaps the Andean group, any tariff agreements would have to be on a regional, not a country, basis, unless the regions planned to dissolve. Nevertheless, the US initially opposed accepting the regions as competent in the negotiations, and apparently tried to divide members of MERCOSUR. Joint negotiation, however, was finally agreed in the first half of 1997, with members of FTAs remaining free to negotiate jointly or individually according to choice. MERCOSUR and CARICOM have declared that they will negotiate as groups, and Chile and Bolivia are increasingly negotiating with MERCOSUR. Chile has now said that it will do so in the FTAA and also in other negotiations, and it has already informally used MERCOSUR as a sympathetic friend (or even strong ally) in unrelated disputes with the United States (for example, on salmon and wood in 1997). This suggests that the ongoing negotiations for the separate entry of Chile into NAFTA are becoming increasingly unlikely to move ahead of an FTAA. It is not yet clear what the Andean group and CACM will do; this raises questions about their commitment to reaching a common external tariff before the target date for the FTAA, but is probably consistent with their relatively weak non-tariff links. An alternative model would be for MERCOSUR to expand, taking in the Andean countries, into the proposed SAFTA (South American FTA), and then all would negotiate as a group with the NAFTA countries, CACM and CARICOM. NAFTA members will negoti-ate individually, which must imply that the Group of Three will also do so, subject to any Andean alliance with MERCOSUR.

In spite of the establishment of the working groups, there has been disagreement over whether the negotiations should proceed on all top-ics simultaneously, or concentrate on some parts first. As the US and MERCOSUR have disagreed on which would be the priorities, the pre-sent position is that all the negotiations are proceeding. If they are linked, this may make it necessary for integrated groups to negotiate together even on issues not yet covered by the region, and encourage regional coordination, if not harmonization.[3]

This has raised the question for MERCOSUR of how to proceed on matters which are in process of integration in both MERCOSUR and the FTAA. Is it necessary to integrate at the sub-regional level first, in order to preserve a MERCOSUR identity within the FTAA, or are the advantages of larger-scale integration more important? The official view, in Argentina and Brazil at least, is that greater integration at the MERCOSUR level should precede the FTAA, for example on areas like services.[4] This

helps to explain the efforts by MERCOSUR to slow the FTAA negotiations by arguing over the sequence of integration. It supports the view
that MERCOSUR is seen as an important grouping for political reasons,
not simply a vehicle for obtaining economic advantages from integration.

It is interesting that MERCOSUR external cooperation has not been
confined to trade negotiations. They 'cooperated in ... the joint condemnation, in June 1992, of a US Supreme Court ruling that endorsed
the US government's claim of the "right to abduct" a suspect from
another country ... despite the fact that the ruling involved a Mexican'
(Zormelo, 1995, p. 33). Chile has also used MERCOSUR in non-MERCO-
SUR matters: in disputes with the US in 1997 over anti-dumping and
subsidy cases, it asked for political support from MERCOSUR.

The CARICOM (and to a lesser extent CACM) countries have already
been negotiating jointly with the US to obtain 'NAFTA parity' for their
exports, especially of processed manufactures. (Mexico now has duty-
free entry for products similar to theirs, and the Caribbean countries
have tried to improve their bilateral preferences in the US to a similar
level.) They thus have experience of negotiating together, even on a
question – preferences in a third country – on which they would not
necessarily be required to have the same policy. They have also negotiated together with the EU (see below).

The FTAA negotiations thus suggest a clear hierarchy in terms of
coordination. MERCOSUR and CARICOM are the clearest examples of
groups with an identity; and NAFTA and the Group of Three can be
seen as preliminary steps to a hemisphere agreement, not as permanent
and integrated units in themselves. The Andean and Central American
countries fall between these.

Other negotiations in Latin America

As the history of membership in the various Latin American groups
indicates, the FTAA is not the only possible change to be foreseen. MER-
COSUR is now legally (after completion of the first five years) open to
any member of LAIA, although it is not clear if it is actually willing to
admit new members. The MERCOSUR countries have negotiated
arrangements with Bolivia and Chile, in each case on what they call a '4
+ 1' basis or, in terms of the introduction to this chapter, hub and
spokes. This suggests both that MERCOSUR has learned how to coordinate negotiations and that it sees its core membership as having a permanent special position relative to the rest. The first gives it a basis for
negotiating with other groups, but it is not clear whether the hub and

spokes basis can be preserved as more countries join. In 1997, it attempted to negotiate an agreement with the remaining Andean Group countries, which would be basically one of free trade, not membership in the customs union. This would be more like the agreement with Chile than the one with Bolivia. Agreement was not reached. It also began negotiations with Mexico but failed to work out a deal. These free trade agreements are in part a rationalization to MERCOSUR level of the existing bilateral agreements which each member country had with other Latin American countries under the LAIA. In their relations with Mexico, however, the MERCOSUR countries have not acted together. Following a failure to negotiate a joint extension of their bilateral agreements with Mexico, Brazil cancelled its agreement in December 1997, while the other three renewed theirs.

Making the MERCOSUR arrangements on a country or region-by-region, not a single FTA, basis can work temporarily because trade between the 'spokes' is limited, and even trade with the hub tends to concentrate on one or two MERCOSUR countries, for example, a clear identification of interest in Venezuela with Brazil and in Chile with Argentina. Although its rules would admit Central American countries, there have been no negotiations north of the Andean Group. It has, however, also signed an agreement with the EU which offers the possibility of an FTA (see below), and talked about links to both ASEAN and SADC. These seem to be more a way of showing an interest in building up alternative trading relations outside Latin America and the FTAA than active initiatives, but confirm MERCOSUR's position as a coherent group able to take joint initiatives.

Chile has FTA agreements with Canada and Mexico, and is still legally in negotiations to enter NAFTA, in addition to its MERCOSUR link.

CACM and CARICOM are more restricted in their accession provisions. Only other Central American or Caribbean countries (listed in the original agreements) may join. CARICOM is also restricted by its preference agreements with the EU, which require it to obtain permission before giving trade privileges to other countries (and could require it to offer the EU equal access). It is similarly constrained by its preferences with the US, although less formally. But in practice, both CARICOM and CACM may be more open than the legal rules suggest. Not only are they both negotiating entry into the FTAA, but they have started consultations with Cuba about a possible Caribbean trade group. CARICOM is also in negotiation with the EU both as part of Lomé and as a potential separate region if the EU proposal to break up relations with the ACP countries into regional agreements is carried through (see below). It has signed bilateral agreements with Colombia and Venezuela, and has proposals with MERCOSUR and other Latin American countries. These negotiations should not be seen as independent of each other. MERCOSUR is seen by countries from Chile to CARICOM as the alternative to NAFTA or FTAA, and there are therefore both economic and bargaining motives for negotiating with both at once. The US has shown willingness to negotiate with the Caribbean countries as a group, at least on their trading interests under the Caribbean Basin Initiative. CACM has been slightly less active, but in addition to its negotiations with the Caribbean countries and FTAA, three members (Guatemala, El Salvador and Honduras) are negotiating with Mexico.

The Andean Group is also open to any LAIA country. The Group of Three is open to both Latin American and Caribbean countries. This could raise questions about meeting the LAIA rules, but reflects the bilateral agreements that members of the Group already had with CARICOM. The Andean Group, individually and jointly, and the Group of Three, individually, are negotiating with MERCOSUR, but more at the latter's initiative than their own.

Legally, NAFTA is the least restrictive. Its members may sign agreements with other countries or regions (as Canada and Mexico have done), and any individual country may join, if it meets the terms and is approved by the present members. But the members are not indifferent to fellow members' links. NAFTA owes its existence to Canadian unwillingness to be left as a 'spoke' when the US began independent negotiations with Mexico. In practice, the conditions and requirements for approval make it as restrictive as the members may want, and there are no formal procedures or criteria for new members. The only current NAFTA negotiation is with Chile, but that is being subsumed into the FTAA.

The groups' negotiations with each other confirm the relative strength of MERCOSUR and CARICOM, but suggest that none of the areas can be considered 'finished', or complete as a unit. Although MERCOSUR is trying to preserve a distinction between the original members and the new agreements, it is not clear how long the other countries will accept this. Chile and Bolivia are increasingly pressing for greater participation in all committees.

Asian negotiations

ASEAN, as seen in Chapter 3, is expanding, but by taking in new countries, not by negotiating with other regions. Its members are part of

APEC, but participate as members, not as a group, making individual commitments in the negotiations. (Similarly NAFTA members do not formally act jointly in APEC.) SAARC countries are not members of APEC, and it is India, not the group as a whole, which has led the lobbying for admission to APEC. APEC has taken initiatives at the multilateral level; as its members include all the major trading partners except the EU, it was able to take the lead in encouraging progress on telecommunications and other matters in the WTO in 1996, but has not negotiated with other groups. This suggests that it has the ability to make a temporary alliance for a specific purpose, but does not have the structure or common interests for a permanent joint position. Its decision in 1997 to close to new members for 10 years makes it now the least open of all the regions. It 'nests' ASEAN and NAFTA, but also overlaps with the Andean Group (Peru), the Group of Three (Mexico), and semi-overlaps with MERCOSUR (Chile).

African negotiations

The AEC is not yet under negotiation, but it has been decided that the African regional groups will be the 'building blocks', the negotiating units, for it (AEC, 1997). These include, in addition to SADC: COMESA, which has some trade liberalization; the Arab Maghreb Union, which has only limited trade liberalization; ECOWAS and ECCAS (the Economic Communities of Western and Central African States), neither of which has made progress on trade liberalization; and the Intergovernment Authority on Development in East Africa. Egypt was the only African country not a member of a region, but decided to join COMESA in 1999. None of these regions has a free trade area, much less a common external tariff or negotiating authority. There is little prospect of effective AEC action.

SADC includes the customs union SACU. Under SACU rules, members cannot give trade concessions to non-members without consulting other members, and current negotiations to revise these rules would forbid any outside agreements. In the SADC trade negotiations, it has been agreed that SACU would negotiate together on granting market access to others, thus preserving the CET. But if there is an asymmetric liberalization within SADC, and the other members liberalize more rapidly to each other than to South Africa, it has been proposed that the SACU members other than South Africa should be allowed to benefit from the more liberal access to the other SADC countries. This would, of course, require enforcement of rules of origin within SACU. It suggests the reverse of the approach of MERCOSUR in the FTAA negotiations, in which preserving and increasing integration within MERCOSUR was considered more important than gaining trade advantages. This may suggest a weaker political commitment to SACU.

Relations of the regions to the multilateral institutions

All the organizations allow individual membership of the global institutions, and in some cases some are members and others not; some of the Latin American members of the early regional groups were members of the GATT when others were not.

One of the difficulties identified by some observers in the Uruguay Round was the large (and growing) number of participants. Bargaining theory and the experience of earlier and shorter Rounds suggest that a smaller number would produce a more manageable negotiating process, although economic arguments against oligopolies suggest that, while the process might be more 'manageable', it might also produce a poorer outcome on welfare. If there is a choice here, it is important to keep in mind that the objective of the international system is not to produce an 'orderly' procedure, but an outcome which maximizes welfare. In practice, however, the type of regionalism observed so far has not reduced the number of participants because countries have maintained independent membership (the participation of the EU in the WTO has in fact increased it by one). Regions have offered some saving in bargaining difficulty and time on non-controversial issues. They can reach agreement within themselves and then operate together. On some issues the EU did this, and there is anecdotal evidence of some priority setting within NAFTA in the late stages of the Uruguay Round. The regulatory question (as for large or monopolistic companies within a country) is whether there is now a need for an additional or different regulatory structure for large members. As mentioned in Chapter 5, the new regime for regional groups in the WTO provides in principle for regular reviews of existing groups as well as the notification review, but this has not been implemented.

The introduction of an additional layer (or in Asia and the Western hemisphere, several additional layers) increases the number of special interests which need reconciliation and of formal legislative commitments which need to be made consistent with any external commitment at global level. A clear example is the offers on services in the WTO, where the US and the EU texts include lists of the state and member-country special rules respectively. Only in areas (like tariffs for these areas) where full harmonization has been achieved is there a reduction in complexity. As each of the regions has different divisions of negotiating power between the centre and the members, the complexity of international negotiations is further increased. For each region, there is a conflict here between choosing the system which seems most appropriate for the region internally and choosing one which is consistent with other regions, and therefore which may do least damage to the international system. Alternatively, the complexity may have the effect for both governments and economic agents of increasing the attractiveness of a simple one-layer international system.

WTO

One argument in favour of regionalization in the late 1980s was as a substitute for the risk of a weakened international system. In that context, the risk of regionalism further weakening the system by introducing complications and obstacles was not seen as a problem. However, with the Uruguay Round settled and the WTO established risks to the WTO become an important concern, particularly for the countries which benefit most from order and rules, which are especially the small, economically or politically weak. This was also seen increasingly as a threat by the WTO itself. In practice, the existence of regions among industrial countries is likely to produce the damaging effects identified here, regardless of whether the developing countries move towards their own integration; the marginal cost to internationalism of regionalism among developing countries may be small.

A spread of regionalism would mean that at any time some countries might be changing their regional systems and therefore wanting either to change their external obligations or to be temporarily 'diverted' from external interests (as the EU was during the early stages of the Uruguay Round and NAFTA was at the end). This would make the Round system increasingly difficult.

There are also strictly legal implications of regions for the international organizations. The WTO and the European Bank for Reconstruction and Development have admitted the EU as a member, but have not otherwise altered their procedures to take account of the fact that it is not a country in the same sense as their other members. Formally the position is that the EU takes on international obligations on the matters in which its members give it competence, but the member states are responsible for obligations in other issues. In contrast, other countries are responsible directly for all their obligations (although even within countries the central or federal government may not have legal responsibility). An increased number of groups with different divisions of responsibilities would put a strain on these *ad hoc* arrangements and reduce the transparency of rules and obligations which is a major benefit of the international system. But adapting formally to regions is problematic where there are groups with changing structures and members. Other organizations which have tried to group countries (the joint executive director system in the international financial institutions, for example) have needed to change the groups to take account of changed interests, although normally at fairly long intervals: the emergence of OPEC as a group in 1974, the acceptability of South Africa as part of Africa in 1994. If regions take on new responsibilities or if the WTO were to move to a similar system, there would be clear problems in defining usable permanent groups.

The EU now has competence within the WTO to negotiate for its members on trade policy for goods. The position on other questions is more complicated. Some services are under EU competence, namely, those which are actually traded; some are shared, particularly those which involve regulation. Until the end of the Uruguay Round some were still reserved to member states, but the adoption of the new provisions, (under Article B3 of the Rome Treaty) removed this (WTO, EU, 1997). Intellectual property is in transition to the EU level. Investment policy, which is now coming onto the multilateral agenda, involves both the EU and the member states. During the Uruguay Round, the EU was not a member, so representatives of individual member states spoke on matters of EU competence, but in principle did so on behalf of the EU, not their own country.

The only other customs union participating in the Uruguay Round was SACU. Here the dominant position of the South African economy meant that South Africa negotiated, and the others then put in almost identical offers. This required all of them to reverse their positions, along with South Africa, in the final year when the new South African regime was putting in a substantially more liberal offer. It also meant that all five were *de facto* treated (by South Africa's choice) as developed countries (with minor exceptions in some implementation periods). As three of the other four are developing countries, and Lesotho is least developed, this imposed significant extra obligations on them. All the other regions examined here also include members at different levels of development, and therefore also face a possible difference in interests where the WTO differentiates among members.

The need to have side negotiations within the EU caused delays and frustrations to other members, while for the major country simply to ignore the smaller countries may have created long-term difficulties for SACU. It will be important for customs unions and the WTO itself to find more satisfactory ways of negotiating in the future. Most of the other regional groups are free trade areas, which do not need to negotiate as a unit, provided they keep their internal rules of origin effective and do not want to assert a regional identity. MERCOSUR, however, will need to act as a customs union in any future negotiation on tariffs. In the services negotiations, so far, there has been no question of joint participation, because these are still matters of national competence, but MERCOSUR is planning to integrate them (see Chapter 10).

The question of whether MERCOSUR should itself be a member of the WTO is not really significant for settling these problems. The EU only became a member in 1994, 30 years after completing the customs union. Nor would a stronger MERCOSUR secretariat be a sufficient solution. Although it could make coming to a joint position more efficient, and signal the need to do so, taking a position is likely to remain a matter of coordinating country policies for some time to come.

MERCOSUR had begun to act jointly: as early as 1992 during the Uruguay Round, its members jointly committed themselves to binding the CET at 35 per cent (Zormelo, 1995, p. 32). It is currently being studied as a new regional group by the Committee on Regions, and for this it has formed an *ad hoc* MERCOSUR–WTO group (IDB INTAL, 1996, p. 49).

The WTO treats the three customs unions differently in its Trade Policy Reviews. The EU has been reviewed as a single customs area since the first review under the GATT, before the EU was itself a member of the WTO (it was the old GATT concept, 'a customs area'). The first review of South Africa mentioned SACU, but did not review the other members; the second (1998) reviewed all five members at the same time and with a common discussion in the Council, but as separate countries. The reviews of the MERCOSUR countries have been completely separate.

CARICOM and CACM have coordinated their positions, in the WTO and other trade negotiations. NAFTA had some informal coordination in the Uruguay Round negotiation. Mexico only joined the GATT during the Round, so recently that it probably still regards its WTO membership as too important to be delegated to a joint negotiation, especially as it sees encouraging new markets as a parallel objective with NAFTA (Ernesto Zedillo, speech in London, 29 January 1996).

It is not only regions which face the difficulty of determining how to negotiate as a group at the multilateral level. Groups like OPEC, the International Textiles and Clothing Bureau, and the Cairns group of agricultural exporters in the Uruguay Round have negotiated jointly. The difference for regions is that there are potentially conflicting legal obligations, not just common interests.

Other international institutions

The only other multilateral institution to have a region as a member is the EBRD, of which the EU is again a member in addition to, not instead of, its member states. As in the joint membership of the WTO, this can be justified because the countries and the EU share responsibility for policy towards assisting the East European countries. Similar arguments could justify regional membership of functional organizations like the World Intellectual Property Organisation (WIPO) or the various organizations with responsibility for transportation services, or for energy, but they have not been used. Nor have they been used for the other regional banks or the World Bank. The difference is probably more one of timing than principle: the others were formed when the EU was less integrated than it is now, and only the WTO (when it replaced the GATT) and the EBRD offered the chance of a new organization to make new rules. Up to now, the regions have not had competence in the areas of assistance, monetary and exchange management, and security that would make joint membership in the World Bank, the IMF, or the UN agencies appropriate. The EU's move to a common currency and an agreed external security policy could mark a change in this position. Legally, the IMF has countries, not currencies, as members, but as the obligations which the EU member states have to the IMF shift to a European level, there could be room for change. Unlike the WTO, IMF country reviews are still of the individual countries, not the EU, but again this will be less suitable in a common exchange-rate area. The question of representation in the IMF and other international financial institutions after monetary union is still under discussion by the finance ministers; it has been agreed that one will speak for all, but membership is still in question.

Relations of the EU with other regions

Its size, level of development, and now age have given the EU a particular role in relation to other regions, not only as a model (or anti-model), but also as a trading partner and aid donor with a strong commitment to a regional approach. The EU, as a region itself, takes a strong view that economic linkages should be, perhaps need to be, reinforced by institutional linkages. This means that it not only accepts regions as trading partners or joint recipients for aid, but encourages their institutional strengthening.[5] The EU also applies its interpretation of its own experience – that forming a region promoted growth, efficiency, and also intra-regional security and peace – to other regions, and therefore sees this as a reason to encourage countries to form regions.

> The community-perhaps not surprisingly given its own history-has always regarded this [regional cooperation] as a key area. It is viewed as one of the most promising ways of contributing to growth in the developing countries, and particularly those in sub-Saharan Africa. That is why significant resources have always been specifically reserved under the Lomé conventions for regional projects and programmes. (Smidt, 1996, p. 8)

It pointed out (EC, Brussels 16 June 1995, p. 1) that the EC has encouraged, partly by example, partly through direct support, many of the new regional groupings in the developing world', and 'all major strategy documents and undertakings of the European Commission addressing the problems of developing countries and the EU's relations with them, place a high priority on the support of regional initiatives'. This has been a long-standing policy towards the developing countries , and more recently in relations with the East European countries. It is only recently, however, that the EU has moved beyond its encouragement of regional integration among developing countries to encouraging region-to-region trading arrangements in its relations with them.

Latin America

This is the area with the longest history of EU encouragement of local regions. While Latin America is not a major recipient of EU aid, the aid has been highly concentrated on technical and financial aid for regional initiatives.

In the 1970s and 1980s, the European Community defined its priorities in cooperation agreements with Latin America and Asia as (i) combating poverty, and in particular assisting rural development, and (ii) promoting regional integration. For Latin America regional integration was the main objective. Assistance began with the first EC/Latin America Joint Committee in 1970, following which the EC established direct relations with the Andean Pact, which was regarded by the Commission as potentially similar to the EC and therefore received substantial assistance. It is probable that EC assistance kept the Pact alive through the late 1970s and 1980s when there was little active local integration. The first cooperation agreement with the Andean countries was in December 1983. Projects to help regional integration accounted for 85 per cent of the funding of the Pact (Retout, 1990). Assistance included briefing officials on the procedures for integrating and assistance in the administrative and technical elements of regional organizations, as well as in transportation and communications regional infrastructure. Bilateral aid from the member states has also been substantially higher for the Andeans than for any other sub-region of Latin America: a third of the total for the region was directed to these countries.

In Central America, there was strong support, including in the late 1970s and early 1980s. An agreement was signed in 1985, when the CACM might otherwise have collapsed, and when internal integration was very limited. It involved not only economic cooperation but the San José peace and consultation process (the first meeting was in 1984), which set up a 'political dialogue' between the European Community and Central America. In addition to its economic interests, the EC played an active role as a peacekeeper in the area. As with the Andean Pact, although quantitatively most funds went to conventional development projects, some of the assistance was directly to the regional organization, including, in 1989, assistance in setting up a regional payments system. In its assistance to regional groups, the EU is also willing to consider financing costs like the loss of internal tariff revenues (OECD, New Generation, 1996). Bilateral donors within the EU have also promoted regional development in Central America. On a regional level the EC has been conducting formal political dialogue in the Rio Group since 1990.

More than a third (35 per cent) of the EC's total spending on financial and technical cooperation in Latin America between 1976 and 1989 (about 20 per cent in the 1990s) was on regional programmes. Programmes for the Andean Group took 20 per cent of EC aid to the region between 1976 and 1994; half went to Central America; and there was substantial aid associated with the creation of MERCOSUR. The agreements the EU has with MERCOSUR specify helping with integration, including appropriate infrastructure, as an essential part of the programme. Statements from the European Commission emphasized that this would be a continuing motive (Smidt, 1996; Lowe, 1996), and current proposals to reform the Lomé programme for the ACP countries along regional lines are consistent with this priority. It is clear from the agreements with Latin American countries that encouraging them into regional organizations remains a motive for assistance. The clearest statement of the EU's view is in the agreement with Argentina, 'Considering that Argentina is engaged in a process of regional integration with Latin American countries which is bound to be conducive to progress, economic reform and political stability' (EC Argentina 1990): this reveals an enthusiasm for regions which goes well beyond what can be demonstrated by economic or political analysis. More concretely, the attitude is manifest in the fact that agreements have been signed with the Central American countries as a group and with the Andean and MERCOSUR (organizations, as well as jointly with the member countries). The EU's commitment to strengthen relations with regional groups of the region is also evident in a document prepared by the Commission in 1994:

> we seek to intensify the dialogue and cooperation between the EU, the Rio-Group, Central America (San José) and MERCOSUR, broaden the agenda and enhance the political aspects of this dialogue. We are prepared to take up and strengthen dialogue and cooperation with other regional and sub-regional groupings, as well as with individual countries.

The importance of regions is mentioned in all the agreements, and in most of them provision is made for technical assistance in implementing them. The agreement with MERCOSUR reiterates the importance of regionalism in promoting international integration and notes the common interests and experiences of the EU and MERCOSUR. It is explicitly mentioned as a priority for development cooperation in the MERCOSUR, Andean Pact, and Central American agreements, as well as those with Argentina and Chile.

The EU negotiated an interregional framework agreement with MERCOSUR in 1995 and in 1997 a parallel agreement with Chile. In the agreement with MERCOSUR, preparing the conditions for an interregional association is one of the declared objectives, with a mention of the possibility of an EU–MERCOSUR free trade area. The regional priority is reflected in some of the specific commitments, for example customs cooperation, and also the promotion of joint ventures and regional activities generally. The agreement provides specifically for the EU to give technical assistance in the implementation of the MERCOSUR institutions. A 1997 agreement with Mexico also provides for negotiating an FTA. A first agreement had been signed in 1975; after some lapses in the 1970s, it was revived from 1983 (at the same time as other agreements), and a new agreement was signed in 1991. The 1997 agreement introduced 'political dialogue', as well as the FTA proposal. Like the

Chile agreement, it is exceptional for the EU in being much like the MERCOSUR agreements, but with a single country.

The idea of FTAs between the EU and MERCOSUR or Mexico would be a new form of interregional link, but it is not clear if this is feasible. Sensitive products on both sides and commitments by MERCOSUR and Mexico to the LAIA, which should preclude external agreements, suggest that there will be difficulty in turning this from an expression of friendship into a practical proposal. In 1997, negotiations with MER-COSUR only reached the point of agreeing on data on trade flows and discussing European agricultural subsidies. The EU target year is 2000 (thus, before the 2005 target for the FTAA). With Mexico, discussions began in 1996, and a preliminary EU study found that 10–11 per cent of EU imports from Mexico would be sensitive (Sanahuja, 1997, p. 20). Some members have already opposed an FTA with either MERCOSUR or Mexico.

There are, however, strict limits to the regionalism promoted by the agreements. The agreement with Mexico (EC, 1995, Mexico) explicitly mentions only existing regional agreements (which would include those with Latin America, but not, at 1991, the time of the agreement, NAFTA), and both the Brazil and the Paraguay agreements explicitly encourage agreements only in their region. This is not defined, but it seems clear that it is intended to exclude arrangements with the US. It is argued that other agreements would reduce member countries' interest in purely Latin American agreements, and potentially reduce their benefits.

The history of Latin American regions and the EU prompts a question: How far is the regional movement in Latin America the result of EU targeting? The Andean Pact (founded in 1967) and the CACM (in 1960) both preceded Europe's move into assisting Latin America; the only influence would be example. But in the late 1970s and early 1980s, European encouragement and financial assistance probably preserved the regions long after they were effectively dead, and made their revival in the late 1980s easier. The additional preferences which the EC offered the Andean countries to encourage them away from exporting drugs were specified in terms of membership in the Group, and have thus had the effect of encouraging Peru to remain a member in order to receive the preferences, even when it was unwilling to participate actively in the region. The EU is not the only reason for the Group's revival, but it may be important for preserving the form of institutions. The regionally driven revival has come in the form of side agreements, with Colombia and Venezuela, then with the addition of Ecuador and Mexico, and not from the traditional Group, which has been kept legally in existence to preserve privileged GSP status. The major region, MERCO-SUR, was not a European initiative, although it has been strongly encouraged and assisted. Europe and Latin America are the two areas where regions have a long history, so what we see is a common interest, not direct causation.

Asia

The only Asian region with which the EU has had long-term relations is ASEAN, plus *ad hoc* groups in the EU–Asian summit. The formal basis for ASEAN–EU relations is a cooperation agreement, with a foreign ministers' conference every two years, and official meetings every year. There are no economic ties to the region, and the EU's aid programmes are by country and not tied to regional projects, as in Latin America and Africa. Political cooperation with Asia, however, has gone further, with the first Asia–EU summit in Bangkok in March 1996, including Japan, China, and South Korea, as well as ASEAN. This had primarily political motives, with trade initiatives confined to encouraging a joint approach to multilateral negotiations. The summit, however, did not correspond to any institutional link, either between Asia and the EU or within Asia. The Asian group was larger than ASEAN, but smaller than APEC. In its relations with ASEAN, the EU tried to prevent Burma from becoming a member, and, when it was admitted, tried to avoid meeting it at EU–ASEAN meetings.

North Africa and the Middle East

The European Community originally signed separate agreements with these countries, and only started to promote a regional area in the 1990s. The agreements follow a common pattern, however, and they have thus had the effect of encouraging the individual countries to coordinate their approaches. Tunisia was the first country to sign a new trade agreement, in 1995, and it has been followed by Morocco, Israel, and other countries. There is a proposal, the Barcelona declaration of 1995, for an EU–Mediterranean FTA by 2010, but the work programme so far is directed more to physical integration and lowering legal barriers to investment, than to trade barriers.

ACP

The exception to the EU's regional approach in the past has been the countries involved in the Lomé Convention for Africa, the Caribbean and the Pacific. These have been treated as a single group, even where regions existed, as in the Caribbean. Negotiations have been between the EU and the ACP jointly. The Lomé arrangement cannot be considered the equivalent of a region (and has not been accepted by the WTO; it has a waiver). It is time-bound (five years for the first three conventions, ten for the fourth, from 1990 to 2000), non-reciprocal, and does not include free trade among the ACP members. It is defined in terms of their relations to the EU, and thus is a variant of the hub and spoke model. The EU has encouraged regional free trade areas within the group but these have not been incorporated directly into the Lomé arrangements. In Southern Africa, it first helped the Preferential Trading Area (PTA), now COMESA. It has provided direct support for SADC from its foundation (to resist the old South Africa) and continues to support the administration and studies on how to integrate the different sectors. It has also provided more general support (the Cross Border Initiative) for removing practical and legal barriers to trade in order to encourage trade and investment. This, however, has a more limited membership than either COMESA or SADC, so it is not consistent with strengthening the groups.

The EU's proposals for a programme to succeed the current Lomé Convention include four options. Three are continuation, abolition, and *ad hoc* arrangements with different groups. The only alternative seriously suggested is to divide the ACP countries into three groups, or possibly more with African sub-groups, and encourage each region to form itself into a FTA and then negotiate an FTA with the EU. There are practical problems, not least the absence of regions in the Pacific or in Africa other than the SADC region.There are no precedents for an FTA to negotiate a joint link. Having a preferential link with groups which are mixed in terms of development raises the same problem as is seen in relations between regions and the WTO. SADC has considered the possibility of negotiation with the EU, if such a reform went through, but could not do so at present because it contains one member with only GSP access to the EU (South Africa, although it is negotiating a FTA with the EU), while the other members come under Lomé. The proposal, however, is evidence of the EU's assumption that any geographical group of countries will want to form a region, especially if given encouragement and an incentive in terms of trade preferences, as well as its preference for negotiating with regions rather than individual countries. If this alternative is chosen, the resulting regions will be clearer evidence than from Latin America or ASEAN of the EU as a major explanation of the growth of regionalism.

Eastern Europe

Although the East European regions are not included in this analysis, it can be noted that, in spite of the fact that both these countries and the EU see membership in the EU as a short- to medium-term goal, the EU is encouraging them to form regions, even in the temporary waiting period (the principal one is the Central European FTA, CEFTA).

Conclusion on EU

The assistance of the EU to regions, and its implicit encouragement through its preference for negotiating with regions on economic and political subjects, has offered strong incentives for regional groups to remain in existence (and for individual countries to remain in them). The EU has not yet, however, created regions where they did not exist before its intervention or created trade/FTA links between regions and the EU. These two steps are now being proposed, the first in the context of the reform of Lomé and the second for MERCOSUR. These would be a major extension of EU impact on regions, but, for this reason, it cannot be inferred from the past success in encouraging regions that the new projects will succeed.

US relations with regions

The history of US relations with regions is very different. Until the agreements with Canada and then Mexico, the US did not participate in any regions, and even in its relations with the EU, it has been very reluctant to deal with it as a group. Its position in the FTAA negotiations was initially that it would negotiate only with individual Latin American countries, not groups like MERCOSUR, and it has not offered the type of institutional support which the EU has given. Its attitude remains that regions are only useful as steps toward multilateral integration, and recent policy statements stress fear of other regions: 'countries . . . creating new exclusive trade alliances to the potential detriment of U.S. prosperity and leadership. More than 20 such agreements have been concluded without the United States since 1992 alone and the trend continues' (Barshefsky, 1997). This US position might make it surprising that the developing region most associated with the US – Latin America – has been the most enthusiastic about regions. One possible explanation is that the regions are in part intended to avoid dependence on and dominance by the US. Another is that in recent years official assistance from the EU has actually exceeded that from the

US, and for the MERCOSUR countries, trade with the EU is greater than with the US. The explanation should probably be found, however, more in the characteristics of the countries. Europe is also the major trading partner and donor in Africa, where regions have been much less successful.

Regional relations

The EU and MERCOSUR both have the competence to negotiate with other regions, and the agreement between them is one sign of this. Nevertheless, Brazil and Argentina still take independent initiatives, and have not yet become accustomed to acting only through MERCOSUR. Even when it is MERCOSUR which is acting, this is still, under the present administrative structure, implemented by one of the members, not by an equivalent of the European Commission. CARICOM normally does negotiate as a group, but like MERCOSUR does this less formally that in the EU. The negotiations with Chile and Bolivia, and more recently with the Andean countries, however, are examples of coordinated action by MERCOSUR. The agreement with Chile provides for five classes of goods according to sensitivity, giving a transition period for the most sensitive of 18 years. This implies that there will be continuing negotiations between MERCOSUR and Chile. Chile, however, 'only became an associate to MERCOSUR in order to maintain its independence regarding trade policy formulation towards third countries' (WTO, 1997, Chile, p. 27). This is given as a reason additional to reluctance to accept the (higher) MERCOSUR common external tariff.

SACU is different. The external trade relations of South Africa are not the same as those of the other members. South Africa has always been a 'developed' country, although it was admitted to the GSP in 1994. The other four members are developing or least developed countries, eligible for GSP from all the developed countries, and members of Lomé in their relations with the EU. In the period of sanctions, the divide was even sharper, and an informal negotiating group of the other four emerged. Although South Africa is now negotiating jointly with the others for some purposes, even when this occurs (as noted for SADC), the interests are still distinct. Formally, SACU trade policy is entirely in the hands of the South African Government, with as yet only proposals for an observer from the other countries. On the other hand, any member may sign an agreement with a third country provided it consults the others and does not allow trade to evade tariffs. The differences in interests and the South African unwillingness to surrender its dominant position have made it difficult to find a satisfactory reform of this situation. Coordination on bilateral arrangements may now be increasing. Until recently, there were several bilateral arrangements by members of SACU with other southern African countries. But the most recent attempt, by Namibia to sign an agreement with Zambia in 1997, was moved (at South African insistence) to SACU level, and the agreement will be signed with SACU.

CARICOM has negotiated with the Central American countries, to form the beginnings of a Caribbean area, and also, more recently, with Colombia and Venezuela. It would become one of the regions of the former Lomé countries, if the Lomé reform is adopted, but has not up to now negotiated as a group with the EU. Members are required to 'seek' progressive coordination of trade relations, but may undertake separate negotiations with notification to the Secretariat. CACM members are also permitted to negotiate separately, provided they notify the Executive Committee (OAS Compendium). That such latitude for separate arrangements is still possible suggests that such customs unions are intended only to provide a common stimulus at domestic level, and not seen as vehicles for relations with the rest of the world. For MERCOSUR and the EU, the external policy side is significant. CARICOM and CACM are perhaps closer to SACU. CACM has also made agreements as a group, with Mexico, Colombia, and Venezuela. The Andean group negotiated some of its non-trade initiatives of the early 1970s, for example on investment and industrial planning, with potential investors and their countries.

Many of the regions have exchanged information and informal suggestions of cooperation with each other. In this context, ASEAN has been more important than it has been in other areas, partly because the economic success of its members has made it a tempting model for the Latin American and African countries. But there has also been exchange of information between MERCOSUR and SADC.

Summary

The EU acts as a group externally and internally; there are no other economic regions of which it is a member, or which are members of it (see Table 11.1 for summary). It is therefore a clear stage between country and the world. MERCOSUR is the nearest parallel, but its relation to the FTAA is still unclear, and it has a less clear position in the WTO, of which only the EU is a group member. SACU does not have the administrative structure to act as MERCOSUR and the EU do, and the other customs unions are less integrated internally and united externally. The frequently mentioned problem of complex and overlapping regions proves to be quite limited, if ineffectual regions and *ad hoc* bilateral agreements are excluded. The Andean Pact overlaps with MERCOSUR, but this is clearly a transition to consolidation. The proposed continental schemes for the Americas and Africa would include the relevant regions, but are being designed explicitly to be based on regions, either as well as (FTAA) or instead of (AEC) countries. The exception is APEC, which contains some of the proposed FTAA countries, but not all, and an associated member of MERCOSUR. Although it has subsidiary regions, it does not have a structure to deal with them. This corresponds to its internal institutional weakness. As long as APEC has no institutional structure or obligations internally or externally, its overlap does not seem a major problem.

Notes

1 Cuba is not included, so if it were to join a Caribbean area with Central America and CARICOM, this would create an anomaly.

2 This gives the executive the ability to present a trade bill for approval or rejection, but without amendment.

3 The obvious analogy is the EU's parallel negotiations as a group and as member states in the Uruguay Round which included tariffs (EC competence), investment (country competence) and services (mixed).

4 'On 19 June [1997], during the MERCOSUR summit, Argentina's Secretary for International Economic Relations, Jorge Campbell, stated that "the existence of negotiations on the FTAA requires us to deepen MERCOSUR in order to survive with a real identity"' (IRELA, MERCOSUR, 1997, p. 27).

5 In this, it is following the example of the former colonial powers. As Viner (1950, pp. 70–1) points out, a customs union between Tanganyika and Kenya was first created by the UK in 1923, to bring Tanganyika to the higher Kenya level 'to create a protected market in Tanganyika for the produce of the small colony of British planters in Kenya, for whose welfare the British Government has shown a constant and marked solicitude'. Subsequent to this, the UK carried the East African Community forward to the post-colonial period, and also created a Federation of Rhodesia and Nyasaland. Of these customs unions, only SACU, dominated by one country, survived.

Table 11.1 External relations of regions

	EU	SACU	MER-COSUR	CARI-COM	Andean	CACM	NAFTA	G3	ANZC	ASEAN	SAARC	SADC	LAIA	FTAA	APEC	AEC
Does region negotiate?	yes	partially	yes	no	no	yes	no	no	no	no	no	no	no	no	no	
Does it coordinate a position?	yes	partially	yes	yes	no	yes	yes	no	yes	yes	no	no	no		yes	
Is it expanding?	yes	contract	yes	no	contract	no	prob no	no	no	yes	no	yes	no		no	
Is it open?	yes	no	yes	no	yes	no	yes	yes	no	yes	no	yes	no	yes	no	no
Does it contain regions?	no	no	no	no	no	no	no	no	no	no	no	yes	yes	yes	yes	yes
Are they in as regions or countries?	–	–	–	–	–	–	–	–	–	–	–	countries	countries	either countries	countries	regions
Is it in a region?	no	SADC, AEC	LAIA, FTAA	FTAA	LAIA, FTAA	FTAA	FTAA, APEC	LAIA, FTAA	APEC	APEC	no	AEC	FTAA	no	no	no
Is it in as region or country?	–	country	region	country	country	country	country	country	country	country	–	region	country	–	–	–
Does it overlap?	no	yes	yes	country	yes	no	yes	yes	no	no	no	yes	country	country	yes	–
In WTO?	reg & cou	country	country	no	country	country	country	yes	no	country	country	country	country	country	some country	country
In TPRC?	reg	jointly	country	country	–	–	–	country	country	–	–	–	–	–	–	–

	EU	SACU	MER-COSUR	CARI-COM	Andean	CACM	NAFTA	G3	ANZC	ASEAN	SAARC	SADC	LAIA	FTAA	APEC	AEC
Other multilateral organisations as region?	yes	no	no	no	no	no	no	no	no	no	no	no	no	no	no	no
Negotiating with EU?		yes	yes	yes	no	yes	no	no	no	yes	no	yes	no	no	no	no
Region supported by EU?		lim-ited	yes	yes	yes	yes	no	no	no	limited	no	yes	no	no	no	no
Are members feds?	some	no	limited	no	no	no	yes	some	yes	no	no	no	lim-ited	some	some	no

Part IV
Conclusion

12
Regionalism: the Stages between Countries and the World

What are the conditions for success of a region?

Success has been defined as surviving and evolving. Which of the regions considered here seem likely to achieve this, and what do they have in common? This question has two parts: success in doing what the region was designed to do, which may be very limited, and surviving; and success in creating a new economic or political unit, effectively the second part of the definition. The objectives of a region at any stage are evidence, but not sufficient. A region with limited objectives may evolve over time; more extensive immediate objectives may indicate a desire to write a final agreement, and then not expect it to change.

Chapter 3 indicated that the EU, SACU, CARICOM and SADC had a wide range of motives for intergration (Table 12.1), while the EU, MERCOSUR, CARICOM and CACM had the strongest basis in common characteristics or background. On trade integration, measured by policy and intentions or achievements, the customs unions, the EU, SACU and MERCOSUR, lead, with the other Latin American groups in general more integrated than the Asian or African; investment measures in general give the same answer as trade. The other linkages are more variable; the EU is the only group integrated by all measures, and the least integrated are SAARC and the continental schemes. The intermediate groups, however, show a variety of patterns of what is integrated, and how far in their relations with others. The disparity between the measures of size in Chapter 4 and those of the economic importance of the region to its members: the intensity measures in Chapter 7 or the indications of other linkages found in Chapter 10, suggest that enhancing

Table 12.1 Summary of linkages

	EU	SACU	MER-COSUR	CARI-COM	Andean	CACM	NAFTA	G3	ASEAN	SAARC	SADC	LAIA	FTAA	APEC	AEC
Motives for regions	high	high	middle	high	middle	middle	middle	low	middle	low	high	low	low	middle	middle
Adaptability	high	low	high	high	high	middle	low	low	high	low	high	low	low	middle	low
Common characteristics	high	middle	high	high	middle	high	middle	low	middle	low	middle	middle	middle	middle	middle
Formal trade	high	high	high	high	middle	middle	middle	middle	low	low	low	low	low	low	low
Trade integration	high	high	high	middle	middle	high	high	middle	low	low	middle	high	high	high	low
Investment integration	yes	yes	yes	no	some	no	yes	no	some	no	yes	no	no	no	no
Services	high	high	middle	middle	low	low	middle	low	low	low	low	low	low	low	low
Business conditions	high	high	middle	middle	low	low	middle	low	low	low	low	low	low	low	low
Policy	high	high	middle	low	low	low	middle	low	low	low	low	low	low	low	low
Institutional	high	low	high	high	high	high	middle	middle	middle	low	middle	low	low	low	low
Other	high	middle	middle	high	middle	high	middle	low	low	low	low	low	low	middle	low
Average, 'others'	high	high	middle	middle	middle	middle	middle	low	low	low	low	low	low	low	low
Relations with others	high	middle	high	middle	low	middle	low	low	middle	low	middle	low	low	low	low
Summary	high	high	high	middle	middle	middle	middle	low	low	low	middle	middle	middle	middle	low

the importance of the members in the world economy is not the most important role of a region. Trade policies and intensity of trade relations are not sufficient to hold an area together. The gains from trade are likely to be uncertain, small, unevenly distributed and unpredictable in the long run. Therefore it is the other objectives of a trading group which must be significant. If these are not equally strong for all members, then it may be necessary for those which want the region to survive to 'pay' the other members. This may be direct or by including additional forms of integration which are more important to the others.

The regions we observe here which are not at present very integrated may be a temporary alliance of countries with common economic interests, or a step to greater multilateral integration or perhaps to a broader region, or a step to fuller integration at the regional level. A judgement now can only be provisional. In the past, when developing countries had very high tariffs and actively used tariff policy in development, the shifts to an FTA and then beyond that to a customs union were major changes in policy, and therefore could be considered significant indications of regional commitment. At current levels of tariffs, and with the shift to less government intervention, in trade policy or other forms, an FTA is not necessarily as strong a gesture of liberalization and discrimination among its members and a customs union is not as much of a commitment to joint policy. The purely trade groups, like SAARC, and APEC, which does not even include full conventional trade integration, seem less integrated than those with other objectives, including some where trade has come after other objectives. The Latin American groups, even those of the 1960s which had fluctuations in their substance, preserve at least the shell of cooperation. They supplemented trade with objectives of industrial planning, security, and stronger integration. SADC (originally SADCC) started with non-trade objectives, of security.

It is difficult to draw conclusions about regions' commitment on the basis of how rapidly they are moving to integration, or to find rules about how rapidly new groups should integrate. The old ones have taken well over the WTO's new limit of 10 years to reach full trade integration, and only one has approached services integration. In contrast, some newer ones, like MERCOSUR and SADC, have set shorter periods. Is it necessary to take a gradual approach, to give time for governments and economic actors to develop the system and learn how to operate it, and to give time for economies to adjust to closer integration, or is it better to take advantage of the commitment to regionalism (which is strong at the outset) to achieve deeper integration before difficulties (and protectionism) emerge? The differences in the degree of initial integration might suggest one criterion for speed, but comparing Europe, already integrated but slow, and MERCOSUR, exceptionally unintegrated but fast, suggests that this is too simple. An important difference is the stage in the history of regions at which a new region emerges. The post-EU regions all have its example before them, whether as a target or a warning. Expectations of integration are greater, and the base-line of the international system, of what is 'normal' integration even outside regions, is much higher.

Does strong leadership in the member countries help the evolution of a region? The evidence is against this. In the EU and MERCOSUR, regions were formed when countries were emerging from political and security conflicts: the region was more a part of national strengthening and confidence-building than a sequel to this. In NAFTA, the concentration of political and economic power in Mexico (and their close relationship) made the acceptance of NAFTA more straightforward, once these interests had been convinced that it was desirable (Oman, 1994, pp. 119–120). But NAFTA came when Mexico was economically weaker than it had been in the 1960s or 1970s (at that time it had stayed out of Latin American integration), and the 'policy-locking-in' arguments for NAFTA suggest that it was supported because it strengthened policy, not because it reflected strong policy. In contrast, the EU now demands a minimum level of economic and political development and stability for entry into membership. The SACU countries were, until the change of government in South Africa, an alliance of political weakness (South Africa) with economic weakness (the others). Economically, the ASEAN countries were stronger in the 1980s and early 1990s than the Latin American, but less integrated. Is integration the reverse, a sign of weakness? The strong support by the US Government for NAFTA and the continued membership of the major European countries in the EU make such an argument equally difficult to sustain. There does not seem to be a simple rule here.

Does a region require a very strong initial stimulus, whether from interest groups or by an initiative from the governments of one (or a few) members? The history of existing regions and international integration may have reduced the 'barriers to entry'. The suggestion of a region must be made, so some initiative is necessary, but it is now sufficiently normal that it is becoming difficult to find a grouping where the suggestion has never been made. The levels of commitment and types of integration are so varied, and evolve so much over time, that it is difficult to find a general rule for the beginning.

Judgements on each region

MERCOSUR is integrated across a range of activities, but with continuing gaps and exceptions, and its administration is still underdeveloped. It has moved from one step to another, with some overall objective, but no detailed programme. Thus it extended from Argentina and Brazil to Paraguay and Uruguay, then to associate members, then to giving these members a bigger role within the basic group while seeking also to add more associates. It is still integrating on trade, but has now moved to services.

CARICOM, the Andean Group and CACM are integrated on trade, but have made (and intend) less progress on other links. Their small size means that these regions will never be as important to their members as are the larger regions, and therefore relations with others, not exclusive concessions, will be important.

The trade integration of NAFTA, the width of its coverage and its administrative strength place it among the most integrated regions, but it is also the nearest to the model of a one-off, static arrangement. There are no plans or administrative provisions to move into new areas. A characteristic which weakens it is the fact that all the members are taking initiatives to make agreements with non-members (Mexico in the Group of Three, but also Canada with Chile, all three in APEC, the US initiative of the FTAA, among others). These links strongly suggest that for all three, NAFTA is seen as only one step towards more general integration, useful at the time, perhaps because the multilateral system was stalled (as was arguable during the negotiation of NAFTA) or unlikely to move on areas which the members want to include in trade agreements (notably labour and the environment for the US), or simply seen as slow.

The very low intensity of trade in the Group of Three, before and after its formation, combined with a relatively advanced administrative structure and range of integration on non-trade elements, suggests that non-trade motives explain it. For Mexico, it fits into the strategy of increasing linkages in all directions, following its shift from an internally based trade policy. For Colombia and Venezuela, there is an element of this, although their bilateral arrangements and integration in the Andean Pact are much more significant for actual trade flows. For both sides, it also offers an alternative link to what are likely to be their major trade links: NAFTA or a potential South American-wide extension of MERCOSUR. This suggests, therefore, that for none of them is NAFTA, the Group of Three or MERCOSUR seen as the basis of a closely integrated common market. There is also an additional objective for Colombia and Venezuela: both have a potential interest in an FTAA, which they expect to be closely modelled on NAFTA. The Group of Three follows the NAFTA model very closely, and has given its members experience in negotiating and administering its commitments.

ASEAN seems relatively unintegrated, both economically and institutionally. Against this, are its continuity and its security role. The deliberate attempts to take on new elements suggest that there is a sense of regional common interest or identity. Moving from the informal ASEAN group to ASEAN trade can thus be seen as a result, not a cause, of regional ties. Accepting regional responsibility for intervention in Cambodia and Burma, while rejecting extra-regional criticism of Burma, also supports this regional identity. SAARC is an important political initiative among countries in conflict, but so far has little economic or administrative content.

SADC is at too early a stage to make a firm judgement. The interests of the countries are not particularly close in relation to development or to external countries. They concern regional questions, of relations among themselves, regional infrastructure, etc. The member countries are of very different sizes, levels of development, and sectoral composition. There is a history of common commitments, and a sense of regional identity at least as strong as in ASEAN. SADC's direct links among populations and economic sectors may be stronger (given its level of development) than those of newer groups like MERCOSUR. If SADC is not a commitment to permanent regional discrimination, but more of a first step to multilateralism, the lack of detailed rules, the weak administrative and institutional structures, and the apparent lack of serious non-economic structures are not a serious disadvantage, and some (the lack of administrative rigidities and the limited number of special regional rules) may prove an advantage. If, however, it is to be a more permanent organization, it will need to clarify what its real objectives are: these could include regional security or negotiating power in a world of regions, as well as regional trade and infrastructure.

South Africa may have a commitment to the poorer countries of the region, both as possible allies against the rest of the world and as inevitable dependants. The other members may want to secure a voice in the activities of a major trading partner and regional power; they have a direct interest in its internal peace. But it is not yet clear that the countervailing influences, the smaller countries' fear of South African domination and South Africa's fear of giving up its ability to pursue an independent trade and foreign policy, are sufficiently weaker to permit the emergence of a region. At this stage, it is also unclear that the countries agree (internally or among themselves) on the appropriate form for government policy, and therefore the role of trade policy. The central problem behind these uncertainties may be that they are all developing, and they face major structural change, both economic and political. It is unlikely that all will develop at the same rate, or following the same pattern. Divergences in performance, and probably in structural change, are likely to put a severe strain on any plans or strategies adopted on the basis of present structures. These impose greater pressures than in a more advanced and stable group, and therefore require greater noneconomic cohesion.

Judging the success of APEC, which has no formal objectives, is difficult. A view that the only objective is growth (Yamazawa, 1996 p. 121) suggested that it was a purely *ad hoc* group, but the agreement in 1997 that members had to accept the goal of free trade by 2020 is a major innovation. It was accompanied by the setting of membership criteria with an emphasis on Asian membership, and the decision to limit numbers and rate of increase. All these indicate that there is now a desire to deepen integration. Some members may want APEC to become a more conventional region.

One assessment is that 'the three most significant developments that can be specifically attributed to APEC [are] . . . the inclusion of the "three Chinas" in one international forum, the endorsement of the Non-Binding Investment Principles and the Bogor Declaration [the objective of free trade by 2020]. None of these, however, can be claimed to have generated substantial progress on economic indicators, nor in terms of output,' (Bora, 1995, p. 23). These are all processes, not achievements. This seems a reasonable assessment of APEC, as more a consultative and advisory organization than a region. It could be considered a trivial club (presenting a declaration specifically called 'non-binding' invites ridicule). But the fact that it presents itself as a regional organization with a voice, if not a policy, in trade and investment suggests that at least some of the members want it to be taken seriously in the context of other regions and the multilateral system. This implies that it does have some 'identity', although perhaps of more importance for the members which are not members of other significant regions than for the others. This could create future conflicts, if NAFTA, ASEAN, and MERCOSUR command increased loyalty and perhaps divert attention from APEC for their members. The other continental regions represent political aspirations, but, in both, other smaller regions are necessary preliminary steps. The step to the continent would be important economically in Latin America, and could be an outcome of current intiatives. In Africa, the sub-regions are still at too early a stage to consider a next step.

The interaction between regions and development

The economic advantages of regions are clear, but very limited for the small countries with small shares of regional trade. There are exceptions: NAFTA, for Mexico, is the largest. But for the others, the share of the increase in intra-regional trade is too low relative to total output to have a major direct impact. The shift to a less interventionist style of development limits both the potential advantages of regions (of offering a larger, perhaps more integrated, field for development) and the disadvantages of loss of policy independence. The development of regional institutions can encourage (or require) strengthening of national institutions, to provide the administrative and legal basis. The EU has a long history of the 'levelling up' of national institutions, This may be occurring in MERCOSUR; it has been important in NAFTA, notably with regard to intellectual property, the environment, and labour legislation. It may have had some influence in the early stages of the Andean Pact. It is arguable that regions have had at least an effect of example in CARICOM and SACU. The difference in the nature of the regions means that it would be impossible to expect any correlation between economic performance and regional integration, and none can be found.

Do regions increase the stability of the external environment for developing countries, and is this an advantage? Or does integrating with an unstable partner (and developing countries' performance is on average more variable than the world average) increase instability? The first point to make on both these questions is that it is not clear that stability is itself a benefit for development. There is strong empirical and theoretical support for liberalization having beneficial effects on income and probably on development, but it is difficult to model effects of instability, distinguishing it from simple poor performance. If there is a trade-off between liberalization and stability, liberalization has more certain advantages. Secondly, binding tariffs or other policies within a region increases their predictability, but not by as much as at the multilateral level; for the low trade shares typically found here, it is much less. Liberalizing to all countries, rather than the region, may give gains both from greater openness and from openness to, on average, a more stable environment[1] If stability is an important influence on development, this suggests that, for a small region of developing countries, there is a risk that the benefits of regional liberalization will bring potential costs of greater exposure to a more unstable set of trading partners.

The increase in countries' vulnerability to a few other countries when they become members of a region may encourage greater interest and pressure among the members for stable, predictable policies, even if there is no formal coordination of macroeconomic or development policies. If members exercise such 'peer pressure' on each other, it would be expected that countries in regions would, at least after some period of adjustment and development, have better policies than if they were not members. This is a difficult proposition to test. It does not mean that they would have better policies than countries not in regions (because of the other, much more significant, determinants of policy), and the need for changing responses means that policies before countries joined a region (or after they left) are not a good measure of what the policies would have been in the absence of the region. What can be observed are direct interventions, for example, to preserve constitutional government. The success here is mixed, with MERCOSUR better than SADC or ASEAN. Only in the EU has there been a further move to coordination. This may have very different consequences: encouraging countries to provide a favourable environment for their neighbours, i.e. to offer stable growth, is very different from imposing common policies: in the latter case, if countries are mistaken in the policies, the whole region suffers.

Only the EU, MERCOSUR, and NAFTA have labour or social aspects. This means the other regions have (or are intended to have) effects on only part of what is normally included in development, on the growth of sectors or total income, not on individuals or distribution.

Regions and the multilateral system

The intention of the new WTO regime for regions, and in particular the new Committee on Regions, is to regulate regions which do not conform to the model of an FTA or a customs union that moves to full internal free trade (at least in goods; potentially in services) within ten years. This could force a region without a strong trade motivation either to remove the trade element or to complete trade integration, with its probable implication of trade discrimination against the rest of the world, sooner or more fully than it would otherwise do. If it follows the first path, of deleting trade, the region, under present rules, is effectively removed from international supervision. There is no way of regulating the other policy elements which a region may include, although all of these have the potential to set up barriers against, or to disadvantage, non-member countries, and there is no obligation for a region without trade elements to give information to the WTO or any other multilateral institution. APEC, which already considers itself exempt from WTO rules because it has only a distant and non-binding trade policy target, might be joined by other non-trade regions. Information about the regions would, of course, still be available, but there would be no regular reporting or outside appraisal. The alternative response, of full track integration, could damage not only excluded countries but the region itself (trade diversion).

Improving the regulation of the trade policies of regions, and extending this to all the possible types of integration which have been considered here, and which also have effects on the rest of the world, is desirable in order to reveal, and if possible mitigate or prevent, trade diversion or other damage to excluded countries. But it also has the potential effect of encouraging regions to integrate according to the international rules, rather than the particular interests or needs of the members. It may alternatively lead them to find new ways of integrating, if their objective is to disadvantage the rest of the world.

The most efficient and welfare-efficient way of setting the boundary between countries' freedom to choose policies including those that discriminate against the rest of the world and international regulation of policies is always difficult to define. The boundary has been moving increasingly into the realm of country policies. Policy on new areas like intellectual property, standards, public procurement, etc. has gone beyond demands for MFN, non-discrimination among non-nationals, to first: national treatment, non-discrimination between nationals and the rest of the world, and then to internationally set minimum standards of treatment. How do the rules for regions fit into this? Effectively regions can discriminate in favour of their members only if they follow particular forms (at least for matters covered by the multilateral system), and as the coverage extends, the scope for regions diminishes. This is an inevitable conflict. All rules have costs, in creating rigidities and in encouraging distortions to find ways to avoid or circumvent them. The question for the international system is whether the objective of avoiding diversion (in trade or other forms) is worth the distortions. So far, the central objective has been fairly well preserved, and regions have moved more in the direction of extending their liberalization to the rest of the world than finding ways of discriminating more tightly.

The MFN rules and the permitted derogation from them provided for in Article XXIV depend on clear definitions of nation and region. The preference derogation for developing countries has already led to some problems here (the controversy over whether Lomé should be treated as a preference area or a region, for example), but the potential for conflict is now much greater, as the definition of 'trade' and 'trade-related' has expanded, which widens the scope of WTO regulation. Concepts like the Asian 'open regionalism' and partial reciprocity further blur distinctions. The questions have been postponed for services by the system of permitting derogations from MFN, but this only allows existing discrimination, not future developments. These difficulties are most likely to affect developing countries: their regions are more likely to be changing and 'messy'; and their economies are more likely to undergo structural changes, leading to changes in trade patterns, policies, and partners; they could not register the need to make future exceptions to services MFN treatment. They can no longer expect full exemption under the Enabling Clause, as MERCOSUR was refused this.

A subsidiary question is the effect of relations among regions on the regions and on the system. The discussion of specific issues like rules of origin and of the more general question of how to make further progress in integration in more than one region at a time strongly suggests that having a range of regional affiliations can become increasingly costly in terms of regulation and that negotiations on one can delay or discourage integration in another, or hinder policy development at the national or multilateral levels. Multiple levels of decision-making are difficult to manage, as has been demonstrated within countries. They normally work acceptably if there are clear divisions of responsibilities and clear hierarchies (whether from the bottom up in a federal system or from the centre out in a more centralized one), and if changes in the division and the scope of responsibilities are not too frequent. The recent history of regions and the multilateral system showed that the limits on consistent simultaneous evolution were being reached during the Uruguay Round, when developments in NAFTA and the EU were seen to be potentially delaying or conflicting with those in the WTO. The current developments in the Americas, with regions like MERCO-SUR both deepening and widening while there are simultaneous negotiations for a FTAA, suggest potential conflicts in priorities. In Asia, the roles of APEC and the sub-regional groups like ASEAN have been sufficiently limited for conflict to be unlikely. There is, however, also a possibility that progress at one level can encourage faster negotiations at a different level. If a region wants to remain more integrated than the rest of the world or than a higher-level region, it may be encouraged to go further to keep ahead; this is the experience of MERCOSUR in the FTAA, perhaps of the EU in the GATT, and potentially of ASEAN in APEC. These interactions make it difficult to reach a general conclusion on whether regions help or obstruct multilateralism. The basic opposition of the multilateral system to regions is justified by the measurable costs of trade diversion. But there are potential costs for the members in their relations with the multilateral system and in any existing agreements they have: the costs to their trading partners of the administration of their agreements and also the cost of examining and regulating these. What is perhaps surprising, therefore, is how limited and inconsistent the regulation of regions by the WTO has been. As indicated in the previous chapter, only one customs union is regularly reviewed as a unit (or customs area); other regions are reviewed only on their formation. The treatment of regional initiatives and obligations in the country trade policy reviews does not reflect their importance to the multilateral system.

One type of regulation which is clearly unrealistic, however, is for the international system to set standards for the membership of regions. The descriptions of the regions here make it clear that the range of different objectives and coverage would make it impossible to set a standard for all regions; alternatively, any such standard would simply lead to their relabelling as other types of group. The evolutionary nature of groups is a further obstacle: no rule could hold over time. Entry to the GATT/WTO has meant different conditions at different periods, and it has also meant different conditions for different countries. These vary partly according to current policies and views of trade, but also according to the interests of the existing members in allowing the new member to join. If regions are not allowed to retain the same discretion, the international system will be sidelined.

The non-trade responsibilities of many of the groups raise problems of cooperation among the international institutions. These are not new. On trade policy, there is already the need to reconcile the IMF principles on payments regimes, the IMF and World Bank policies on fiscal balance (for countries often dependent on tariff revenues), the World Bank support for trade liberalization, and the WTO methods and regulation of tariff changes. The potential regulatory overlap of the WTO with the ILO on labour standards or with environmental conventions is already an issue. The acceleration of regulation and integration at the international level has left few areas where regions have moved which are not at least proposed for the WTO. The regions are, however, illustrating the need for an integrated global regulatory system.

There is one possible outcome of greater regionalization which has not been discussed, but which already appears to be emerging. In the face of the complexity of different regional obligations, there are pressures to reduce other sources of complexity and special trading arrangements, in particular those with developing countries. An alternative way of viewing this is to argue that, on the simplistic model that policy-makers can only deal with a small number of divisions, regionalization is a substitute for the pre-1989 division of the world into North, South and East; with the 'East' gone, the 'South' does not fit into a new continental model. A reduction in preferences for developing countries results automatically from the reduction in relative preferences when developed members of a region lower tariffs to each other. A growth in geographical regionalization could lead to a review of non-geographical preference schemes (the reform of the ACP scheme of the EU) to 'rationalize' treatment by rearranging the countries into regions. Requirements of reciprocity or of permission to negotiate with other schemes also suggest that there will be difficulties in maintaining special preference regimes alongside regional groups. New regions joining developing and developed members pose new difficulties for preference regimes between the developed members and non-member developing countries. (The Caribbean countries' concern about NAFTA is a notable example, but the expansion of EU membership to the southern European members and the agreements with the East European countries are also relevant.) The outcome, however, will depend on bargaining, rather than simply calculating the apparent loss or compression of preferences. There are precedents for 'messy preferences' and 'messy regions' where preference donors and recipients have had a joint interest. But the potential inconsistency between preferences and regions does provide an additional reason for expecting the effects of regionalism to be negative for developing countries.

Do regions matter? Are there policy conclusions?

The regionalism which is observed is complex, and there are strong reasons to believe that it will remain so. Regional trading groups either move towards more integration (culminating, at least in the past, in what are now federal countries) or prove to be unstable temporary alliances of countries whose common interests diverge as they diverge economically or in policy approach (the experience of past developing country groups). Experience at international level confirms this.

Regions have not weakened the WTO: there is a strong case for saying that it is the most successful group of the past 50 years. It has expanded its membership, the coverage of its rules, and its powers. The extension of its responsibilities means that in practice it embraces many of the areas that the EU's adoption of the Single European Market and the formation of NAFTA were intended to integrate: services, national treatment for foreign investment, intellectual property, dispute resolution, and potentially environmental, labour and business regulation questions. Its rules on services have neglected migration up to now, but the framework is there. This means that the present regions need to be looked at individually, not as part of a global process. A few have probably appeared only in response to the apparent regionalization of the 1980s (as others did in the 1960s), but these will not permanently affect their members or the international system.

For regions which form to attain particular advantages of integration, progress at a higher level will make further progress at the regional level unnecessary. Only if the purpose is specifically to be a separate entity is there an incentive to go further.

The discussion of regions in the early 1990s suggested a world which was rapidly dividing into regions. The analysis of regions here suggests that this is a not a true picture: the 'real', integrated regions are still found in only three continents – Europe, North and South America – that is, basically in one political–economic tradition. 'A history or tradition of regionalism and cooperation has been an important contributing factor in the formation of trade blocs such as those in Western Europe, Latin America, the English-speaking Caribbean, and the Andean Pact' (Bernal, *Trade blocs*, 1997, p. 27). The Australia–New Zealand experience is well short of a region but could fall in that tradition. Africa and Asia are without integrated regions. SACU is a relic of history, and may dissolve into SADC; ASEAN is a political force, with little economic content. The countries not in regions include some of the largest in the world: most of the largest continent, and substantial numbers in other areas.

Less than a third of total world trade takes place within the regions, and this share has fallen since 1990 (Table 12.2). This includes the EU, MERCOSUR (including Bolivia and Chile), CARICOM, Andean Group, CACM, NAFTA, Group of Three, ANZCERTA, ASEAN including Singapore, SAARC and SADC. Of this, 24 per cent, i.e. three-quarters, is accounted for by the EU and 7–8 per cent by NAFTA. All other regions are too small or have too low a share of intra-regional trade to matter. These low numbers also indicate that the effect of regions other than

Table 12.2 Share of intra-regional trade
in world trade (%)

Exports		Imports	
1990	1996	1990	1996
37.2	34.1	35.9	32.1

Source: Table 7.1

the EU on world output is small, although clearly trade diversion or income effects could be important for major trading partners.[2]

One argument for regions was that they provided a more stable environment within a changing multilateral system, but the arguments and evidence suggest that developing countries are likely to produce unstable regions. The advantage of greater integration over the greater certainty of the present WTO structure is limited. The large number and the importance of the non-joiners also suggest that any regions which do form will face the likelihood of challenge under the new WTO Article XXIV and dispute procedures if they seem likely to have any adverse effect on the rest of the world. Thus regions now face more serious institutional obstacles to any special arrangements than earlier groups faced. This may make the early stages of a region, when it is least integrated and most vulnerable to outside pressures and internal differences, more difficult.

The lowering of trade barriers and the inclusion of many new areas in the WTO make it harder to find special roles for regions. Existing ones may continue to advance slightly faster, as their greater integration leads to identification of new needs for regulation earlier than in other countries; new regional organizations, unless formed in response to a special problem, are likely to struggle to keep up, unless there is serious 'policy diversion' into regions and away from the multilateral system. The placing of the environment, labour standards, and business regulation on the WTO agenda and the completion of negotiations on areas like financial services further reduce any role for regions. This suggests that the argument that regions are needed to make faster progress on issues than the international system can achieve has a limited and decreasing validity.

But the regions which do exist and those which may form do offer a challenge for the international organisations. Both they and the regions will need to accept that there is a conflict between fully flexible systems and transparency. The advantages for economic agents of transparency and certainty may be greater than they seem to policy-makers (and some academic writers). The advantages of flexibility for regions may be greater than they seem to the WTO.

For developing countries, the shift to looking at the system in terms of regions and non-members and different levels of integration among countries, rather than of industrial and developing countries, confirms the ending of their special position as a group in the international system. They remain a group, however, although one with various subgroups, some overlapping with developed countries, with common interests over wide or narrow bands of economic and other issues. An international system which is more adapted to deal with such groups, some of which may be based in geographic regions, others defined by income, type of economic structure, or other characteristics, may offer different advantages for development, including greater flexibility as countries' development needs and their groupings change. Developing country groups which do not have the institutional strength and identity of the more advanced regions will have the disadvantage of being fluctuating groups, without internal stability or the external negotiating power given by a mature regional group, but the corresponding advantage of not needing to seek group agreement on all issues. It is unrealistic to require a simple structure or even a tidy or logical one. To do so would be to put 'managing' the structure of the system ahead of development or welfare as an objective. It would also be different from the 'messy' solutions invariably found at national level (and in the EU). But it is not wrong to seek to make any solution as simple as possible, for the sake of those not involved: for countries excluded from the region, in the case of the regions which do exist; for participants who are excluded because they are economic agents, not countries, in the case of all institutions.

For the regions, there is the question of where they stand in what is now a continuum, not a sharp divide, from countries to the international system. In the most mature region, the EU, this range is being extended in the other direction as well, to sub-country regions: these are reviving within countries, and forming informal (up to now) alliances within the European region. It may be not only the international system, but national systems and analysis of political actors which need to be adapted. In a more regulated and organized international system, it may be possible to accept actors with different obligations to the world system and to other countries or regions; the old simplicities of countries may no longer be sufficient. The history of regions here does not provide sufficient evidence for this. It would be possible to regard the EU as now effectively moving into the role of a (loose, federal) country, SACU as perhaps moving away from this, while many of the others are temporary alliances, economic or political. The simple country structure is too new to be regarded as immutable. Regions may be a return to the more irregular structure of the past. The emergence of new arrangements of partial autonomy within countries would be the counterpart of the partial unification represented by regions. Is this reconcilable with the criterion of 'identity': can it hold simultaneously for different levels, of sub-country region, country, region, the world? Clearly it can, because it already exists at different levels within a country, not only geographic, but of interest groups or other social groupings.

Notes

1 Even if the potential partners are not exceptionally unstable, preferential exposure to one group of countries reduces the stability gained from the counterbalancing peaks and troughs which follow from exposure to a wide range of countries; if the region encourages greater intensity of trade, it may increase the risk of exposure to instability from a concentrated trading area.

2 Assertions that 'virtually every WTO member belongs to at least one regional economic grouping' (WTO Annual Report 1997) are meaningless because they include organizations without content like APEC. The high number of notifications of regions to GATT or WTO largely reflects agreements within or by the EU.

References and Bibliography

Abreu, Marcelo de Paiva (1993) *Brazil–US Relations and the Enterprise for the Americas Initiative*, Texto para Discussão 296, Rio de Janeiro: Pontificia Universidade Católica do Rio de Janeiro.

Abreu, Marcelo de Paiva (1997) 'Financial Integration in MERCOSUR Countries', *Integration and Trade*, April: 79–94.

Acuerdo de Cartagena (1987) *Bases para una estrategía integrada de cooperación con la comunidad económica europea*, Guayaquil, October.

Agosín, Manuel R. (1994) 'Free Trade Agreements for Chile: Potential Benefits and Costs', *Transnational Law and Contemporary Problems* 4(1): 21–46.

Alonso-Gamo, Patricia, Fennell, Susan and Sakr, Khaled (1997) *Adjusting to New Realities: MENA, The Uruguay Round, and the EU-Mediterranean Initiative*, IMF Working Paper. Washington, DC: International Monetary Fund.

Amjadi, Azita and Winters, Alan (1997) *Transport Costs and 'Natural' Integration in MERCOSUR*, International Trade Division Working Paper. Washington, DC: World Bank.

Anderson, Kym and Blackhurst, Richard (eds) (1993) *Regional Integration and the Global Trading System*, New York and London: Harvester Wheatsheaf.

APEC Eminent Persons Group (1995) *Implementing the APEC Vision*, Third Report, August. Singapore: APEC Secretariat.

Ariff, Mohamed (1992) 'AFTA and Malaysia: Opportunities and Challenges', 17th Conference of the Federation of ASEAN Economic Association, Indonesia.

Ariff, Mohamed (1995) 'The Prospects for an ASEAN Free Trade Area', *World Economy*, Annual supplement.

Arndt, H. (1993) 'Anatomy of Regionalism', *Journal of Asian Economics* 42(2): 272–82.

Bagwell, Kyle and Staiger, Robert W. (1993) 'Multilateral Tariff Cooperation during the Formation of Customs Unions', manuscript, November.

Baldwin, Richard E. (1997) 'The Causes of Regionalism', *World Economy* 20(5): 865–88.

Balze, Felipe A. M. de la (ed.) (1995) *Argentina y Brasil Enfrentando el Siglo XXI*, Buenos Aires: Consejo Argentino para las Relaciones Internacionales.

Bannister, Geoffrey and Primo Braga, Carlos A. (1990) 'East-Asian Investment and Trade: Prospects for Growing Regionalization in the 1990s', unpublished, Washington, DC: World Bank.

Barshefsky, Charlene (1997) 'Testimony on Fast Track Trade Negotiating Authority', Washington, DC: website.

Bárta, Vít and Richter, Sándor (1996) 'Eastern Enlargement of the European Union from a Western and Near Eastern Perspective', *Research Reports* No. 227, Vienna: Vienna Institute for Comparative Economic Studies (WIIW).

Bataller, M. Francisco (1994) 'La Transformación Política y Económica de América Latina y la Contribución de la Comunidad Europea a la Democratización y a la Protección de los derechos humanos en la Región', in *Los Derechos humanos en América*, Valladolid: Cortes de Castilla y León.

Baumann, Renato (1991) 'Intra-industry Trade: A comparison between Latin America and some industrial countries', manuscript, Santiago: UN ECLAC.

Baumann, Renato (1992) 'An Appraisal of recent intra-industry trade for Latin America', *Cepal Review* 48 (December): 83–94.

Baumann, Renato (1993) 'Integration and trade diversion', *CEPAL Review* 51 (December): 133–47.

Baumann, Renato and Carvalho, Alexandre (1997) *Simulação dos Efeitos Comerciais da ALCA para o Brasil*, Brasilia: UN ECLAC.

Bayoumi, Tamim and Lipworth, Gabrielle (1997) *Japanese Foreign Direct Investment and Regional Trade*, IMF Working Paper. Washington, DC: International Monetary Fund.

Bernal, Richard L. (1993) 'The Caribbean and Hemispheric Free Trade', *The Caribbean Basin: Economic and Security Issues I*, study papers, Joint Economic Committee, Congress of the United States, January.

Bernal, Richard L. (1994) 'The Compatibility of Caribbean Membership in Lomé, Nafta, and GATT', *Social and Economic Studies* 43 (2).

Bernal, Richard L. (1996) 'Regional Trade Arreangements and the Establishment of a Free Trade Area of the Americas', *Law and Policy in International Business* 27(4): 945–62.

Bernal, Richard L. (1997) *Paths to the Free Trade Area of the Americas*, Washington, DC: Center for Strategic and International Studies.

Bernal, Richard L. (1997) *Trade Blocs: A Regionally Specific Phenomenon or a Global Trend?* Washington, DC: National Policy Association.

Bhagwati, Jagdish and Panagariya, Arvind (1995) *Preferential Trading Areas and Multilateralism: Strangers, Friends or Foes?* Paper prepared for Conference on Regionalism, AEI, June.

Bhalla, A. and Bhalla, P. (1996) 'ASEAN and SAARC', *RIS Digest* 13(2–4): 55–90.

Blancher, N. and Mainguy, C. (1997) 'Comparaison des Processus de Régionalisation', *Revue Analytique de la Littérature*, Strasbourg.

Bliss, Christopher (1994) *Economic Theory and Policy for Trading Blocks*, Manchester: Manchester University Press.

Blomström, Magnus and Kokko, Ari (1997) *Regional Integration and Foreign Direct Investment*, World Bank Policy Research Working Paper No. 1750. Washington, DC: World Bank.

Bloom, David E. (1995) *Is an Integrated Regional Labor Market Emerging in East and Southeast Asia?* NBER Working Paper No. 5174, Cambridge, MA: NBER.

Bond, Eric W., Syropoulos, Constantinos and Winters, L. Alan (1995) *Deepening of Regional Integration and Multilateral Trade Agreements*, Internal paper, November. Washington, DC: World Bank.

Bond, Eric (1997) *Using Tariff Indices to Evaluate Preferential Trading Arrangements: An Application to Chile*, World Bank Policy Research Working Paper No. 1751. Washington, DC: World Bank.

Bora, Bijit (1997) *Potential for Investment Liberalization between AFTA and CER*, Policy Discussion Paper No. 97/13. Adelaide: Centre for International Economic Studies.

Bora, Bijit (1995) *The Asia Pacific Economic Cooperation Process*, Policy Discussion Paper No. 95/12, Adelaide: Centre for International Economic Studies.

Bora, Bijit (1995) 'Trade and Investment in the APEC Region: 1980–1993', paper, Adelaide.

Borrmann, Axel and Koopmann, Georg (1994) 'Regionalisation and Regionalism in World Trade', *Intereconomics*, July/August.

Bouzas, Roberto (1995) 'Mercosur and Preferential Trade Liberalisation in South America', *Record, Issues and Prospects*, Documentos e informes de investigación 176, Buenos Aires: FLACSO.

Bouzas, Roberto (1996) 'MERCOSUR's Economic Agenda: Short- and Medium-term Policy Challenges', *Integration and Trade* 0: 97–79.

Brandão, Antoñio Salazar P. and Pereira, Lia Valls (1996) *MERCOSUL: Perspectivas da Integração*. Rio de Janeiro: Fundação Getulio Vargas.

Brun, Julio de (1997) 'Trade in Services in the MERCOSUR Area', paper, Montevideo: Universidad ORT.

Caballeros Otero, Rómulo (1992) 'Reorientation of Central American Integration', *CEPAL Review* 46 (April).

Calfat, Germán and Flôres, Renato (1995) *Northwards or across the Ocean? MERCOSUR Free Trade Options*, Antwerp: University of Antwerp, Centre for Development Studies.

Cassim, Rashad (1995) 'Rethinking Economic Integration in Southern Africa', *Trade Monitor* 10 (September).

CEFIR (1995) *La Dimensión Social de la Integración*, Report of conference, Santiago, April.

CEPAL (1993) *Directorio sobre Inversión Extranjera en América Latina y el Caribe 1993: Marco Legal e Información Estadistica*, Santiago: CEPAL.

CEPAL (1996) *La Inversión Extranjera en América Latina y el Caribe*, Santiago: CEPAL.

Chia, Siow Yue (1992) 'Capital Flows, FDI and the Role of Multinationals in an AFTA', 17th conference of the Federation of ASEAN Economic Associations, Indonesia.

Chirathivat, Suthiphand (1996) 'ASEAN Economic Integration with the World through AFTA' in J.L.H. Tan (ed.) *AFTA in the Changing International Economy*, Singapore: Institute of Southeast Asian Studies.

Chudnovsky, Daniel (1989) 'Latin American Economic Integration and Multinational Enterprises: Issues in the Integration of Argentina with Brazil' in Sylvain Plasschaert (ed.) *Multinational Enterprises and National Policies*, Rome: Herder, International Federation of Catholic Universities.

Chudnovsky, Daniel (ed.) (1996) *Los limites de la apertura*, Buenos Aires: Alianza Editorial/CENIT.

Coase, R.H. (1960) 'The Problem of Social Cost', *The Journal of Law and Economics* III (October): 1–44.

COMESA (1994) *Trade Policy Issues and Recommendations on Agricultural Integration and Development in Eastern and Southern Africa*, Consultancy Report, September.

COMESA (1994) *Report of the First Meeting of the COMESA Council of Ministers*, December. Lilongwe: COMESA/CMI/5.

COMESA (1993) *Treaty Establishing the Common Market for Eastern and Southern Africa*.

Commission of the European Communities (1997) Extract from the draft minutes of the Council (General Affairs), 2003rd meeting, Luxembourg, 29 April.

Commission of the European Communities (1997) 'WTO Aspects of EU's Preferential Trade Agreements with Third Countries', Communication from the Commission, 10 June.

Commission of the European Communities (1995) 'G-24 High Level Meeting: Background Documents and Working Documents'. Communication from the Commission, Brussels, 10 March.

Commission of the European Communities (1995) 'Towards Closer Relations between the European Union and Mexico'. Communication from the Commission to the Council and the European Parliament, Brussels, 2 August (mimeo).

Commission of the European Communities (1995) 'Acuerdo marco interregional de cooperación entre le communidad Europea y sus estados miembros y el mercado común del sur y sus estados partes.'

Commission of the European Communities (1995) *Communication from the Commission: European Community support for regional Economic integration efforts among developing countries*, COM(95)219 final, Brussels, 16 June.

Commission of the European Communities (1994) 'Report on the Implementation of Macro-Financial Assistance to Third Countries'. Communication from the Commission to the Council and the European Parliament, *European Economy*, Part B, No.58.

Commission of the European Communities (1993) Framework Agreement for Cooperation between the European Economic Community and the Cartegena Agreement and its member countries, namely Bolivia, Colombia, Ecuador, Peru and Venezela. *Official Journal of the European Communities*, January.

Commission of the European Communities (1993) Proposal for a Council Decision concerning the conclusion of a framework Cooperation Agreement between the European Economic Community and the Republics of Costa Rica, El Salvador, Guatemala, Honduras, Nicaragua and Panama. *Official Journal of the European Communities*, March.

Commission of the European Communities (1992) Council decision concerning the conclusion of the Framework Agreement for cooperation between the European Economic Community and the Eastern Republic of Uruguay. *Official Journal of the European Communities*, April.

Commission of the European Communities (1992) Council decision concerning the conclusion of the Framework Agreement for cooperation between the European Community and the Republic of Paraguay. *Official Journal of the European Communities*, October.

Commission of the European Communities (1992) Proposal for a Council decision concerning the conclusion of the Framework Agreement for cooperation between the European Economic Community and the Federative Republic of Brazil. *Official Journal of the European Communities*, June.

Commission of the European Communities (1991) Council decision concerning the conclusion of the Framework Agreement for cooperation between the European Economic Community and the Republic of Chile. *Official Journal of the European Communities*, March.

Commission of the European Communities (1991) Council decision concerning the conclusion of the Framework Agreement for cooperation between the European Economic Community and the United Mexican States. *Official Journal of the European Communities*, March.

Commission of the European Communities (1990) Council decision concerning the conclusion of the Framework Agreement for cooperation between the European Economic Community and the Argentine Republic. *Official Journal of the European Communities*, October.

302   References and Bibliography

Confederação Nacional da Industria (1995) *Abertura Comercial & Estratégia Tecnológica*, 5th survey, Rio de Janeiro.

Confederação Nacional da Industria (1994) *Abertura Comercial & Estratégia Tecnológica*, 4th survey, Rio de Janeiro.

Cox, Ronald W. (1995) 'Corporate Coalitions and Industrial Restructuring: Explaining Regional Trade Agreements', *Competition and Change* 1(1): 13–30.

David, Maria Beatriz de Albuquerque and Nonnenburg, Marcelo José Braga (1997) *MERCOSUL: Integração Regionale o Comércio de Productos Agrícolas*, Rio de Janeiro: IPEA.

de Melo, Jaime and Panagariya, Arvind (eds) (1993) *New Dimensions in Regional Integration*, Cambridge: Cambridge University Press.

DeRosa, Dean A. (1995) *Regional Trading Arrangements among Developing Countries: The ASEAN Example*, Washington, DC: International Food Policy Research Institute.

DeRosa, Dean A. (1996) 'Regionalism and the Bias Against Agriculture in Less Developed Countries', *The World Economy*: 45–66.

Devos, Serge, 'Regional Integration', *OECD Observer* 192 (February/March).

Dollar, David (1996) 'Economic Reform, Openness, and Vietnam's Entry into ASEAN', *ASEAN Economic Bulletin* 13(2): 169–84.

Eichengreen, Barrry (1997) 'Free Trade and Macroeconomic Policy', Paper for World Bank Annual Latin American Conference on Development Economics, Montevideo.

Eichengreen, Barry and Irwin, Douglas A. (1993) *Trade Blocs, Currency Blocs and the Disintegration of World Trade in the 1930s*, CEPR Discussion Paper No. 837.

El-Agraa, Ali M. (1989) *The Theory and Measurement of International Economic Integration*, London: Macmillan.

Emecz, Steven (1993) 'The Maquiladora Programme and the NAFTA', Thesis, Bristol Business School.

Endsley, Harry B. (1995) 'Dispute Settlement Under the CFTA and NAFTA: From Eleventh-Hour Innovation to Accepted Institution', *Hastings International and Comparative Law Review* 18(4): 659–711.

Erzan, Refik and Yeats, Alexander (1992) *Free Trade Agreements with the United States: What's in it for Latin America?* Working Paper No. 827. Washington, DC: World Bank.

Estévez, Eduardo R. (1996) 'MERCOSUR: El Mercado de América Latina', mimeo. Buenos Aires.

Fairlie Reinoso, Alan (1996) 'Comunidad Andina, regionalismo abierto y comercio intraindustrial', *Fondo Editorial de la Fundación Academia Diplomática del Perú* 43 (January/March): 53–71.

Fairlie Reinoso, Alan (1996) 'Intra-Industry Trade in the Andean Group in the 1980s', in Weine Karlsson and Akhil Malaki (eds) *Growth, Trade and Integration in Latin America*, Stockholm: Institute of Latin American Studies.

Fairlie Reinoso, Alan (1994) 'Comercio intraindustrial en el Grupo Andino en la década 1980', *Integración latinoamericana* 204 (October): 25–41.

Fairlie Reinoso, Alan (1992) 'Crisis, Integración y Desarrollo en América Latina', for Conference, Buenos Aires.

Fawcett, Louise and Hurrell, Andrew (eds) (1995) *Regionalism in World Politics*, Oxford: Oxford University Press.

Fernández, Raquel (1997) *Returns to Regionalism: An Evaluation of Nontraditional Gains from Regional Trade Agreements*, Policy Research Working Paper No. 1816. Washington, DC: World Bank.

Fieleke, Norman S. (1992) 'One Trading World, or Many? The Issue of Regional Trading Blocs', *New England Economic Review* (May/June).

Frankel, Jeffrey (1991) 'Is a Yen Bloc Forming in Pacific Asia?' *Finance and the International Economy 5*. AMEX Bank Review Prize Essays, Oxford for AMEX.

Frankel, Jeffrey, Stein, Ernesto and Wei, Shang-Jin (1995) 'Trading Blocs and the Americas: the Natural, the Unnatural, and the Super-natural', *Journal of Development Economics* 47.

Fundação Getulio Vargas (1997) *Analise Comparativa dos Ganhos de Integração: Alca e União Européia*, Rio de Janeiro.

Fundación Invertir Argentina (1996) *Invertir*, June.

Gana, Eduardo (1997) *Promoción de los Vínculos Económicos entre los Esquemas de Integración de América Latina y el Caribe*, Santiago: UN ECLAC.

Garay, Luis Jorge and Estevadeordal, Antonio (1996) 'Protection, Preferential Tariff Elimination and Rules of Origin in the Americas', *Integration and Trade* 0:2–25.

Garnaut, Ross and Drysdale, Peter (1994) *Asia Pacific Regionalism*, Pymble, Australia: Harper Educational.

Garriga, Marcelo and Sanguinetti, Pablo (1997) 'The Determinants of Regional Trade in MERCOSUR: Geography and Commercial Liberalization', mimeo. Buenos Aires: Universidad Torcuato di Tella.

GATT (1993) *Final Act Embodying the Results of the Uruguay Round of Multilateral Trade Negotiations*, Geneva: GATT.

GATT (1986) *The Text of The General Agreement on Tariffs and Trade*, Geneva: GATT.

Gereffi, Gary and Wyman, Donald L. (eds) (1990) *Manufacturing Miracles Paths of Industrialization in Latin America and East Asia*, Princeton, NJ: Princeton University Press.

Gibb, Richard (1997) 'Regional Integration in Post-Apartheid Southern Africa: The Case of Renegotiating the Southern African Customs Union', *Journal of Southern African Studies* 23(1): 67–86.

Gibb, Richard (1969) 'Regionalism in the World Economy', *Area* 28(4): 446–58.

Gonçalves, José Botafogo (1996) 'MERCOSUR, SAFTA, NAFTA: A Converging Overview on Hemispherical Integration'. Brazil: Ministry of External Relations.

Goto, Junichi (1997) 'Regional Economic Integration and Agricultural Trade', Policy Research Working Paper No. 1805, Washington, DC: World Bank.

Gould, David M. (1998) 'Has NAFTA Changed North American Trade', *Economic Review*, Federal Reserve Bank of Dallas, First Quarter: 12–23.

Gould, David M. (1996) 'Distinguishing NAFTA from the Peso Crisis', *Southwest Economy* (September–October): 6–10. Dallas: Federal Reserve Bank of Dallas.

Gratius, Susanne (1993) *El MERCOSUR y la Comunidad Europea: Una Guía para la Investigación*, Documento de Trabajo No. 37. Madrid: IRELA.

Gruben, William C. and Welch, John H. (1994) 'Is NAFTA Economic Integration?', *Economic Review*: 35–51. Dallas: Federal Reserve Bank of Dallas.

Gruben, William C. and Welch, John H. (1993) 'Is NAFTA more than Free Trade Agreement?'. Paper from conference 'Mexico and the NAFTA: Who Will Benefit?', London: Institute of Latin American Studies, 12–14 May.

Hall, Derek (1993) 'Two Phases of Foreign Direct Investment in Eastern Asia', manuscript.

Haines-Ferrari, Marta (1993) 'MERCOSUR: A New Model of Latin American Economic Integration?', *Journal of International Law* 25(3): 413–48.

Harmsen, Richard and Leidy, Michael (1994) 'Regional Trading Arrangements' in IMF, *International Trade Policies: The Uruguay Round and Beyond*, vol. II, Washington, DC: International Monetary Fund.

Higgott, Richard (1996) 'Understanding Regional Integration in the Asia Pacific: Towards an Integrated Approach', LSE workshop on regionalism, London, July.

Higgott, Richard (1995) 'Regional Integration, Economic Cooperation and Economic Policy Coordination in the Asia Pacific: Unpacking APEC, EAEC, and AFTA'. Paper for GEI seminar, 14 November.

Higgott, Richard, Leaver, Richard and Ravenhill, John (eds) (1993) *Pacific Economic Relations in the 1990s: Cooperation or Conflict*, St Leonards: Allen & Unwin.

Hinojosa-Ojeda, Raúl, Lewis, Jeffrey D. and Robinson, Sherman (1997) 'Simon Bolivar Rides Again? Pathways Toward Integration between NAFTA MERCOSUR, and the Greater Andean Region', *Integration and Trade* 1 (April): 95–122.

Hirst, Mónica (1995) *La Dimensión Política del MERCOSUR: Actores, Politización e Ideologia*, Documentos e Informes de Investigación No. 198. Buenos Aires: FLACSO.

Hirst, Mónica (1992) 'MERCOSUR and the New Circumstances for its Integration', *CEPAL Review* 46 (April).

Hoekman, Bernard M. (1992) *Regional versus Multilateral Liberalization of Trade in Services*, London: CEPR Discussion paper No. 749.

Hoekman, Bernard M. and Djankov, Simeon (1996) *Catching Up with Eastern Europe? The European Union's Mediterranean Free Trade Initiative*, Policy Research Paper No. 1562, Washington, DC: World Bank.

Hoekman, Bernard M. and Leidy, Michael P. (1992) *Holes and Loopholes in Integration Agreements: History and Prospects*, London: CEPR Discussion Paper No. 748.

Hufbauer, Gary Clyde and Schott, Jeffrey J. (1994) *Western Hemisphere Economic Integration*, Washington, DC: Institute for International Economics.

Hurrell, Andrew (1996) 'The Case of MERCOSUR', LSE workshop on regionalism, London, July.

Hurrell, Andrew (1995) 'Explaining the Resurgence of Regionalism in World Politics', *Review of International Studies* 21.

Iglesias, Enrique V. (1997) 'The New Face of Regional Integration in Latin America and the Caribbean'. Paper for Third Annual World Bank Conference on Development in Latin America and the Caribbean, Montevideo.

Imada, Pearl and Naya, Seiji (eds) (1992) *AFTA the Way Ahead*. Singapore: ISEAS.

Imani Development Ltd (1997) *Study on the Economic Impact of the Proposed EU–SA Free Trade Agreeement on Botswana, Lesotho, Namibia and Swaziland*, Harare.

IMF (1997) 'Asian Financial Deputies Agree on Framework for Regional Cooperation'. IMF survey, December, Washington, DC: International Monetary Fund.

IMF *Direction of Trade Statistics Yearbook*. Various issues. Washington, DC: International Monetary Fund.

IMF *International Financial Statistics*. Various issues. Washington, DC: International Monetary Fund.

Institute for European–Latin American Relations (1997) *MERCOSUR: Prospects for an Emerging Bloc*. Madrid: IRELA.

Institute for European–Latin American Relations (1997) 'Constructing the Free trade Area of the Americas', Briefing, June.

Institute for European–Latin American Relations (1995) 'The European Union and the Rio Group: The Biregional Agenda'. Base document prepared for the European Commission on the occasion of the V Institutionalised Ministerial Meeting between the European Union and the Rio Group, Paris, 16–17 March.

Institute for European–Latin American Relations (1994) 'European Cooperation with Latin America in the 1990s: A Relationship in Transition'. Dossier No. 51. Madrid, December.

Institute for European–Latin American Relations and Commission of the European Communities (1994) 'Europe and Latin America: A Partnership for Action'. Basic document on the relations of the European Union with Latin America and the Caribbean, October.

Insulza, José Miguel (1997) Key note address given at Canning House, London, 29 October.

Inter-American Development Bank (1997) *Intal Monthly Newsletter* (March). INTAL.

Inter-American Development Bank (1997) *Report: MERCOSUR 3*. INTAL. Buenos Aires: IDB.

Inter-American Development Bank (1996) *Report: MERCOSUR 1*. INTAL. Buenos Aires: IDB.

Inter-American Development Bank (1996) Newsletter.

Inter-American Development Bank and Institute for European–Latin American Relations (1996) *Foreign Direct Investment in Latin America in the 1990s*. Madrid: IRELA.

Inter-American Development Bank and UN Economic Commission for Latin America and the Caribbean (1995) *Trade Liberalization in the Western Hemisphere*. Washington.

International Trade Centre (1995) *PC/TAS, International Trade Statistics*. Geneva: UNCTAD/WTO.

Izam, Miguel (1997) *Evolución, Análisis y Perspectivas del Mercado Común del Sur*, Santiago: UN ECLAC.

Izam, Miguel (1994) 'European integration and Latin American Trade', *CEPAL Review* 51: 149–62.

James, William E. (1997) 'APEC and Preferential Rules of Origin', *Journal of World Trade* 31(3): 113–34.

Junguito, Roberto (1997) 'Roundtable on Agriculture Policy and Integration'. Paper for Third Annual World Bank Conference on the Development of Latin America and the Caribbean, Montevideo.

Kelegama, Saman (1997) 'Risks to the Sri Lankan Garment Industry from Trade Diversion Effects of NAFTA', *Development Policy Review* 15(3): 227–49.

Khan, Ashfaque H. (1995) 'Intra-Regional Trade in South Asia: Problems and Prospects'. Paper prepared for workshop on SAARC, December.

Kouparitsas, Michael A. (1997) 'A Dynamic Macroeconomic Analysis of NAFTA', *Economic Perspectives*, Chicago: Chicago Federal Reserve Bank (January–February).

Köves, András and Oblath, Gábor (1994) *The Regional Role of the Former Soviet Union and the CMEA: A Net Assessment*. Kopint-Datorg Discussion Papers No. 24, Budapest.

Kreinin, Mordechai E. And Plummer, Michael G. (1992) 'Effects of Economic Integration in Industrial Countries on ASEAN and the Asian NIEs', *World Development* 20(9): 1345–66.

Krugman, Paul (1991) *Geography and Trade*, Cambridge, MA: MIT Press.

Kume, Honorio (1995) 'Uma Nota sobre o Regime de Origem no MERCOSUL', Working Paper No. 373. Rio De Janeiro: Ipea.

Laird, Samuel (1997) *Mercosur: Objectives and Achievements*. Paper for Third Annual World Bank Conference on Development in Latin America and the Caribbean, Montevideo.

Langhammer, Rolf and Hiemenz, Ulrich (1990) *Regional Integration among Developing Countries*. Kiel Studies No. 232. Tubingen.

Langhammer, Rolf (1992) *The NAFTA: Another Futile Trade Area (AFTA) or a Serious Approach Towards Regionalism?* Kiel Discussion Papers No. 192.

Langhammer, Rolf (1995) 'Regional Integration in East Asia from Market-Driven Regionalisation to Institutionalised Regionalism', *Weltwirtschaftliches Archiv* 1 (131).

Lawrence, Robert Z. (1996) *Regionalism, Multilateralism, and Deeper Integration*, Washington, DC: The Brookings Institution.

Leidy, Michael P. and Hoekman, Bernard M. (1992) *What to Expect From Regional and Multilateral Trade Negotiations: A Public Choice Perspective*. London: CEPR Discussion Paper No. 747.

Leipziger, Danny M., Frischtak, Claudio, Kharas, Homi J. and Normand, John F. (1997) 'Mercosur: Integration and Industrial Policy', *World Economy* 20(5):585–603. Oxford: Blackwell Publishers.

León, Judyth de (1994) 'La Cuenca del Pacífico', *Mercado de Valores* (January): 56–9.

Lipsey, Richard G. and Meller, Patricio (eds) (1996) *NAFTA y MERCOSUR*. Santiago: CIEPLAN/Dolmen.

Lopez, David (1997) 'Dispute Resolution Under MERCOSUR from 1991 to 1996: Implications for the Formation of a Free Trade Area of the Americas', *Kluwer Law International*, III, 2, Spring.

Low, Linda (1991) 'The East Asian Economic Grouping', *The Pacific Review* 4(4).

Lowe, Michele A.M. (1996) *Europe and the Caribbean: Planning for a 'Partnership 2000'*, Caribbean Council for Europe.

Lucángeli, Jorge (1995) 'Hacia una nueva relación en la construcción de un espacio competitivo común'. Brasilia: Embajada Argentina en Brasil.

Lucángeli, Jorge (1996) 'Reflexiones sobre la Necesidad de Profundizar el proceso de Integración del MERCOSUR'. Buenos Aires: Centro de Economía Internacional.

Lucángeli, Jorge (1997) 'Argentina and the Challenge of MERCOSUR', mimeo.

Machado, João Bosco (1996) 'Dilemas da Consolidação de uma União Aduaneira', *Revista Brasileira de Comércio Exterior* 49 (October–December): 44–53.

Machado, João Bosco and Veiga, Pedro da Motta (1997) *A ALCA e a Estratégia Negociadora Brasileira*, Texto para Discussão No. 127. Rio de Janeiro: Fundação Centro de Estudos do Comércio Exterior.

Mangkusuwondo, Suhadi (1992) 'AFTA as seen by individual ASEAN countries: a view from Indonesia', 17th Conference of the Federation of ASEAN Economic Association, Indonesia.

Mangkusuwondo, Suhadi (1995) 'The APEC Vision: The Second EPG Report, *RIS Digest* (March).

Mehta, Rajesh (1995) 'Effects of NAFTA on Developing Countries: A Brief Summary of Recent Literature', *RIS Digest* (March).

Mercado de Valores (1993) 'Acuerdos Paralelos al Tratado de Libre Comercio', October.

Mercado de Valores. Data on investment in Mexico, April 1994, pp. 45–53; April 1995, pp. 64–7; May 1996, pp. 44–5; September 1996, p. 45.

MERCOSUR (1994) *Protocol of Ouro Preto,* www.Brazil.org.uk/ouropreto.zip.

MERCOSUR (1991) Asunción Treaty, www.Brazil.org.uk/asuncion.zip.

Mexican Investment Board (1994) *Mexico Your Partner for Growth NAFTA,* Mexico City.

Mistry, Percy (1996) *Regional Integration Arrangements in Economic Development,* The Hague: FONDAD.

Mohanty, S.K. (1995) 'Trade Cooperation in the Indian Ocean Rim Countries: Issues and Prospects', *RIS Digest* (March).

Mortimore, Michael (1997) 'Dimensions of Latin American Integration: the NAFTA and MERCOSUR Automobile Industries'. Paper for CEPAL. Santiago: CEPAL.

Mytelka, Lynn K. (1994) *South–South Co-operation in a Global Perspective,* Paris: OECD Development Centre Documents.

Nabli, Mustapha K. (1997) 'The European Union–Tunisia Free Trade Area Agreement and Some Lessons for South Africa'. Paper given at TIPS 1997 Annual Forum, Muldersdrift, South Africa, September.

Nadal, Egea, Alejandro (1995) *Technology, Trade, and NAFTA's Environmental Regime.* Working Paper No. 15. Intech.

Ndlela, Daniel B. (1997) *A Study on the COMESA–SADC Relations and Implications for Zimbabwean Economy,* Harare: Zimconsult for Government of Zimbabwe.

Neto, Raul de Gouvea and Bannister, Geoffrey (1997) 'Trading Blocs: Incubators for Emerging Multinationals?', unpublished paper. Albuquerque: University of New Mexico.

Nogueira, Uziel (1997) *The Integration Movement in the Caribbean at Crossroads.* Working paper No. 1. Buenos Aires: Intal.

OAU/African Economic Community (1997) *AEC Newsletter* 1(4):3.

OECD (1996) *Development Cooperation: Annual Report 1995.* Paris: OECD.

OECD (1996) *Geographical Distribution of Financial Flows to Aid Recipients.* Paris: OECD.

OECD (1996) 'The New Generation of Regional Initiatives and Donors Responses'. Paris: OECD.

OECD (1995) *Development Cooperation: Annual Report 1994.* Paris: OECD.

OECD (1995) *Geographical Distribution of Financial Flows to Aid Recipients.* Paris: OECD.

Ohno, Koichi and Okamoto, Yumiko (eds) (1994) *Regional Integration and Foreign Direct Investment: Implications for Developing Countries,* Tokyo: Institute of Developing Economies.

Olarreaga, Marcelo and Soloaga, Isidro (1997) *Endogenous Tariff Formation: The Case of MERCOSUR.* Working paper ERAD-97–003. Geneva: WTO.

Oman, Charles (1994) *Globalisation and Regionalisation: The Challenge for Developing Countries,* Paris: OECD.

Panagariya, Arvind (1996) 'The Free Trade Area of the Americas: Good for Latin America?', *The World Economy* 19(5): 485–515.

Panagariya, Arvind (1993) *Should East Asia Go Regional?: No, No, and Maybe.* Working Paper No. 1209. Washington, DC: World Bank.

Pangestu, Mari and Bora, Bijit (1996) *Evolution of Liberalization Policies Affecting Investment Flows in the Asia Pacific.* Policy Discussion Paper 96/01. Adelaide: Centre for International Economic Studies.

Panić, M. (1988) *National Management of the International Economy*, London: Macmillan.

Parra, Antonio R. (1993) 'A Comparison of the NAFTA Investment Chapter with Other International Investment Instruments'. Paper presented at training programme for Mexican NAFTA Panelists, Mexico City, December.

Parrenas, Julius Caesar (1995) *Rapidly Emerging Regional Integration Systems: Implications for the Asian Developing Countries and Possible Policy Responses.* UNCTAD/ITD/19, December.

Peña, Felix (1997) 'Reglas de Juego e Instituciones en el MERCOSUR', mimeo, Buenos Aires.

Peña Alfaro, Ricardo (1986) 'Ventajas y desventajas del ingreso de México al GATT', *Comercio Exterior* 36(1): 33–45.

Pereira, Lia Valls (1997) 'MERCOSUL: Resultados e Perspectivas do ponto de vista Brasileiro'. Rio de Janeiro: Fundação Getulio Vargas.

Peres Nunez, Wilson (1990) *From Globalization to Regionalization: The Mexican Case.* Technical Paper No. 24. Paris: OECD.

Perez del Castillo, Santiago (1993) 'MERCOSUR: History and aims', *International Labour Review* 132(5–6): 639–53.

Perroni, Carlo and Whalley, John (1994) 'The New Regionalism: Trade Liberalization or Insurance?', mimeo, NBER conference paper, September, and also at Warwick summer 1995 conference.

Piani, Buida (1996) 'O NAFTA e o MERCOSUL: Implicações sobre o Comércio com os Estados Unidos' in *Perspectivas da Economia Brasileira 1996.* Rio de Janerio: IPEA.

Piei, Mohd. Haflah and Khalifah, Noor Aini (1996) 'Vietnam in ASEAN', *ASEAN Economic Bulletin* 13(2): 200–11.

Plummer, Michael G. (1994) 'U.S. Policy Coherence and ASEAN Economic Development'. Workshop on OECD and ASEAN, 22–4 June. Singapore: Institute of Southeast Asian Studies.

Podestá, Bruno (1997) 'Globalización Integración y Sociedad', for seminar, Montevideo.

Podestá, Bruno (1995) 'La representación socio-profesional en los países de Mercosur en relación al CES', *Revista de Trabajo* 2(6): 229–35.

Polak, Jacques J. (1996) 'Is APEC a Natural Regional Trading Bloc? A Critique of the "Gravity Model" of International Trade', *The World Economy* 19(5): 533–43.

Preusse, Heinz G. (1994) 'Regional Integration in the Nineties – Stimulation or Threat to the Multilateral Trading System', *Journal of World Trade* 28(4): 147–64.

Primo Braga, Carlos and Low, Patrick (1994) 'The New Regionalism and its Consequences'. World Bank paper. Washington, DC: World Bank.

Primo Braga, Carlos, Safadi, Raed and Yeats, Alexander (1994) *NAFTA's Implications for East Asian Exports.* Policy Research Working Paper No. 1351. Washington, DC: World Bank.

Primo Braga, Carlos and de Brun, Julio (1997) 'Services in MERCOSUR'. World Bank paper.

Puyana, Alicia (c. 1993) 'Latin American Economic Integration in the 1990s: Is there still any hope?',draft, mimeo.

Rajapatirana, Sarath (1994) *The Evolution of Trade Treaties and Trade Creation.* Policy Research Working Paper No. 1371. Washington, DC: World Bank.

Rao, V.L. (1995) 'Regional Integration in Latin America and the Caribbean', *RIS Digest* (March).

Retout, Oliver (1990) *Le Dialogue Europe–Amérique Latin–Asie: La Coopération Financière et Technique 1976–89*. Brussels: EC.

Rieger, Hans Christoph and Tan Loong-Hoe (1987) 'The Problems of Economic Cooperation', *Regional Cooperation: Recent Developments* (April–September). London: Commonwealth Secretariat.

Roberts, Adam and Kingsbury, Benedict (eds) (1993) *United Nations, Divided World*, Oxford: Clarendon Press.

Ronderos, Carlos T., Correa, Patricia B., Ramírez, Jorge O. and Reina, Mauricio E. (1997) '¿Tiene Colombia una política de integración?', *Debates de Coyuntura Económica* 43 (September).

Rosenthal, Gert (1993) 'Regional Integration in the 1990s', *CEPAL Review* 50 (August): 11–19.

Rowat, Malcolm (1997) 'Competition Policy and MERCOSUR'. Washington, DC: World Bank, Technical Department Latin America and Caribbean Region.

Sampson, Gary P. (1996) 'Compatibility of Regional and Multilateral Trading Arrangements: Reforming the WTO Process', *The American Economic Review* 86 (2):88–92. American Economic Association.

Sanahuja, José Antonio (1997) 'Mexico y la Unión Europea, ¿Hacia un nuevo modelo de relación?' Paper from the Departamento de Relaciones Internacionales, Madrid Universidad Complutense, January.

Schaper, Marianne (1997) 'Situación del Mercosur en temas ambientales: perspectivas y desafios'. Santiago: CEPAL.

Schiff, Maurice (1996) *Small is Beautiful*. Working Paper No. 1668, October. Washington, DC: World Bank.

Schiff, Maurice and Winters, L. Alan (1997) *Regional Integration as Diplomacy*. Policy Research Working Paper No. 1801. Washington, DC: World Bank.

Schott, Jeffrey, J. (1997) 'NAFTA: An Interim Report'. Paper for Third Annual World Bank Conference on Development in Latin America and the Caribbean', Montevideo.

Serra, Jaime (ed.) (1997) *Reflections on Regionalism*. Washington, DC: Carnegie Endowment for International Peace.

Sinclair, Peter and Vines, David (1994) 'Do fewer, larger trade blocs imply greater protection? The good news and the bad news about regional trading blocs'. IESG seminar, 17 June.

Smidt, Steffen (1996) 'The Maastricht Treaty, the Lomé Convention and the future of EU Aid'. Talk at Overseas Development Institute, London, March.

Smith, Peter H. (ed.) (1993) *The Challenge of Integration: Europe and the Americas*, London: Transaction Publishers.

Southern African Customs Union, *Agreement*, 1969, revised 1976.

Southern African Development Community (1996) *Draft Trade Protocol*, Revised Version, June.

Stallings, Barbara (ed.) (1995) *Global Change, Regional Response*, Cambridge: Cambridge University Press.

Tan, Kong Yam (1992) 'AFTA as seen by individual ASEAN countries: A View from Singapore', 17th Conference of the Federation of ASEAN Economic Association, Indonesia.

Tavares de Araujo Jr. and Tineo, Luis (1997) *The Harmonization of Competition Policies among MERCOSUR Countries*, Santiago: Organization of American States Trade Unit.

Teunissen, Jan Joost (ed.) (1996) *Regionalism and the Global Economy: The Case of Africa*, The Hague: Forum on Debt and Development.

Teunissen, Jan Joost (ed.) (1996) *Regionalism and the Global Economy: The Case of Central and Eastern Europe*, The Hague: Forum on Debt and Deveopment.

Teunissen, Jan Joost (ed.) (1995) *Regionalism and the Global Economy: The Case of Latin America and the Caribbean*, The Hague: Forum on Debt and Development.

Thisen, Jean (1995) 'Elements of a Model Convention for Subregional Common Markets in Africa', for UN LINK September.

Trebilcock, Michael J. and House, Robert (1995) *The Regulation of International Trade*, London: Routledge.

United Nations (various) *Monthly Bulletin of Statistics*, New York: United Nations.

UNCTAD (1997) *World Investment Report 1996*. Geneva: UNCTAD.

UNCTAD (1996) *World Investment Directory, Africa*. Geneva: UNCTAD.

UNCTAD (1995) *Currency Convertibility and Monetary Cooperation within Integration Groupings of Developing Countries*. Geneva: UNCTAD/ECDC/250, May.

UNCTAD (1995) *Implications of the Dynamism of Large Economic Spaces*. Geneva: TD/B/SEM.1/2 and Statistical Annex.

UNCTAD (1995) *State of South–South Cooperation*. New York and Geneva: UNCTAD.

UNCTAD (1995) *World Investment Report 1995*. Geneva: UNCTAD.

UNCTAD (1994) *Clearing and Payments Arrangements among Developing Countries*. Geneva: UNCTAD/ECDC/238, February.

UNCTAD (1994) *World Investment Directory, Latin America and the Caribbean*. Geneva: UNCTAD.

UNECA (1994) *The Uruguay Round Agreement and its Possible Impact on Regional Economic Integration in Africa in the light of the Abuja Treaty*. Conference on the Uruguay Round, Tunis, October.

UN ECLAC (1997) *La Inversión extranjera en América Latina y el Caribe*, Santiago: ECLAC.

UN ECLAC (1997) *Centroamérica: Evolución de la Integración Económica durante 1996*, Mexico City: ECLAC.

UN ECLAC (1996) *Panorama de la Inserción Internacional de América Latina y el Caribe*, Santiago: ECLAC.

UN ECLAC (1995) *Centroamérica y el TLCAN: Efectos inmediatos e implicaciones futuras*, Santiago: ECLAC.

UN ECLAC (1995) *Recent Economic Trends in People's Republic of China: Implications for sino-Latinoamerican trade*, Santiago: ECLAC.

UN ECLAC (1995) *Factors Affecting the Participation of Caribbean Countries in the Free Trade Area of the Americas*, Caribbean Development and Cooperation Committee, Port of Spain: ECLAC.

UN ECLAC (1995) *Integration and Caribbean Development*, Port of Spain: ECLAC.

UN ECLAC (1995) *Desenvolvimiento de los procesos de integracion en America Latina y el Caribe*, Santiago: ECLAC.

UN ECLAC (1994) *La nueva integración regional en el marco de la asociacion latinoamericana de integración (ALADI)*, Santiago: ECLAC.

UN ECLAC (1993) *Directorio sobre Inversión Extranjera en América Latina y el Caribe 1993: Marco Legal e Información Estadística*, Santiago: ECLAC.

UN ECLAC (1990) *Latin American Trade with Other Economic Blocs: The Experience of the 1970s and 1980s*, Santiago: ECLAC.

UN ESCAP (1994) 'The Implications of NAFTA for the Asia and Pacific Region: Regional Perspective', Symposium on implications of NAFTA for the Asia and Pacific Region, Bangkok, September.

UN ESCAP (1992) *Studies in Regional Economic Cooperation in the ESCAP Region.*

United States (various), *Survey of Current Business.*

United States Government (1997) *Study on the Operation and Effect of the North American Free Trade Agreement (NAFTA)*, Washington, DC: US Government.

United States International Trade Commission (1997) *The Impact of the North American Free Trade Agreement on the U.S. Economy and Industries: A Three-Year Review*, Washington, DC: US Government.

United States Trade Representative (1997) *Future Free Trade Area Negotiations: Report on Significant Market Opening*, Washington, DC: US Government.

van Dijk, Meine Pieter and Sideri, Sandro (eds) (1996) *Multilateralism versus Regionalism: Trade Issues after the Uruguay Round*, London: Frank Cass for EADI.

van Klaveren, Alberto (1997) 'The Impact of Globalisation on Chile'. Paper presented at Canning House, London, 29 October.

Vega Canovas, Gustavo (c. 1993) 'Mexico, el tratado de comercio libre de América del Norte y el Grupo de los tres', mimeo.

Vernon, Raymond (1996) 'Passing Through Regionalism: The Transition to Global Markets', *The World Economy* 19(6): 621–33.

Viner, Jacob (1950) *The Customs Union Issue*, New York: Carnegie Endowment for International Peace.

Vines, David (1996) 'What is Asia–Pacific Open Regionalism, and what are its implications?' Paper for FCO conference, January.

Vines, David (1996) 'Linkages and Interactions between Global Economic Institutions'. Paper for Institutional Aspects of the World Trade Organization's Effectiveness, Stanford, CA, September.

Wei, Shang-Jin and Frankel, Jeffrey A. (1995) *Open Regionalism in a World of Continental Trade Blocs*. NBER Working Paper No. 5272. Cambridge, MA: NBER.

Weibe, M. (1997) 'ASEAN and environment', manuscript, Buenos Aires: FLACSO.

Weston, Ann (1994) *The NAFTA Papers: Implications for Canada, Mexico, and Developing Countries*, Toronto: North–South Institute.

Williamson, Jeffrey G. (1995) *Globalization, Convergence, and History*. NBER Working Paper No. 5259. Cambridge, MA: NBER.

Winters, L. Alan (1997) 'Assessing Regional Integration Arrangements', for World Bank Latin American conference on Development, Montevideo.

Winters, L. Alan (1997) 'What can European Experience Teach Developing Countries about Integration?', *World Economy* 20(5): 889–912.

Winters, L. Alan (1996) *Regionalism versus Multilateralism*. Policy Research Working Paper No.1687. Washington, DC: World Bank.

Winters, L. Alan (1993) 'The EC and World Protectionism: Dimensions of the Political Economy', draft. London: CEPR, November.

Winters, L. Alan and Chang, Won (1997) *Regional Integration and the Prices of Imports*. Policy Research Working Paper No. 1782. Washington, DC: World Bank.

Wolf, Martin (1994) *The Resistible Appeal of Fortress Europe*. Rochester Paper 1. London: Centre for Policy Studies.

312 *References and Bibliography*

Wonnacott, R. (1995) 'Merchandise Trade in the APEC Region: Is There Scope for Liberalization on an MFN Basis?', *World Economy*, Annual Supplement in APEC.
World Bank (1995) *Global Economic Prospects*. Washington, DC: World Bank.
World Trade Organization (1997) *Annual Report*. Geneva: WTO.
World Trade Organization (1997) 'Non-attributable summary of the main improvements in the new financial services commitments', December, Internet. wto.org.
World Trade Organization (1997) *Trade Policy Review: Brazil*. Geneva: WTO.
World Trade Organization (1997) *Trade Policy Review: European Union*. Geneva: WTO.
World Trade Organization (1997) *Trade Policy Review: Paraguay*. Geneva: WTO.
World Trade Organization (1997) *Trade Policy Review: Mexico*. Geneva: WTO.
World Trade Organization (1997) *Trade Policy Review: Chile*. Geneva: WTO.
World Trade Organization (1996) *Trade and Foreign Direct Investment*. Geneva: WTO.
World Trade Organization (1995) *Regionalism and the World Trading System*. Geneva: WTO.
Yamazawa, Ippei (1996) 'APEC's New Development and its Implications for Nonmember Developing Countries', *The Developing Economies* XXXIV(2): 113–37.
Yeats, Alexander (1997) *Does Mercosur's Trade Performance Raise Concerns about the Effects of Regional Trade Arrangements?* Policy Research Working Paper No. 1729. Washington, DC: World Bank.
Zahler, Roberto and Budnevich, Carlos (1997) 'Integration of Financial Services in Latin America'. Paper prepared for Third Annual World Bank Conference on the Development of Latin America and the Caribbean, Montevideo.
Zormelo, Douglas (1995) *Regional Integration in Latin America: Is MERCOSUR a New Approach?* ODI Working Paper No. 84. London: Overseas Development Institute.

Web resources

Organization of American States Foreign Trade Information System:	www.sice.oas.org/root/datae.stm
	www.sice.oas.org/root/tradee.stm
	www.sice.oas.org/root/bitse.stm
OAS Compendium:	www.sice.oas.org/cp061096/english/toc.stm
Inter-American Development Bank:	www.iadb.org
World Trade Organization:	www.wto.org
ASEAN data:	coombs.anu.edu.au/wwwvL-AsianStudies.html
US International Trade Commission:	www.usitc.gov/tr/tr.htm
United Nations:	www.un.org
World Bank, Latin American Dept:	www.worldbank.org/html/lat/english/default.htm
World Bank, Research Dept:	www.worldbank.org/iecit/iecit.html
Africa News:	www.africanews.org/south/southernafrica
NAFTA agreement:	the-tech.mit.edu/bulletins/na fta.html
MERCOSUR:	www.dpr.mre.gov.br/dpg/merc00-i.htm
MERCOSUR:	www.brazil.org.uk
ASEAN:	www.aseansec.org
NAFTA:	www.dallasfed.org/fedhome.html
Trade Statistics:	dtiinfo1.dti.gov.uk/ots/emic/WEB PAGES/

Index

Abreu, Marcelo de Paiva, 214
accession, of new members, 41, 52, 57,
    251–61 passim
ACP, 8, 49, 258, 267, 270–1, 293
acquis, 40–1
administration, of trade, 224–5,
    236–41, 247
AEC, 47, 48, 50, 59, 89, 90, 260,
    275–7, 282; and trade, 98, 100,
    121, 147, 149, 150
Africa, 5, 9, 88, 92, 115, 147, 149, 177,
    195, 196, 234, 260–1, 271, 272,
    288, 294 (see also individual
    entries); Development Bank, 90;
    North, 47, 270
Agosín, Manuel R., 144
agriculture, 39, 43, 56, 103, 104, 106,
    116–17, 122, 137, 172, 210, 211,
    227, 234
aid, 266–7, 269, 270
air services, 90, 214, 238
Akrasanee, N., 63
Andean group/Pact, 9, 14, 48, 50,
    52–4, 56, 62, 63, 68–71 passim,
    75, 77, 89, 90, 92, 221, 223, 228,
    232, 233, 235, 241, 242, 245, 246,
    254, 266–70, 273–7 passim, 282,
    285, 288, 294; and investment,
    167, 170, 173, 182–7 passim, 198,
    199, 202–3; and labour 216, 219;
    and negotiations, 256, 258, 259;
    and services, 214; and trade, 98,
    104, 107, 110, 111, 118, 130–1,
    142, 148–50 passim, 154;
    institutions, 238
Angola, 195, 204
ANZCERTA, 47–50 passim, 61, 63, 68,
    70, 71, 73, 76, 77, 79, 89, 90, 216,
    220, 222, 224, 226, 275, 276, 294;
    and investment, 167, 171–2,
    191–2, 197–9 passim; and labour,
    216; and services, 213; and trade,

98, 102, 107, 111, 119, 136–7,
    149, 150, 156
APEC, 39, 47–50 passim, 58, 61–2,
    68–73 passim, 89, 92, 122, 224,
    225, 231, 235, 239–40, 244–6
    passim, 252, 260, 275–7 passim,
    282, 283, 285, 287, 290–2 passim;
    and investment, 192, 193, 195–7;
    and services, 216; and trade,
    100–1, 121, 147, 149, 150, 161–2
Arab Maghreb Union, 260
Argentina, 143–6 passim, 148, 158,
    169, 223, 226–9 passim, 231, 232,
    243, 245, 267–8, 273; and Brazil,
    52, 55, 63, 105, 123, 177–81
    passim, 234; and MERCOSUR, 55,
    56, 104, 105, 110, 123–9 passim,
    152, 177–81, 201, 214, 228, 229,
    232–5 passim, 256, 258
Ariff, Mohamed, 75
ASEAN, 31, 47, 48, 50, 59–61 passim,
    63, 69, 70, 73, 75, 76, 79, 89,
    90, 169, 185, 222, 224, 229–31
    passim, 234, 239, 243–5, 258–60
    passim, 270, 274–6 passim, 282,
    284, 286, 289, 291, 292, 294; and
    investment, 167, 172, 173, 187,
    192–4, 197–9 passim, 203–4;
    and services, 215–16; and trade,
    98, 102, 107, 109, 111, 119, 122,
    135, 137–40, 149, 150, 156–7;
    institutions, 239
Asia, 5, 20, 22, 29, 32, 38, 60–2 passim,
    69, 76, 88, 92, 175, 198, 222, 228,
    240, 250–2, 254, 259–60, 270,
    291, 294 (see also individual
    entries)
Australia, 11, 39, 61, 68, 71, 76, 137,
    156, 161, 171–2, 191–2, 231; and
    New Zealand, 30, 73, 91, 252, 294
    (see also ANZCERTA)
Austria, 51, 151, 230